AMERICAN COMPOSERS

AMS PRESS
NEW YORK

FREDERICK SHEPHERD CONVERSE.

(*See page 457.*)

AMERICAN COMPOSERS

A STUDY OF THE MUSIC OF THIS COUNTRY, AND OF ITS FUTURE, WITH BIOGRAPHIES OF THE LEADING COMPOSERS OF THE PRESENT TIME

BEING A NEW REVISED EDITION OF CONTEMPORARY AMERICAN COMPOSERS

BY

RUPERT HUGHES

Author of "Love Affairs of Great Musicians," etc.

WITH ADDITIONAL CHAPTERS BY

ARTHUR ELSON

Author of "The Modern Composers of Europe, "Woman's Work in Music," etc.

ILLUSTRATED

THE PAGE COMPANY

BOSTON ❦ ❦ ❦ MDCCCCXIV

Library of Congress Cataloging in Publication Data

Hughes, Rupert, 1872-1956.
    American composers.

    Original ed. issued in series: The Music lovers'
series.
    1. Composers, America. 2. Music, American.
I. Elson, Arthur, 1873-1940. I. Series: The Music
lovers' series.
ML390.H89 1973   780'.973   72-1618
ISBN 0-404-09905-X

780.97
H894a

Reprinted from an original copy in the collections
of the Newark Public Library

84-8873

Reprinted from the edition of 1914, Boston
First AMS edition published in 1973
Manufactured in the United States of America

AMS PRESS INC.
NEW YORK, N. Y.   10003

PREFACE

MR. HUGHES originally planned to undertake himself the preparation of this new edition, but pressure of labor in other fields
forced him to give up the project. He,
consequently, turned over the large amount
of material which he had collected to Mr.
Elson, whose experience in the field of
musical criticism has made him well fitted
for the task of reviewing the progress of
American Composers since the publication
of the first edition.

CONTENTS.

Part I.

LIST OF MUSIC.

———•———

LIST OF ILLUSTRATIONS.

xi

PART I.

AMERICAN COMPOSERS TO
1900
BY RUPERT HUGHES

FOREWORD.

ONE day there came into Robert Schumann's ken the work of a young fellow named Brahms, and the master cried aloud in the wilderness, "Behold, the new Messiah of music!" Many have refused to accept Brahms at this rating, and I confess to being one of the unregenerate, but the spirit that kept Schumann's heart open to the appeal of any stranger, that led him into instant enthusiasms of which he was neither afraid nor ashamed, enthusiasms in which the whole world has generally followed his leading — that spirit it is that proves his true musicianship, and makes him a place forever among the great critics of music, — a small, small crowd they are, too.

It is inevitable that a pioneer like Schumann should make many mistakes, but he escaped the one great fatal mistake of those who are not open to conviction, nor alert for new beauty and fresh truth, who are willing to take art to their affections or respect only when it has lost its bloom and has been duly appraised and ticketed by other generations or foreign scholars. And yet, even worse than this languorous inanition is the active policy of those who despise everything contemporary or native, and substitute sciolism for catholicity, contempt for analysis.

While the greater part of the world has stayed aloof, the problem of a national American music has been solving itself. Aside from occasional attentions evoked by chance performances, it may be said in general that the growth of our music has been unloved and unheeded by anybody except a few plodding composers, their wives, and a retainer or two. The only thing that inclines me to invade the privacy of the American com-

poser and publish his secrets, is my hearty
belief, lo, these many years! that some of
the best music in the world is being written
here at home, and that it only needs the light
to win its meed of praise.

Owing to the scarcity of printed matter
relating to native composers, and the utter
incompleteness and bias of what exists, I have
based this book almost altogether on my own
research. I studied the catalogues of all the
respectable music publishers, and selected
such composers as seemed to have any serious intentions. When I heard of a composer whose work, though earnest, had not
been able to find a publisher, I sought him
out and read his manuscripts (a hideous task
which might be substituted for the comparative pastime of breaking rocks, as punishment
for misdemeanors). In every case I secured
as many of each composer's works as could
be had in print or in manuscript, and endeavored to digest them. Thousands of

pieces of music, from short songs to operatic
and orchestral scores, I studied with all avail-
able conscience. The fact that after going
through at least a ton of American compositions, I am still an enthusiast, is surely a
proof of some virtue in native music.

A portion of the result of this study was
published *au courant* in a magazine, awakening so much attention that I have at length
decided to yield to constant requests and
publish the articles in more accessible form.
The necessity for revising many of the
opinions formed hastily and published imme-
diately, the possibility now of taking the work
of our musicians in some perspective, and the
opportunity of bringing my information up
to date, have meant so much revision, exci-
sion, and addition, that this book is really a
new work.

The biographical data have been furnished
in practically every case by the composers
themselves, and are, therefore, reliable in

everything except possibly the date of birth. The critical opinions gain their possibly dogmatic tone rather from a desire for brevity than from any hope — or wish — that they should be swallowed whole. No attempt to set up a standard of comparative merit or precedence has been made, though it is inevitable that certain music-makers should interest one more than certain others even more worthy in the eyes of eminent judges.

It may be that some inspectors of this book will complain of the omission of names they had expected to find here. Others will feel a sense of disproportion. To them there is no reply but a pathetic allusion to the inevitable incompleteness and asymmetry of all things human.

Many will look with skepticism at the large number of composers I have thought worthy of inclusion. I can only say that the fact that an artist has created one work of high merit makes him a good composer in my opinion, whether or no he has ever written another, and whether or no he has afterward fallen into the sere and yellow school of trash. So Gray's fame is perennial, — one poem among many banalities.

Besides, I do not concur in that most commonplace fallacy of criticism, the belief that not more than one genius is vouchsafed to any one period of an art, though this opinion can be justified, of course, by a very exclusive definition of the word genius. To the average mind, for instance, the whole literary achievement of the Elizabethan era is condensed into the name of Shakespeare. Contemporary with him, however, there were, of course, thirty or forty writers whose best works the scholar would be most unwilling to let die. There were, for instance, a dozen playwrights, like Jonson, Fletcher, Ford, Marlowe, and Greene, in whose works can be found literary and dramatic touches of the very highest order. There were poets less prolific than

Spenser, and yet to be credited with a few works of the utmost beauty, minor geniuses like Ralegh, Sidney, Lodge, Shirley, Lyly, Wotton, Wither, John Donne, Bishop Hall, Drayton, Drummond, Herbert, Carew, Herrick, Breton, Allison, Byrd, Dowland, Campion — so one might run on without naming one man who had not written something the world was better for.

All periods of great art activity are similarly marked by a large number of geniuses whose ability is not disproved, because overshadowed by the presence of some titanic contemporary. It would be a mere impertinence to state such an axiom of art as this, were it not the plain truth that almost all criticism of contemporaries is based upon an arrant neglect of it ; and if it were not for the fact that I am about to string out a long, long list of American music-makers whose ability I think noteworthy, — a list whose length may lead many a wiseacre to pull a longer face.

Parts of this book have been reprinted from *Godey's Magazine,* the *Century Magazine,* and the *Criterion,* to whose publishers I am indebted for permission. For the music reproduced here I have to thank the publishers whose copyrights were loaned for the occasion.

If the book shall only succeed in arousing in some minds an interest or a curiosity that shall set them to the study of American music (as I have studied it, with infinite pleasure), then this fine white paper and this beautiful black ink will not have been wasted.

AMERICAN COMPOSERS

———◆———

CHAPTER I.

A GENERAL SURVEY.

CODDLING is no longer the chief need of the American composer. While he still wants encouragement in his good tendencies, — much more encouragement than he gets, too, — he is now strong enough to profit by the discouragement of his evil tendencies.

In other words, the American composer is ready for criticism.

The first and most vital flaw of which his work will be accused is the lack of nationalism. This I should like to combat after the sophistric fashion of Zeno, — showing, first, why we lack that desideratum, a strictly national school ; secondly, that a strictly national school is not desirable ; and thirdly, that we most assuredly have a national school.

In building a national individuality, as in building a personal individuality, there is always a period of discipleship under some older power. When the rudiments and the essentials are once thoroughly mastered, the shackles of discipleship are thrown off, and personal expression in an original way begins. This is the story of every master in every art : The younger Raphael was only Perugino junior. Beethoven's first sonatas were more completely Haydn's than the word "gewidmet" would declare. The youthful Canova was swept off his feet by the unearthing of old Greek masterpieces. Stevenson confesses frankly his early efforts to copy the mannerisms of Scott and others. Nations are only clusters of individuals, and subject to the same rules. Italy borrowed its beginnings from Byzantium; Germany and France took theirs from Italy; we, ours, from them.

It was inconceivable that America should produce an autocthonous art. The race is one great mixture of more or less digested foreign elements; and it is not possible to draw a declaration of artistic, as of political, independence, and thenceforward be truly free.

Centuries of differentiated environment (in all the senses of the word environment) are needed to produce a new language or a new art; and it was inevitable that American music should for long be only a more or less successful employment of European methods. And there was little possibility, according to all precedents in art history, that any striking individuality should rise suddenly to found a school based upon his own mannerism.

Especially was this improbable, since we are in a large sense of English lineage. As the co-heirs, with those who remain in the British Isles, of the magnificent prose and poetry of England, it was possible for us to produce early in our own history a Hawthorne and a Poe and an Emerson and a Whitman. But we have had more hindrance than help from our heritage of English music, in which there has never been a master of the first rank, Purcell and the rest being, after all, brilliants of the lesser magnitude (with the permission of that electric Englishman, Mr. John F. Runciman).

A further hindrance was the creed of the Puritan fathers of our civilization; they had a granite heart, and a suspicious eye for music. Here is a cheerful example of congregational lyricism, and a lofty inspiration for musical treatment (the hymn refers to the fate of unbaptized infants):

> " A crime it is !   Therefore in Bliss
> You may not hope to dwell;
> But unto you I shall allow
> The easiest room in Hell."

It was only at the end of the seventeenth century that singing by note began to supplant the " lining-out " barbarism, and to provoke such fierce opposition as this :

" First, it is a new way — an unknown tongue; 2d, it is not so melodious as the old way; 3d, there are so many tunes that nobody can learn them; 4th, the new way makes a disturbance in churches, grieves good men, exasperates them, and causes them to behave disorderly; 5th, it is popish; 6th, it will introduce instruments; 7th, the names of the notes are blasphemous; 8th, it is needless, the old way being good enough; 9th, it requires too much time to learn it; 10th, it makes the young disorderly."

At the time when such puerility was disturbing this cradle of freedom and cacophony, Bach and Händel were at work in their contrapuntal webs, the Scarlattis, Corelli and Tartini and Porpora were alive. Peri, Josquin and Willaert and Lassus were dead, and the church had had its last mass from the most famous citizen of the town of Palestrina.   Monteverde was no longer inventing like an Edison; Lulli had gone to France and died; and Rameau and Couperin were alive.

At this time in the world's art, the Americans were squabbling over the blasphemy of instruments and of notation! This is not the place to treat the history of our music. The curious can find enlightenment at such sources as Mr. Louis C. Elson's "National Music of America." It must be enough for me to say that the throttling hands of Puritanism are only now fully loosened. Some of our living composers recall the parental opposition that met their first inclinations to a musical career, opposition based upon the disgracefulness, the heathenishness, of music as a profession.

The youthfulness of our school of music can be emphasized further by a simple statement that, with the exception of a few names like Lowell Mason, Louis Moreau Gottschalk, Stephen A. Emery (a graceful writer as well as a theorist), and George F. Bristow, practically every American composer of even the faintest importance is now living.

The influences that finally made American music are chiefly German. Almost all of our composers have studied in Germany, or from teachers trained there; very few of them turning aside to Paris, and almost none to Italy. The prominent teachers, too, that have come from abroad have been trained in the German school, whatever their nationality. The growth of a national school has been necessarily slow, therefore, for its necessary and complete submission to German influences.

It has been further delayed by the meagre native encouragement to effort of the better sort. The populace has been largely indifferent, — the inertia of all large bodies would explain that. A national, a constructive, and collaborative criticism has been conspicuously absent.

The leaders of orchestras have also offered an almost insurmountable obstacle to the production of any work from an American hand until very recently.   The Boston Symphony Orchestra has been a noble exception to this rule, and has given about the only opening possible to the native writer.   The Chicago Orchestra, in eight seasons under Theodore Thomas, devoted, out of a total of 925 numbers, only eighteen, or something less than two per cent., to native music.   Yet time shows a gradual improvement, and in 1899, out of twenty-seven orchestral numbers performed, three were by Americans, which makes a liberal tithe.   The Boston Symphony has played the compositions of John Knowles Paine alone more than eighteen times, and those of George W. Chadwick the same number, while E. A. MacDowell and Arthur Foote each appeared on the programs fourteen times. The Kaltenborn Orchestra has made an active effort at the promulgation of our music, and especial honor is due to Frank Van der Stucken, himself a composer of marked abilities ; he was among the first to give orchestral production to American works, and he was, perhaps, the very first to introduce American orchestral work abroad. Like his offices, in spirit and effect, have been the invaluable services of our most eminent pianist, Wm. H. Sherwood, who was for many years the only prominent performer of American piano compositions.

Public singers also have been most unpatriotic in preferring endless repetition of dry foreign arias to fresh compositions from home. The little encore song, which generally appeared anonymously, was the opening wedge for the American lyrist.

Upon the horizon of this gloom, however, there is a tremor of a dawning interest in national music. Large vocal societies are giving an increasing number of native part songs and cantatas ; prizes are being awarded in various places, and composers find some financial encouragement for appearing in concerts of their own work. Manuscript societies are organized in many of the larger cities, and these clubs offer hearing to novelty. There have latterly appeared, from various publishers, special catalogues vaunting the large number of American composers represented on their lists.

Another, and a most important sign of the growing influence of music upon American life, is seen in the place it is gaining in the college curriculum ; new chairs have been established, and prominent composers called to fill them, or old professorships that held merely nominal places in the catalogue have been enlarged in scope. In this way music is reëstablishing itself in something like its ancient glory; for the Greeks not only grouped all culture under the general term of "Music," but gave voice and instrument a vital place in education. Three of our most prominent composers fill the chairs at three of the most important universities. In all these cases, however, music is an elective study, while the rudiments of the art should, I am convinced, be a required study in every college curriculum, and in the common schools as well.

Assuming then, for the nonce, the birth — we are too new a country to speak of a Renascence — of a large interest in national music, there is large disappointment in many quarters, because our American music is not more American. I have argued above that a race transplanted from other soils must still retain most of the old modes of expression, or, varying them, change slowly. But many who excuse us for the present lack of a natural nationalism, are so eager for such a differentiation that they would have us borrow what we cannot breed.

The folk-music of the negro slaves is most frequently mentioned as the right foundation for a strictly American school.   A somewhat misunderstood statement advanced by Dr. Antonin Dvôrák, brought this idea into general prominence, though it had been discussed by American composers, and made use of in compositions of all grades long before he came here.

The vital objection, however, to the general adoption of negro music as a base for an American school of composition is that it is in no sense a national expression.   It is not even a sectional expression, for the white Southerners among whose slaves this music grew, as well as the people of the North, have always looked upon negro music as an exotic and curious thing.   Familiar as it is to us, it is yet as foreign a music as any Tyrolean jodel or Hungarian czardas.

The music of the American Indian, often strangely beautiful and impressive, would be

as reasonably chosen as that of these im-
ported Africs. E. A. MacDowell had, indeed,
written a picturesque and impressive Indian
suite, some time before the Dvôrákian invasion. He asserts that the Indian music is
preferable to the Ethopian, because its sturdi-
ness and force are more congenial with the
national mood.

But the true hope for a national spirit in
American music surely lies, not in the arbitrary seizure of some musical dialect, but in
the development of just such a quality as
gives us an individuality among the nations
of the world in respect to our character as a
people ; and that is a Cosmopolitanism made
up of elements from all the world, and yet, in
its unified qualities, unlike any one element.
Thus our music should, and undoubtedly will,
be the gathering into the spirit of the voices
of all the nations, and the use of all their
expressions in an assimilated, a personal, a
spontaneous manner. This need not, by any

means, be a dry, academic eclecticism. The Yankee, a composite of all peoples, yet differs from them all, and owns a sturdy individuality. His music must follow the same fate.

As our governmental theories are the out-growth of the experiments and experiences of all previous history, why should not our music, voicing as it must the passions of a cosmopolitan people, use cosmopolitan ex-pressions? The main thing is the individu-ality of each artist. To be a citizen of the world, provided one is yet spontaneous and sincere and original, is the best thing. The whole is greater than any of its parts.

Along just these lines of individualized cosmopolitanism the American school is working out its identity. Some of our com-posers have shown themselves the heirs of European lore by work of true excellence in the larger classic and romantic forms.

The complaint might be made, indeed, that the empty, incorrect period of previous American music has given place to too much correctness and too close formation on the old models. This is undoubtedly the result of the long and faithful discipleship under German methods, and need not be made much of in view of the tendency among a few masters toward original expression. For, after all, even in the heyday of the greatest art periods, only a handful of artists have ever stood out as strongly individual; the rest have done good work as faithful imitators and past masters in technic. It is, then, fortunate that there is any tendency at all among any of our composers to forsake academic content with classical forms and text-book development of ideas.

Two things, however, are matters for very serious disappointment: the surprising paucity of musical composition displaying the national sense of humor, and the surprising abundance of purest namby-pamby. The presence of the latter class might be explained by the absence of the former, for namby-pamby cannot exist along with a healthy sense of the ludicrous. There has been a persistent craze among native song-writers for little flower-dramas and bird-trage-dies, which, aiming at exquisiteness, fall far short of that dangerous goal and land in flagrant silliness. This weakness, however, will surely disappear in time, or at least diminish, until it holds no more prominent place than it does in all the foreign schools, where it exists to a certain extent.

The scherzo, however, must grow in favor. It is impossible that the most jocose of races, a nation that has given the world an original school of humor, should not carry this spirit over into its music. And yet almost none of the comparatively few scherzos that have been written here have had any sense of the hilarious jollity that makes Beethoven's wit side-shaking. They have been rather of the Chopinesque sort, mere fantasy. To the composers deserving this generalization I recall only two important exceptions, Edgar S. Kelley and Harvey Worthington Loomis.

The opportunities before the American composer are enormous, and only half appreciated. Whereas, in other arts, the text-book claims only to be a chronicle of what has been done before, in music the text-book is set up as the very gospel and decalogue of the art. The theorists have so thoroughly mapped out the legitimate resources of the composer, and have so prescribed his course in nearly every possible position, that music is made almost more of a mathematical problem than the free expression of emotions and æsthetics. " Correct " music has now hardly more liberty than Egyptian sculpture or Byzantine painting once had. Certain dissonances are permitted, and certain others, no more dissonant, forbidden, quite arbitrarily, or on hair-splitting theories. It is as if one should write down in a book a number of charts, giving every scheme of color and every juxtaposition of values permissible to a painter. The music of certain Oriental nations, in which the religious orders are the art censors, has stuck fast in its rut because of the observance of rules purely arbitrary. Many of the conventions of modern European music are no more scientific or original or consistent ; most of them are based upon the principle that the whim of a great dead composer is worthy to be the law of any living composer. These Blue Laws of music are constantly assailed surreptitiously and in detail ; and yet they are too little attacked as a whole. But music should be a democracy and not an aristocracy, or, still less, a hierarchy.

There is a great opportunity for America to carry its political principles into this youngest of the arts. It is a gratifying sign that one of the most prominent theorists of the time, an American scholar, A. J. Goodrich, is adopting some such attitude toward music. He carries dogma to the minimum, and accepts success in the individual instance as sufficient authority for overstepping any general principle. He refers to a contemporary American composer for authority and example of some successful unconventionality with the same respect with which he would quote a European's disregard of convention. His pioneering is watched with interest abroad as well as here.

Worthy of mention along with Mr. Goodrich' original work is the effort of Homer A. Norris to instil French ideas of musical theory. As a counterweight to the German monopoly of our attention, his influence is to be cordially welcomed.

Now that Americanism is rife in the land, some of the glowing interest in things national might well be turned toward an art that has been too much and too long neglected among us.

The time has come to take American music seriously. The day for boasting is not yet here, — if indeed it ever comes; but the day of penitent humility is surely past.

A student of the times, Mr. E. S. Martin, shortly before the Spanish War, commented on the radical change that had come over the spirit of American self-regard. We were notorious in the earlier half of the century for boasting, not only of the virtues we indubitably had, but of qualities that existed solely in our own imagination. We sounded our barbaric yawp over the roofs of the world. A century of almost unanimous European disapproval, particularly of our artistic estate, finally converted us from this attitude to one of deprecation almost abject. Having learned the habit of modesty, it has clung to us even now, when some of the foremost artists in the world are Americans.

Modesty, is, of course, one of the most beautiful of the virtues, but excess is possible and dangerous. As Shakespeare's Florio's Montaigne has it: "We may so seize on vertue, that if we embrace it with an over-greedy and violent desire, it may become vitious." In the case of the American composer it is certainly true that we "excessively demeane ourselves in a good action." If, then, the glory of our late successes in the field of battle shall bring about a recrudescence of our old vanity, it will at least have its compensations.

Meanwhile, the American artist, having long ago ceased to credit himself with all the virtues, has been for years earnestly working out his own salvation in that spirit of solemn determination which makes it proverbial for the American to get anything he sets his heart on. He has submitted himself to a devout study of the Old Masters and the New; he has made pilgrimage after pilgrimage to the ancient temples of art, and has brought home influences that cannot but work for good.

The American painter has won more European acceptance than any of our other artists, though this is partly due to his persistence in knocking at the doors of the Paris salons, and gaining the universal prestige of admission there.   There is, unfortunately, no such place to focus the attention of the world on a musician.   Yet, through the success of American musical students among their rivals abroad ; through the concerts they are giving more and more frequently in foreign countries ; through the fact that a number of European music houses are publishing increasing quantities of American compositions, he is making his way to foreign esteem almost more rapidly than at home.

A prominent German critic, indeed, has recently put himself on record as accepting the founding of an American school of music as a *fait accompli*.   And no student of the times, who will take the trouble to seek the sources of our art, and observe its actual vitality, need be ashamed of looking at the present state of music in America with a substantial pride and a greater hope for the future.

CHAPTER II.

THE INNOVATORS.

Edward Alexander MacDowell.

THE matter of precedence in creative art is as hopeless of solution as it is unimportant. And yet it seems appropriate to say, in writing of E. A. MacDowell, that an almost unanimous vote would grant him rank as the greatest of American composers, while not

EDWARD MACDOWELL

a few ballots would indicate him as the best of living music writers.

But this, to repeat, is not vital, the main thing being that MacDowell has a distinct and impressive individuality, and uses his profound scholarship in the pursuit of novelty that is not cheaply sensational, and is yet novelty. He has, for instance, theories as to the textures of sounds, and his chord-formations and progressions are quite his own.

His compositions are superb processions, in which each participant is got up with the utmost personal splendor. His generalship is great enough to preserve the unity and the progress of the pageant. With him no note in the melody is allowed to go neglected, ill-mounted on common chords in the bass, or cheap-garbed in trite triads. Each tone is made to suggest something of its multitudinous possibilities. Through any geometrical point, an infinite number of lines can be drawn. This is almost the case with any note of a melody. It is the recognition and the practice of this truth that gives the latter-day schools of music such a lusciousness and warmth of harmony. No one is a more earnest student of these effects than Mac-Dowell.

He believes that it is necessary, at this late day, if you would have a chord "bite," to put a trace of acid in its sweetness. With this clue in mind, his unusual procedures become more explicable without losing their charm.

New York is rather the Mecca than the birthplace of artists, but it can boast the nativity of MacDowell, who improvised his first songs here December 18, 1861. He began the study of the piano at an early age. One of his teachers was Mme. Teresa Carreño, to whom he has dedicated his second concerto for the piano.

In 1876 he went to Paris and entered the Conservatoire, where he studied theory under

Savard, and the piano under Marmontel. He
went to Wiesbaden to study with Ehlert in
1879, and then to Frankfort, where Carl
Heyman taught him piano and Joachim Raff
composition. The influence of Raff is of the
utmost importance in MacDowell's music, and
I have been told that the great romancist
made a *protégé* of him, and would lock him in
a room for hours till he had worked out the
most appalling musical problems. Through
Raff's influence he became first piano teacher
at the Darmstadt Conservatorium in 1881.
The next year Raff introduced him to Liszt,
who became so enthusiastic over his compositions that he got him the honor of playing
his first piano suite before the formidable
Allgemeiner Deutscher Musik Verein, which
accorded him a warm reception. The following years were spent in successful concert
work, till 1884, when MacDowell settled
down to teaching and composing in Wiesbaden. Four years later he came to Boston,

writing, teaching, and giving occasional concerts. Thence he returned to New York,
where he was called to the professorship of
music at Columbia University. Princeton
University has given him that unmusical degree, Mus. Doc.

MacDowell has met little or none of that
critical recalcitrance that blocked the early
success of so many masters. His works
succeeded from the first in winning serious
favor; they have been much played in Germany, in Vienna, St. Petersburg, Amsterdam,
and Paris, one of them having been performed
three times in a single season at Breslau.

MacDowell's Scotch ancestry is always
telling tales on him. The "Scotch snap" is
a constant rhythmic device, the old scale and
the old Scottish cadences seem to be native
to his heart. Perhaps one might find some
kinship between MacDowell and the contemporary Glasgow school of painters, that
clique so isolated, so daring, and yet so ear-

nest and solid. Says James Huneker in a monograph published some years ago: " His coloring reminds me at times of Grieg, but when I tracked the resemblance to its lair, I found only Scotch, as Grieg's grand-folk were Greggs, and from Scotland. It is all Northern music with something elemental in it, and absolutely free from the heavy, languorous odors of the South or the morbidezza of Poland.

Some of MacDowell's most direct writing has been in the setting of the poems of Burns, such as " Deserted " ("Ye banks and braes o' bonnie Doon," op. 9), " Menie," and " My Jean " (op. 34). These are strongly marked by that ineffably fine melodic flavor characteristic of Scottish music, while in the accompaniments they admit a touch of the composer's own individuality. In his accompaniments it is noteworthy that he is almost never strictly contramelodic.

The songs of opera 11 and 12 have a

decided Teutonism, but he has found himself
by opus 40, a volume of "Six Love Songs,"
containing half a dozen flawless gems it is a
pity the public should not know more widely.
A later book, "Eight Songs" (op. 47), is also
a cluster of worthies. The lilt and sympathy
of "The Robin Sings in the Apple-tree,"
and its unobtrusive new harmonies and novel
effects, in strange accord with truth of expression, mark all the other songs, particularly the "Midsummer Lullaby," with its
accompaniment as delicately tinted as summer clouds. Especially noble is "The Sea,"
which has all the boom and roll of the deep-
brooding ocean.

His collections of flower-songs (op. 26) I
confess not liking. Though they are not
without a certain exquisiteness, they seem
overdainty and wastefully frail, excepting,
possibly, the "Clover" and the "Blue-bell."
It is not at all their brevity, but their trivial-
ity, that vexes an admirer of the large ability

that labored over them. They are dedicated to Emilio Agramonte, one of MacDowell's first prophets, and one of the earliest and most active agents for the recognition of the American composer.

In the lyrics in opus 56 and opus 58 Mac-Dowell has turned song to the unusual purposes of a landscape impressionism of places and moods rather than people.

For men's voices there are some deftly composed numbers curiously devoted to lullaby subjects. The barcarolle for mixed chorus and accompaniment on the piano for four hands obtains a wealth of color, enhanced by the constant division of the voices.

Studying as he did with Raff, it is but natural that MacDowell should have been influenced strongly toward the poetic and fantastic and programmatic elements that mark the "Forest Symphony" and the "Lenore Overture" of his master.

It is hard to say just how far this descrip-

tive music can go.   The skill of each composer must dictate his own limits.   As an
example of successful pieces of this kind,
consider MacDowell's " The Eagle."   It ıs
the musical realization of Tennyson's well-
known poem :

> " He clasps the crag with crooked hands;
> Close to the sun in lonely lands,
> Ring'd with the azure world, he stands.
> The wrinkled sea beneath him crawls ;
> He watches from his mountain walls,
> And like a thunderbolt he falls."

Of course the crag and the crooked hands
and the azure world must be granted the
composer, but general exaltation and loneliness are expressed in the severe melody of
the opening.   The wrinkling and crawling
of the sea far below are splendidly achieved
in the soft, shimmering liquidity of the music.
Then there are two abrupt, but soft, short
chords that will represent, to the imaginative,
the quick fixing of the eagle's heart on some

prey beneath ; and there follows a sudden precipitation down the keyboard, *fortississime,* that represents the thunderous swoop of the eagle with startling effect.

On the other hand, the " Moonshine " seems to be attempting too much. " Winter " does better, for it has a freezing stream, a mill-wheel, and a " widow bird." These " four little poems " of opus 32 had been preceded by six fine " Idylls " based on lyrics of Goethe's. The first, a forest scene, has a distinct flavor of the woods, the second is all laziness and drowsiness, and the third is moonlight mystery. The fourth is as intense in its suppressed spring ecstasy as the radiant poem itself singing how

> " Soft the ripples spill and hurry
> To the opulent embankment."

The six short " Poems " (op. 31) based on poems of Heine's are particularly successful, especially in the excellent opportunity of the lyric describing the wail of the Scottish woman who plays her harp on the cliff, and sings above the raging of sea and wind. The third catches most happily the whimsicality of the poet's reminiscences of childhood, but hardly, I think, the contrasting depth and wildness of his complaint that, along with childhood's games, have vanished Faith and Love and Truth. In the last, however, the cheery majesty that realizes Heine's likening of Death to a cool night after the sultry day of Life, is superb.

Then there are some four-hand pieces, two collections, that leave no excuse for clinging to the hackneyed classics or modern trash. They are not at all difficult, and the second player has something to employ his mind besides accompanying chords. They are meaty, and effective almost to the point of catchiness. The "Tale of the Knights" is full of chivalric fire and martial swing, while the "Ballad" is as exquisitely dainty as a peach-

blossom. The " Hindoo Maiden " has a deal
of the thoroughly Oriental color and feeling
that distinguish the three solos of " Les
Orientales," of which " Clair de Lune " is
one of his most original and graceful writings.
The duet, " In Tyrol," has a wonderful crystal
carillon and a quaint shepherd piping a faint
reminiscence of the Wagnerian school of
shepherds. This is one of a series of " Moon
Pictures " for four hands, based on Hans
Christian Andersen's lore. Two concertos
for piano and orchestra are dazzling feats of
virtuosity ; one of them is reviewed at length
in A. J. Goodrich' book, " Musical Analysis."
He has written also a book of artistic moment
called " Twelve Virtuoso-Studies," and two
books of actual gymnastics for piano practice.

But MacDowell did not reach his freedom
without a struggle against academia. His
opus 10 is a piano suite published at the age
of twenty-two, and opus 14 is another ; both
contain such obsolescences as a presto, fugue,

CLAIR DE LUNE.

La lune était sereine et jouait sur les flots.
La fenêtre enfin libre est ouverte à la brise,
La sultane regarde, et la mer qui se brise,
Là-bas, d'un flot d'argent brode les noirs flots.
(Victor Hugo, „Les Orientales.")

E. A. MAC DOWELL, OP. 37. Nº 1.

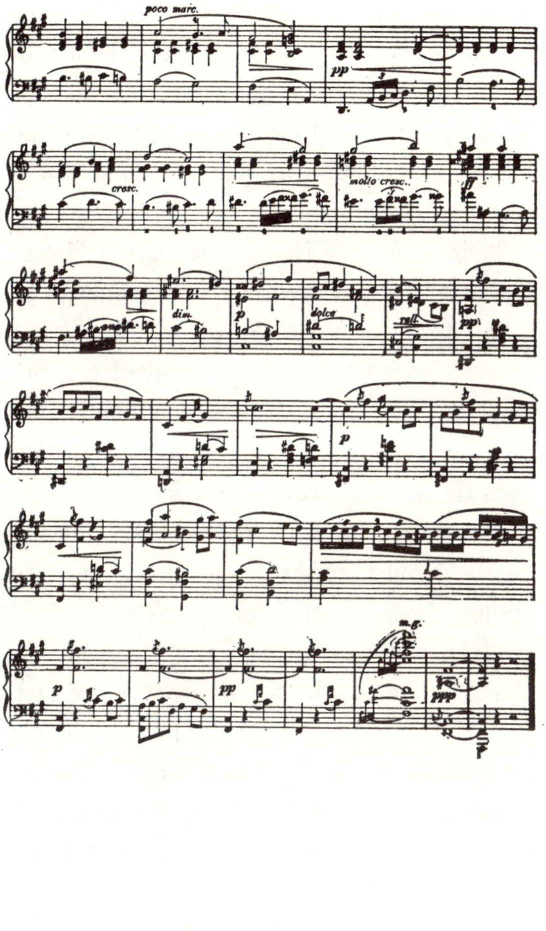
poco marc.
pp
cresc.
molto cresc.
ff
dim.
p
dolce
rall.
pp
p
p
pp
ppp

scherzino, and the like. But for all the classic garb, the hands are the hands of Esau. In one of the pieces there is even a motto tucked, " All hope leave ye behind who enter here ! " Can he have referred to the limbo of classicism ?

It is a far cry from these to the liberality that inspired the new impressionism of " Woodland Sketches " (op. 51) and " Sea Pieces " (op. 55), in which he gives a legitimate musical presentation of a faintly perfumed " Wild Rose " or " Water Lily," but goes farther, and paints, with wonderful tone, the moods inspired by reverie upon the uncouth dignity and stoic savagery of " An Indian Lodge," the lonely New England twilight of " A Deserted Farm," and all the changing humors of the sea, majesty of sunset or star-rise, and even the lucent emerald of an iceberg. His " From Uncle Remus " is not so successful ; indeed, MacDowell is not sympathetic with negro music, and thinks that if we are to found a national school on some local manner, we should find the Indian more congenial than the lazy, sensual slave.

He has carried this belief into action, not only by his scientific interest in the collection and compilation of the folk-music of our prairies, but by his artistic use of actual Indian themes in one of his most important works, his " Indian Suite " for full orchestra, a work that has been often performed, and always with the effect of a new and profound sensation, particularly in the case of the deeply impressive dirge.

A proof of the success of MacDowell as a writer in the large forms is the fact that practically all of his orchestral works are published in Germany and here, not only in full score, but in arrangement for four hands. They include " Hamlet ; " " Ophelia " (op. 22) ; " Launcelot and Elaine " (op. 26), with its strangely mellow and varied use of horns for Launcelot, and the entrusting of the plaintive fate of "the lily maid of Astolat" to the string and wood-wind choirs; "The Saracens" and "The Lovely Alda" (op. 30), two fragments from the Song of Roland; and the Suite (op. 42), which has been played at least eight times in Germany and eleven times here.

The first movement of this last is called "In a Haunted Forest." You are reminded of Siegfried by the very name of the thing, and the music enforces the remembrance somewhat, though very slightly.

Everything reminds one of Wagner nowadays, — even his predecessors. Rudyard Kipling has by his individuality so copyrighted one of the oldest verse-forms, the ballad, that even "Chevy Chace" looks like an advance plagiarism. So it is with Wagner. Almost all later music, and much of the earlier, sounds Wagnerian. But MacDowell has been reminded of Bayreuth very infrequently in this work. The opening move-

ment begins with a *sotto voce* syncopation
that is very presentative of the curious audi-
ble silence of a forest. The wilder moments
are superbly instrumented.

The second movement, "Summer Idyl,"
is delicious, particularly in the chances it
gives the flautist. There is a fragmentary
cantilena which would make the fortune of
a comic opera. The third number, "In October," is particularly welcome in our music,
which is strangely and sadly lacking in
humor. There is fascinating wit throughout this harvest revel. "The Shepherdess'
Song" is the fourth movement. It is not
précieuse, and it is not banal; but its simplicity of pathos is a whit too simple. The
final number, "Forest Spirits," is a brilliant
climax. The Suite as a whole is an important work. It has detail of the most charming art. Best of all, it is staunchly individual.
It is MacDowellian.

While the modern piano sonata is to me

anathema as a rule, there are none of Mac-
Dowell's works that I like better than his
writings in this form. They are to me far
the best since Beethoven, not excepting even
Chopin's (*pace* his greatest prophet, Huneker).
They seem to me to be of such stuff as Beethoven would have woven had he known in
fact the modern piano he saw in fancy.

The "Sonata Tragica" (op. 45) begins in
G minor, with a bigly passionate, slow introduction (metronomed in the composer's copy,
♩-50). The first subject is marked in the
same copy, though not in the printed book,
♩-69, and the appealingly pathetic second
subject is a little slower. The free fantasy is
full of storm and stress, with a fierce pedal-
point on the trilled leading-tone. In the
reprise the second subject, which was at first
in the dominant major, is now in the tonic
major, though the key of the sonata is G
minor. The allegro is metronomed ♩-138,
and it is very short and very wild. Through-

out, the grief is the grief of a strong soul; it never degenerates into whine. Its largo is like the tread of an Æschylean *choros*, its allegro movements are wild with anguish, and the occasional uplifting into the major only emphasizes the sombre whole, like the little rifts of clearer harmony in Beethoven's "Funeral March on the Death of a Hero."

The last movement begins with a ringing *pomposo*, and I cannot explain its meaning better than by quoting Mrs. MacDowell's words: "Mr. MacDowell's idea was, so to speak, as follows: He wished to heighten the darkness of tragedy by making it follow closely on the heels of triumph. Therefore, he attempted to make the last movement a steadily progressive triumph, which, at its climax, is utterly broken and shattered. In doing this he has tried to epitomize the whole work. While in the other movements he aimed at expressing tragic details, in the last he has tried to generalize; thinking that the most poignant tragedy is that of catastrophe in the hour of triumph."

The third sonata (op. 57) is dedicated to Grieg and to the musical exploitation of an old-time Skald reciting glorious battles, loves, and deaths in an ancient castle. The atmosphere of mystery and barbaric grandeur is obtained and sustained by means new to piano literature and potent in color and vigor. The sonata formula is warped to the purpose of the poet, but the themes have the classic ideal of kinship. The battle-power of the work is tremendous. Huneker calls it "an epic of rainbow and thunder," and Henry T. Finck, who has for many years devoted a part of his large ardor to MacDowell's cause, says of the work: "It is MacDowellish, — more MacDowellish than anything he has yet written. It is the work of a musical thinker. There are harmonies as novel as those we encounter in Schubert, Chopin, or Grieg, yet with a stamp of their own."

The " Sonata Eroica " (op. 50) bears the legend " Flos regum Arthurus." It is also in G minor. The spirit of King Arthur dominates the work ideally, and justifies not only the ferocious and warlike first subject with its peculiar and influential rhythm, but the old-fashioned and unadorned folk-tone of the second subject. In the working out there is much bustle and much business of trumpets. In the reprise the folk-song appears in the tonic minor, taken most unconventionally in the bass under elaborate arpeggiations in the right hand. The coda, as in the other sonata, is simply a strong passage of climax. Arthur's supernatural nature doubtless suggested the second movement, with its elfin airs, its flibbertigibbet virtuosity, and its magic of color. The third movement might have been inspired by Tennyson's version of Arthur's farewell to Guinevere, it is such a rich fabric of grief. The finale seems to me to picture the Morte d'Arthur, beginning with the fury of a

storm along the coast, and the battle " on the
waste sand by the waste sea." Moments
of fire are succeeded by exquisite deeps of
quietude, and the death and apotheosis of
Arthur are hinted with daring and complete
equivalence of art with need.

Here is no longer the tinkle and swirl of the
elf dances ; here is no more of the tireless
search for novelty in movement and color.
This is " a flash of the soul that can." Here
is Beethoven *redivivus*. For half a century
we have had so much pioneering and scientific exploration after piano color and tenderness and fire, that men have neglected its
might and its tragic powers. Where is the
piano-piece since Beethoven that has the
depth, the breadth, the height of this huge
solemnity ? Chopin's sensuous wailing does
not afford it. Schumann's complex eccentricities have not given it out. Brahms is too
passionless. Wagner neglected the piano.
It remained for a Yankee to find the austere

peak again! and that, too, when the sonata was supposed to be a form as exhausted as the epic poem. But all this is the praise that one is laughed at for bestowing except on the graves of genius.

The cautious Ben Jonson, when his erstwhile taproom roisterer, Will Shakespeare, was dead, defied "insolent Greece or haughty Rome" to show his superior. With such authority, I feel safe in at least defying the contemporary schools of insolent Russia or haughty Germany to send forth a better musicwright than our fellow townsman, Edward MacDowell.

Edgar Stillman Kelley.[1]

While his name is known wherever American music is known in its better aspects, yet, like many another American, his real art can be discovered only from his manuscripts. In these he shows a very

[1] See p. 485.

munificence of enthusiasm, scholarship, **in-**
vention, humor, and originality.

Kelley is as thorough an American by
descent as one could ask for, his maternal
ancestors having settled in this country in
1630, his paternal progenitors in 1640,
A. D. Indeed, one of the ancestors of his
father made the dies for the pine-tree shil-
ling, and a great-great-grandfather fought in
the Revolution.

Kelley began his terrestrial career April
14, 1857, in Wisconsin. His father was a
revenue officer; his mother a skilled musician, who taught him the piano from his
eighth year to his seventeenth, when he went

EDGAR STILLMAN KELLEY.

to Chicago and studied harmony and counterpoint under Clarence Eddy, and the piano
under Ledochowski. It is interesting to note
that Kelley was diverted into music from
painting by hearing "Blind Tom" play Liszt's
transcription of Mendelssohn's "Midsummer
Night's Dream" music. I imagine that this
idiot-genius had very little other influence of
this sort in his picturesque career.

After two years in Chicago, Kelley went
to Germany, where, in Stuttgart, he studied
the piano with Kruger and Speidel, organ
with Finck, composition and orchestration
with Seiffritz. While in Germany, Kelley
wrote a brilliant and highly successful concert polonaise for four hands, and a composition for strings.

In 1880 he was back in America and
settled in San Francisco, with whose musical
life he was long and prominently identified
as a teacher and critic. Here he wrote his
first large work, the well-known melodramatic

music to "Macbeth." A local benefactor, John Parrot, paid the expenses of a public performance, the great success of which persuaded McKee Rankin, the actor, to make an elaborate production of both play and music. This ran for three weeks in San Francisco to crowded houses, which is a remarkable record for many reasons. A shabby New York production at an ill-chosen theatre failed to give the work an advantageous hearing; but it has been played by orchestras several times since, and William H. Sherwood has made transcriptions of parts of it for piano solo.

The "Macbeth" music is of such solid value that it reaches the dignity of a flowing commentary. Beyond and above this it is an interpretation, making vivid and awesome the deep import of the play, till even the least imaginative auditor must feel its thrill.

Thus the gathering of the witches begins with a slow horror, which is surely Shakespeare's idea, and not the comic-opera *can-can* it is frequently made. As various other elfs and terrors appear, they are appropriately characterized in the music, which also adds mightily to the terror of the murder scene. Throughout, the work is that of a thinker. Like much of Kelley's other music, it is also the work of a fearless and skilled program-matist, especially in the battle-scenes, where it suggests the crash of maces and swords, and the blare of horns, the galloping of horses, and the general din of huge battle. Leading-motives are much used, too, with good effect and most ingenious elaboration, notably the *Banquo* motive. A certain amount of Gaelic color also adds interest to the work, particularly a stirring Gaelic march. The orchestration shows both scholarship and daring.

An interesting subject is suggested by Kelley's experience in hunting out a good motif for the galloping horses of "Macbeth."

He could find nothing suitably representative of storm-hoofed chargers till his dreams came to the rescue with a genuinely inspired theme. Several other exquisite ideas have come to him in his sleep in this way; one of them is set down in the facsimile reproduced herewith. On one occasion he even dreamed an original German poem and a fitting musical setting.

Dr. Wm. A. Hammond, in his book on "Sleep and Its Derangements," is inclined to scout the possibility of a really valuable inspiration in sleep. He finds no satisfactory explanation for Tartini's famous "Devil's Sonata" or Coleridge' proverbial "Kubla Khan." He takes refuge in saying that at least the result could not be equal to the dreamer's capabilities when awake; but Kelley's "Macbeth" music was certainly an improvement on what he could invent out of the land of Nod.

After composing a comic opera, which

was refused by the man for whom it was written because it was too good, he drifted into
journalism, and wrote reviews and critiques
which show a very liberal mind capable
of appreciating things both modern and
classic.

Kelley was again persuaded to write a
comic opera to the artistic libretto, "Puri-
tania," by C. M. S. McLellan, a brilliant
satirist, who has since won fortune by his
highly successful and frequently artistic bur-
lesquery. The work won excellent praise in
Boston, where it had one hundred performances. The work musically was not only
conscientious, but really graceful and captivating. It received the most glowing en-
comiums from people of musical culture, and
largely enhanced Kelley's musical reputation
in its run of something over a year. On its
tour Kelley was also the musical conductor,
in which capacity he has frequently served
elsewhere.

Kelley plainly deserves preëminence among American composers for his devotion to, and skill in, the finer sorts of humorous music. No other American has written so artfully, so happily, or so ambitiously in this field. A humorous symphony and a Chinese suite are his largest works on this order.

The symphony follows the life of " Gulliver in Lilliput." In development and intertwining of themes and in brilliance of orchestration, it maintains symphonic dignity, while in play of fancy, suggestive programmaticism, and rollicking enthusiasm it is infectious with wit. Gulliver himself is richly characterized with a burly, blustering English theme. The storm that throws him on the shores of Lilliput is handled with complete mastery, certain phrases picturing the toss of the billows, another the great roll of the boat, others the rattle of the rigging and the panic of the crew ; and all wrought up to a demoniac climax at the wreck. As the stranded Gulliver falls asleep, the music hints his nodding off graphically. The entrance of the Lilliputians is perhaps the happiest bit of the whole delicious work. By adroit devices in instrumentation, their tiny band toots a minute national hymn of irresistible drollery. The sound of their wee hammers and the rest of the ludicrous adventures are carried off in unfailing good humor. The scene finally changes to the rescuing ship. Here a most hilarious hornpipe is interrupted by the distant call of Gulliver's aria, and the rescue is consummated delightfully.

In nothing has Kelley showed such wanton scholarship and such free-reined fancy as in his Chinese suite for orchestra, " Aladdin." It is certainly one of the most brilliant musical feats of the generation, and rivals Richard Strauss in orchestral virtuosity.

While in San Francisco, where, as every one knows, there is a transplanted corner of China, Kelley sat at the feet of certain Celestial cacophonists, and made himself adept. He fathomed the, to us, obscure laws of their theory, and for this work made a careful selection of Chinese musical ideas, and used what little harmony they approve of with most quaint and suggestive effect upon a splendid background of his own. The result has not been, as is usual in such alien mimicries, a mere success of curiosity.

The work had its first accolade of genius in the wild protests of the music copyists, and in the downright mutiny of orchestral performers.

On the first page of the score is this note : " This should be played with a bow unscrewed, so that the hairs hang loose — thus the bow never leaves the string." This direction is evidently meant to secure the effect of the Chinese violin, in which the string passes between the hair and the wood of the bow, and is played upon the under side. But what self-respecting violinist could endure

such profanation without striking a blow for
his fanes?

The first movement of the suite is made
up of themes actually learned from Chinese
musicians. It represents the "Wedding of
Aladdin and the Princess," a sort of sub-
limated "shivaree" in which oboes quawk,
muted trumpets bray, pizzicato strings flutter, and mandolins (loved of Berlioz) twitter
hilariously.

The second movement, "A Serenade in
the Royal Pear Garden," begins with a lux-
urious tone-poem of moonlight and shadow,
out of which, after a preliminary tuning of
the Chinese lute (or sam-yin), wails a lyric
caterwaul (alternately in 2-4 and 3-4 tempo)
which the Chinese translate as a love-song.
Its amorous grotesque at length subsides into
the majestic night. A part of this altogether
fascinating movement came to Kelley in a
dream.

The third chapter is devoted to the "Flight

of the Genie with the Palace," and there is a wonderfully vivid suggestion of his struggle to wrest loose the foundations of the building. At length he heaves it slowly in the air, and wings majestically away with it.

It has always seemed to me that the purest stroke of genius in instrumentation ever evinced was Wagner's conceit of using tinkling bells to suggest leaping flames. And yet quite comparable with this seems Kelley's device to indicate the oarage of the genie's mighty wings as he disappears into the sky : liquid *glissandos* on the upper harpstrings, with chromatic runs upon the elaborately divided violins, at length changed to sustained and most ethereally fluty harmonics. It is very ravishment.

The last movement, "The Return and Feast of the Lanterns," is on the sonata formula. After an introduction typifying the opening of the temple gates (a gong giving the music further locale), the first theme is announced by harp and mandolin. It is an ancient Chinese air for the yong-kim (a dulcimer-like instrument). The second subject is adapted from the serenade theme. With these two smuggled themes everything contrapuntal (a fugue included) and instrumental is done that technical bravado could suggest or true art license. The result is a carnival of technic that compels the layman to wonder and the scholar to homage.

A transcription for a piano duet has been made of this last movement.

In Chinese-tone also is Kelley's most popular song, "The Lady Picking Mulberries," which brought him not only the enthusiasm of Americans but the high commendation of the Chinese themselves. It is written in the limited Chinese scale, with harmonies of our school; and is a humoresque of such catchiness that it has pervaded even London and Paris.

This song is one of a series of six lyrics

called " The Phases of Love," with this motive
from the " Anatomy of Melancholy : " " I am
resolved, therefore, in this tragi-comedy of
love, to act several parts, some satirically,
some comically, some in a mixed tone." The
poems are all by American poets, and the
group, opus 6, is an invaluable addition to our
musical literature. The first of the series,
" My Silent Song," is a radiantly beautiful
work, with a wondrous tender air to a rapturous accompaniment. The second is a setting
of Edward Rowland Sill's perfect little poem,
" Love's Fillet." The song is as full of art
as it is of feeling and influence. " What the
Man in the Moon Saw " is an engaging satire,
" Love and Sleep " is sombre, and " In a
Garden " is pathetic.

Besides two small sketches, a waltz and a
gavotte, and his own arrangements, for two
and for four hands, of the Gaelic March in
" Macbeth," Kelley has published only three
piano pieces : opus 2, " The Flower Seekers,"

superb with grace, warm harmony, and May ecstasies ; " Confluentia," whose threads of liquidity are eruditely, yet romantically, intertangled to represent the confluence of the Rhine and the Moselle ; and " The Headless Horseman," a masterpiece of burlesque weird ness, representing the wild pursuit of Ichabod Crane and the final hurling of the awful head, — a pumpkin, some say.   It is relieved by Ichabod's tender reminiscences of Katrina Van Tassel at the spinning-wheel, and is dedicated to Joseffy, the pianist, who lives in the region about Sleepy Hollow.

To supplement his successful, humorously melodramatic setting of " The Little Old Woman who Went to the Market her Eggs for to Sell," Kelley is preparing a series of similar pieces called " Tales Retold for Musical Children."   It will include " Gulliver," " Aladdin," and " Beauty and the Beast."

Kelley once wrote music for an adaptation of "Prometheus Bound," made by the late George Parsons Lathrop for that ill-starred experiment, the Theatre of Arts and Letters. The same thoroughness of research that gave Kelley such a command of Chinese theories equipped him in what knowledge we have of Greek and the other ancient music. He has delivered a course of lectures on these subjects, and this learning was put to good and public use in his share in the staging of the novel "Ben Hur." His music had a vital part in carrying the play over the thin ice of sacrilege; it was so reverent and so appealing that the scrubwomen in the theatre were actually moved to tears during its rehearsal, and it gave the scene of the miraculous cure of the lepers a dignity that saved it from either ridicule or reproach.

In the first act there is a suggestion of the slow, soft march of a caravan across the sand, the eleven-toned Greek and Egyptian scale being used. In the tent of the Sheik, an old

Arabian scale is employed. In the elaborate ballets and revels in the " Grove of Daphne " the use of Greek scales, Greek progressions (such as descending parallel fourths long forbidden by the doctors of our era), a trimetrical grouping of measures (instead of our customary fourfold basis), and a suggestion of Hellenic instruments, — all this lore has not robbed the scene in any sense of an irresistible brilliance and spontaneity. The weaving of Arachne's web is pictured with especial power. Greek traditions have, of course, been used only for occasional impressionisms, and not as manacles. Elaborately colored modern instrumentation and all the established devices from canon up are employed. A piano transcription of part of the music is promised. The " Song of Iras " has been published. It is full of home-sickness, and the accompaniment (not used in the production) is a wonderwork of color.

Kelley has two unpublished songs that

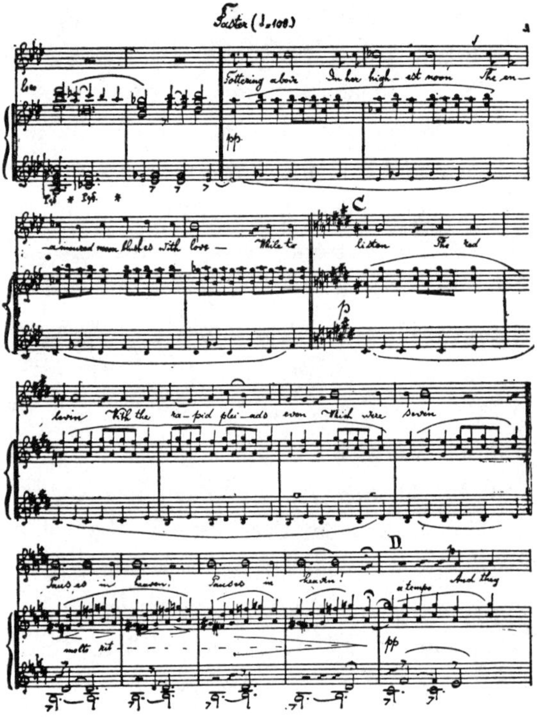

By permission.

FRAGMENT OF "ISRAFEL," BY EDGAR S. KELLEY.

By permission.

show him at his best, both settings of verse
by Poe, — " Eldorado," which vividly develops
the persistence of the knight, and "Israfel."
This latter poem, as you know, concerns the
angel "whose heart-strings are a lute."   After
a rhapsody upon the cosmic spell of the angel's
singing, Poe, with a brave defiance, flings an
implied challenge to him.   The verse marks
one of the highest reaches of a genius honored abroad as a world-great lyrist.   It is,
perhaps, praise enough, then, to say that Kelley's music flags in no wise behind the divine
progress of the words.   The lute idea dictates
an arpeggiated accompaniment, whose harmonic beauty and courage is beyond description and beyond the grasp of the mind at the
first hearing.   The bravery of the climax follows the weird and opiate harmonies of the
middle part with tremendous effect.   The
song is, in my fervent belief, a masterwork
of absolute genius, one of the very greatest
lyrics in the world's music.

Harvey Worthington Loomis.[1]

In the band of pupils that gathered to
the standard of the invader, Antonin Dvôrák,
when, in 1892, he came over here from Mace-
donia to help us, some of the future's best
composers will probably be found.

Of this band was Harvey Worthington
Loomis, who won a three years' scholarship
in Doctor Dvôrák's composition class at the
National Conservatory, by submitting an excellent, but rather uncharacteristic, setting of
Eichendorff's " Frühlingsnacht." Loomis evidently won Doctor Dvôrák's confidence, for
among the tasks imposed on him was a piano
concerto to be built on the lines of so elaborate a model as Rubinstein's in D minor.

[1] See p. 543.

When Loomis' first sketches showed an elaboration even beyond the complex pattern, Dvôrák still advised him to go on. To any one that knows the ways of harmony teachers this will mean much.

Loomis (who was born in Brooklyn, February 5, 1865, and is now a resident of New York) pursued studies in harmony and piano in a desultory way until he entered Doctor Dvôrák's class. For his musical tastes he was indebted to the artistic atmosphere of his home.

Though Loomis has written something over five hundred compositions, only a few works have been published, the most important of which are " Fairy Hill," a cantatilla for children, published in 1896 (it was written on a commission that fortunately allowed him liberty for not a little elaboration and individuality), " Sandalphon," and a few songs and piano pieces.

A field of his art that has won his especial

HARVEY WORTHINGTON LOOMIS.

interest is the use of music as an atmosphere for dramatic expression. Of this sort are a number of pantomimes, produced with much applause in New York by the Academy of Dramatic Arts ; and several musical backgrounds. The 27th of April, 1896, a concert of his works was given by a number of well-known artists.

These musical backgrounds are played in accompaniment to dramatic recitations. Properly managed, the effect is most impressive. Féval's poem, "The Song of the Pear-tree," is a typically handled work. The poem tells the story of a young French fellow, an orphan, who goes to the wars as substitute for his friend Jean. After rising from rank to rank by bravery, he returns to his home just as his sweetheart, Perrine, enters the church to wed Jean. The girl had been his one ambition, and now in his despair he reënlists and begs to be placed in the thickest of danger. When he falls, they find on his breast a withered spray from the pear-tree under which Perrine had first plighted troth. On these simple lines the music builds up a drama. From the opening shimmer and rustle of the garden, through the Gregorian chant that solemnizes the drawing of the lots, and is interrupted by the youth's start of joy at his own luck (an abrupt *glissando*) ; through his sturdy resolve to go to war in his friend's place, on through many battles to his death, all is on a high plane that commands sympathy for the emotion, and enforces unbounded admiration for the art. There is a brief hint of the Marseillaise woven into the finely varied tapestry of martial music, and when the lover comes trudging home, his joy, his sudden knowledge of Perrine's faithlessness, and his overwhelming grief are all built over a long organ-point of three clangorous bride-bells. The *leitmotif* idea is used with suggestive clearness throughout the work.

The background to Longfellow's "Sandalphon" is so fine an arras that it gives the poet a splendor not usual to his bourgeois lays. The music runs through so many phases of emotion, and approves itself so original and exaltedly vivid in each that I put it well to the fore of American compositions.

Hardly less large is the — Loomis calls it "Musical Symbolism," for Adelaide Ann Proctor's "The Story of the Faithful Soul." Of the greatest delicacy imaginable is the music (for piano, violin, and voice) to William Sharp's "Coming of the Prince." The "Watteau Pictures" are poems of Verlaine's variously treated : one as a head-piece to a wayward piano caprice, one to be recited during a picturesque waltz, the last a song with mandolin effects in the accompaniment.

The pantomimes range from grave to gay, most of the librettos in this difficult form being from the clever hand of Edwin Starr

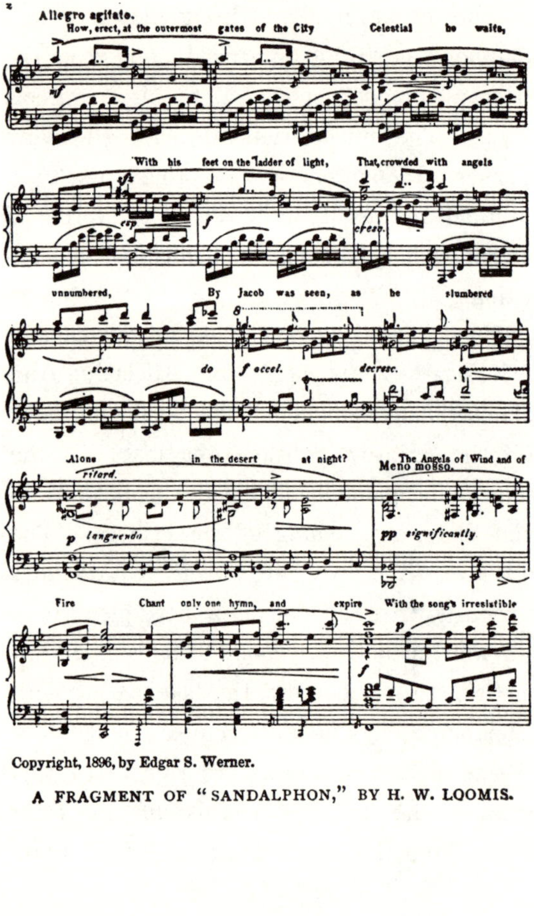

A FRAGMENT OF "SANDALPHON," BY H. W. LOOMIS.

stress, Expire in their rapture and wonder, As harp-strings are broken asunder
dolce
espress.
By music they throb to express. But serene in the rapturous throng, Unmoved
trionfante
by the rush of the song, With eyes unimpassioned and slow, Among the dead
tranquillo
sempre cantabile
tone-sustaining pedal
angels, the deathless Sandalphon stands
listening, breathless, To sounds that ascend from below;
allargando
cresc.
rit.

Belknap. "The Traitor Mandolin," "In Old New Amsterdam," "Put to the Test," "Blanc et Noir," "The Enchanted Fountain," "Her Revenge," "Love and Witchcraft" are their names. The music is full of wit, a quality Loomis possesses in unusual degree. The music mimics everything from the busy feather-duster of the maid to her eavesdropping. Pouring wine, clinking glasses, moving a chair, tearing up a letter, and a rollicking wine-song in pantomime are all hinted with the drollest and most graphic programmism imaginable.

Loomis has also written two burlesque operas, "The Maid of Athens" and "The Burglar's Bride," the libretto of the latter by his brother, Charles Battell Loomis, the well-known humorist. This latter contains some skilful parody on old fogyism.

In the Violin Sonata the piano, while granting precedence to the violin, approaches almost to the dignity of a duet. The finale is captivating and brilliant, and develops some big climaxes. The work as a whole is really superb, and ought to be much played. There are, besides, a "Lyric Finale" to a sonata not yet written, and several songs for violin, voice, and piano.

A suite for four hands, "In Summer Fields," contains some happy manifestations of ability, such as "A June Roundelay," "The Dryad's Grove," and, especially, a humoresque "Junketing," which is surely destined to become a classic. From some of his pantomimes Loomis has made excerpts, and remade them with new elaboration for two pianos, under the name of "Exotics." These are full of variety and of actual novelty, now of startling discord, now of revelatory beauty. A so-called "Norland Epic," freely constructed on the sonata formula, is one of Loomis' most brilliant and personal achievements.

Loomis has an especial aptitude for writing

artistic ballet-music, and for composing in the tone of different nationalities, particularly the Spanish. His pantomimes contain many irresistible dances, one of them including a Chinese dance alternating 4-4 with 3-4 time. His strikingly fleet " Harlequin " has been published.

The gift of adding art to catchiness is a great one. This Loomis seems to have to an unusual degree, as is evidenced by the dances in his pantomimes and his series of six pieces " In Ballet Costume," all of them rich with the finest art along with a Strauss-like spontaneity. These include " L'Amazone," " Pirouette," " Un Pas Seul," " La Coryphée," " The Odalisque," and " The Magyar." One of his largest works is a concert waltz, " Mi-Carême," for two pianos, with elaborate and extended introduction and coda.

A series of Genre Pictures contains such lusciousness of felicity as " At an Italian Festival," and there are a number of musical moments of engaging charm, for instance, "N'Importe Quoi," "From a Conservatory Program," "A Tropical Night," a fascinating "Valsette," a nameless valse, and "Another Scandal," which will prove a gilt-edged speculation for some tardy publisher. It is brimming with the delicious horror of excited gossipry. An example of how thoroughly Loomis is invested with music — how he thinks in it — is his audacious scherzo, "The Town Crier," printed herewith.

In songs Loomis has been most prolific. He has set twenty-two of Shakespeare's lyrics to music of the old English school, such as his uproarious "Let me the cannikin clink," and his dainty "Tell me where is fancy bred."

"The Lark" is written in the pentatonic scale, with accompaniment for two flutes and a harp.

In the same vein are various songs of Herrick, a lyrist whose verse is not usually congenial to the modern music-maker. Loomis' "Epitaph on a Virgin" must be classed as a success.   Indeed, it reaches positive grandeur at its climax, wherein is woven the grim persistence of a tolling bell.   In the same style is a clever setting of Ben Jonson's much music'd "To Celia."

In German-tone are his veritably magnificent "Herbstnacht" and his "At Midnight," two studies after Franz.   Heine's "Des Waldes Kapellmeister" has been made into a most hilarious humoresque.

"Bergerie" is a dozen of Norman Gale's lyrics.   "Andalusia" is a flamboyant duet.

In Scotch songs there is a positive embarrassment of riches, Loomis' fancies finding especial food and freedom in this school.   I find in these settings far more art and grace than I see even in Schumann's many Scotch songs, or those of any other of the Germans. "Oh, for Ane and Twenty" has bagpipe effects.   Such flights of ecstasy as "My

Wife's a Winsome Wee Thing," and "Bonnie Wee Thing," are simply tyrannical in their appeal. Then there is an irresistible "Polly Stewart;" and "My Peggy's Heart" is fairly ambrosial. These and several others, like "There Was a Bonnie Lass," could be made into an album of songs that would delight a whole suite of generations.

A number of his songs are published: they include a "John Anderson, My Jo," that has no particular right to live; a ballad, "Molly," with a touch of art tucked into it; the beautiful "Sylvan Slumbers," and the quaint and fascinating "Dutch Garden."

Aside from an occasional song like "Thistledown," with its brilliantly fleecy accompaniment, and the setting of Browning's famous "The Year' at the Spring," for which Loomis has struck out a superb frenzy, and a group of songs by John Vance Cheney, Loomis has found some of his most powerful inspirations in the work of our lyrist, Aldrich,

—such as the rich carillon of "Wedded," and his "Discipline," one of the best of all humorous songs, a gruesome scherzo all about dead monks, in which the music furnishes out the grim irreverence of the words with the utmost waggery.

Chief among the lyrics by Cheney are three "Spring Songs," in which Loomis has caught the zest of spring with such rapture that, once they are heard, the world seems poor without them in print.   Loomis' literary culture is shown in the sure taste of his selection of lyrics for his music.   He has marked aptitudes, too, in creative literature, and has an excellent idea of the arts kindred to his own, particularly architecture.

Like Chopin, Loomis is largely occupied in mixing rich new colors on the inexhaustible palette of the piano.   Like Chopin, he is not especially called to the orchestra.   What the future may hold for him in this field (by no means so indispensable to classic repute as certain pedants assume) it is impossible to say. In the meantime he is giving most of his time to work in larger forms.

If in his restless hunt for novelty, always novelty, he grows too original, too unconventional, this sin is unusual enough to approach the estate of a virtue. But his oddity is not mere sensation-mongering. It is his individuality. He could make the same reply to such criticism that Schumann made; he thinks in strange rhythms and hunts curious effects, because his tastes are irrevocably so ordained.

But we ought to show a new genius the same generosity toward flaws that we extend toward the masters whose fame is won beyond the patronage of our petty forgiveness. And, all in all, I am impelled to prophesy to Loomis a place very high among the inspired makers of new music. His harmonies, so indefatigably searched out and polished to splendor, so potent in enlarging the color-scale of the piano ; his patient building up, through long neglect and through long silence, of a monumental group of works and of a distinct individuality, must prove at some late day a source of lasting pride to his country, neglectful now in spite of itself.   But better than his patience, than his courage, than his sincerity, better than that insufficient definition of genius, — the capacity for taking infinite pains, — is his inspired felicity.   His genius is the very essence of felicity.

Ethelbert Nevin.

It is refreshing to be able to chronicle the achievements of a composer who has become financially successful without destroying his claim on the respect of the learned and severe, or sacrificing his own artistic conscience and individuality.   Such a composer is Ethelbert Nevin.

His published writings have been altogether

ETHELBERT NEVIN.

along the smaller lines of composition, and he
has won an enviable place as a fervent worker
in diamonds.   None of his gems are paste,
and a few have a perfection, a solidity, and a
fire that fit them for a place in that coronet
one might fancy made up of the richest of

the jewels of the world's music-makers, and
fashioned for the very brows of the Muse
herself.

Nevin was born in 1862, at Vineacre, on
the banks of the Ohio, a few miles from Pittsburgh.   There he spent the first sixteen years
of his life, and received all his schooling,

most of it from his father, Robert P. Nevin, editor and proprietor of a Pittsburgh newspaper, and a contributor to many magazines. It is interesting to note that he also composed several campaign songs, among them the popular " Our Nominee," used in the day of James K. Polk's candidacy. The first grand piano ever taken across the Allegheny Mountains was carted over for Nevin's mother.

From his earliest infancy Nevin was musically inclined, and, at the age of four, was often taken from his cradle to play for admiring visitors. To make up for the deficiency of his little legs, he used to pile cushions on the pedals so that he might manipulate them from afar.

Nevin's father provided for his son both vocal and instrumental instruction, even taking him abroad for two years of travel and music study in Dresden under Von Böhme. Later he studied the piano for two years at

Boston, under B. J. Lang, and composition under Stephen A. Emery, whose little primer on harmony has been to American music almost what Webster's spelling-book was to our letters.

At the end of two years he went to Pittsburgh, where he gave lessons, and saved money enough to take him to Berlin. There he spent the years 1884, 1885, and 1886, placing himself in the hands of Karl Klindworth. Of him Nevin says : "To Herr Klindworth I owe everything that has come to me in my musical life. He was a devoted teacher, and his patience was tireless. His endeavor was not only to develop the student from a musical standpoint, but to enlarge his soul in every way. To do this, he tried to teach one to appreciate and to feel the influence of such great minds of literature as Goethe, Schiller, and Shakespeare. He used to insist that a man does not become a musician by practising so many hours a day at the piano, but by absorbing an influence from all the arts and all the interests of life, from architecture, painting, and even politics."

The effect of such broad training — enjoyed rarely enough by music students — is very evident in Nevin's compositions. They are never narrow or provincial. They are the outpourings of a soul that is not only intense in its activities, but is refined and cultivated in its expressions. This effect is seen, too, in the poems Nevin chooses to set to music, — they are almost without exception verses of literary finish and value. His cosmopolitanism is also remarkable, his songs in French, German, and Italian having no trace of Yankee accent and a great fidelity to their several races.

In 1885, Hans von Bülow incorporated the best four pupils of his friend, Klindworth, into an artist class, which he drilled personally. Nevin was one of the honored four, and appeared at the unique public *Zuhören* of that year, devoted exclusively to the works of Brahms, Liszt, and Raff. Among the forty or fifty studious listeners at these recitals, Frau Cosima Wagner, the violinist Joachim, and many other celebrities were frequently present.

Nevin returned to America in 1887, and took up his residence in Boston, where he taught and played at occasional concerts.

Eighteen hundred and ninety-two found him in Paris, where he taught, winning more pupils than here. He was especially happy in imparting to singers the proper *Auffassung* (grasp, interpretation, finish) of songs, and coached many American and French artists for the operatic stage. In 1893 the restless troubadour moved on to Berlin, where he devoted himself so ardently to composition that his health collapsed, and he was exiled a year to Algiers. The early months of 1895 he spent in concert tours through this country. As Klindworth said of him, "he has a touch that brings tears," and it is in interpretation rather than in bravura that he excels. He plays with that unusual combination of elegance and fervor that so individualizes his composition.

Desirous of finding solitude and atmosphere for composition, he took up his residence in Florence, where he composed his suite, "May in Tuscany" (op. 21). The "Arlecchino" of this work has much sprightliness, and shows the influence of Schumann, who made the harlequin particularly his own ; but there is none of Chopin's nocturnity in the "Notturno," which presents the sussurus and the moonlit, amorous company of "Boccacio's Villa." The suite includes a "Misericordia" depicting a midnight cortège along the Arno, and modelled on Chopin's funeral march in structure with its hoarse dirge and its rich cantilena. The best number of the suite is surely the "Rusignuolo," an exceedingly fluty bird-song.

From Florence, Nevin went to Venice, where he lived in an old *casa* on the Grand Canal, opposite the Browning palazzo, and near the house where Wagner wrote " Tristan und Isolde." One day his man, Guido, took a day off, and brought to Venice an Italian sweetheart, who had lived a few miles from the old dream-city and had never visited it. The day these two spent gondoliering through the waterways, where romance hides in every nook, is imaginatively narrated in tone in Nevin's suite, " Un Giorno in Venezia," a book more handsomely published even than the others of his works, which have been among the earliest to throw off the disgraceful weeds of type and design formerly worn by native compositions.

The Venetian suite gains a distinctly Italian color from its ingenuously sweet harmonies in thirds and sixths, and its frankly lyric nature, and " The Day in Venice " begins logically with the dawn, which is ushered

in with pink and stealthy harmonies, then
"The Gondoliers" have a morning mood of
gaiety that makes a charming composition.
There is a "Canzone Amorosa" of deep fervor, with interjections of "Io t'amo!" and
"Amore" (which has the excellent authority
of Beethoven's Sonata, op. 81, with its "Lebe
wohl"). The suite ends deliciously with a
night scene in Venice, beginning with a choral
"Ave Maria," and ending with a campanella
of the utmost delicacy.

After a year in Venice Nevin made Paris
his home for a year, returning to America
then, where he has since remained.

Though he has dabbled somewhat in orchestration, he has been wisely devoting his
genius, with an almost Chopin-like singleness
of mind, to songs and piano pieces. His
piano works are what would be called *morceaux*. He has never written a sonata, or
anything approaching the classical forms,
nearer than a gavotte or two. He is very

modern in his harmonies, the favorite colors on his palette being the warmer keys, which are constantly blended enharmonically. He "swims in a sea of tone," being particularly fond of those suspensions and inversions in which the intervals of the second clash passionately, strongly compelling resolution. For all his gracefulness and lyricism, he makes a sturdy and constant use of dissonance; in his song "Herbstgefühl" the dissonance is fearlessly defiant of conventions.

Nevin's songs, whose only littleness is in their length, though treated with notable individuality, are founded in principle on the *Lieder* of Schumann and Franz. That is to say, they are written with a high poetical feeling inspired by the verses they sing, and, while melodious enough to justify them as lyrics, yet are near enough to impassioned recitative to do justice to the words on which they are built. Nevin is also an enthusi-

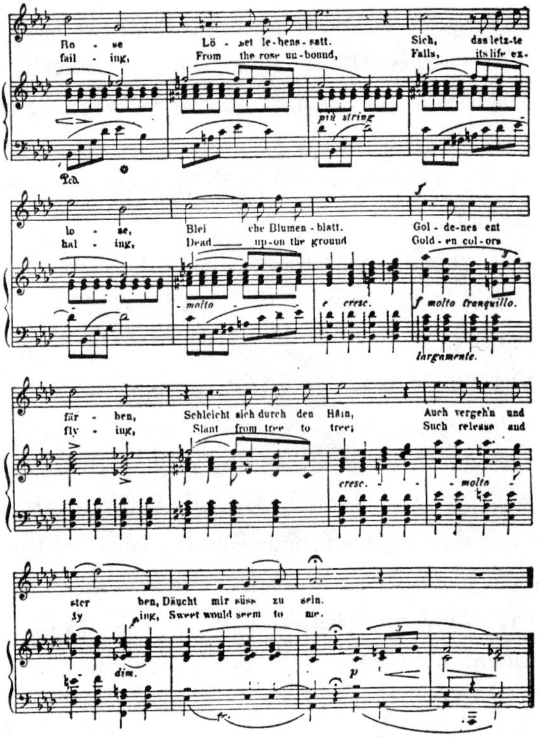

A FRAGMENT FROM "HERBSTGEFÜHL."

astic devotee of the position these masters,
after Schubert, took on the question of the
accompaniment. This is no longer a slavish
thumping of a few chords, now and then, to
keep the voice on the key, with outbursts
of real expression only at the interludes ; but
it is a free instrumental composition with a
meaning of its own and an integral value,
truly accompanying, not merely supporting
and serving, the voice. Indeed, one of
Nevin's best songs, — " Lehn deine Wang an
meine Wang," — is actually little more than
a vocal accompaniment to a piano solo. His
accompaniments are always richly colored
and generally individualized with a strong
contramelody, a descending chromatic scale
in octaves making an especially frequent
appearance. Design, though not classical,
is always present and distinct.

Nevin's first published work was a modest
" Serenade," with a neat touch of syncopation, which he wrote at the age of eighteen.

His "Sketch-Book," a collection of thirteen songs and piano pieces found an immediate and remarkable sale that has removed the ban formerly existing over books of native compositions.

The contents of the "Sketch-Book" display unusual versatility. It opens with a bright gavotte, in which adherence to the classic spirit compels a certain reminiscence of tone. The second piece, a song, "I' the Wondrous Month o' May," has such a spring-tide fire and frenzy in the turbulent accompaniment, and such a fervent reiterance, that it becomes, in my opinion, the best of all the settings of this poem of Heine's, not excluding even Schumann's or that of Franz. The "Love Song," though a piano solo, is in reality a duet between two lovers. It is to me finer than Henselt's perfect "Liebeslied," possibly because the ravishing sweetness of the woman's voice answering the sombre plea of the man gives it a double claim on the heart. The setting of " Du bist wie eine Blume," however, hardly does justice either to Heine's poem, or to Nevin's art. The " Serenade " is an original bit of work, but the song, " Oh, that We Two were Maying ! " with a voice in the accompaniment making it the duet it should be, — that song can have no higher praise than this, that it is the complete, the final musical fulfilment of one of the rarest lyrics in our language. A striking contrast to the keen white regret of this song is the setting of a group of " Children's Songs," by Robert Louis Stevenson. Nevin's child-songs have a peculiar and charming place. He has not been stingy of either his abundant art or his abundant humanity in writing them. They include four of Stevenson's, the best being the captivating " In Winter I get up at Night," and a setting of Eugene Field's " Little Boy Blue," in which a trumpet figure is used with delicate pathos.

Nevin's third opus included three exquisite songs of a pastoral nature, Goethe's rollicking " One Spring Morning " having an immense sale. Opus 5 contained five songs, of which the ecstatic " 'Twas April " reached the largest popularity. Possibly the smallest sale was enjoyed by " Herbstgefühl." Many years have not availed to shake my allegiance to this song, as one of the noblest songs in the world's music. It is to me, in all soberness, as great as the greatest of the *Lieder* of Schubert, Schumann or Franz. In " Herbstgefühl " (or " Autumn-mood ") Gerok's superb poem bewails the death of the leaves and the failing of the year, and cries out in sympathy :

> " Such release and dying
> Sweet would seem to me ! "

Deeper passion and wilder despair could not be crowded into so short a song, and the whole brief tragedy is wrought with a grandeur and climax positively epic. It is a flash of sheer genius.

Three piano duets make up opus 5; and other charming works, songs, piano pieces, and violin solos, kept pouring from a pen whose apparent ease concealed a vast deal of studious labor, until the lucky 13, the opus-number of a bundle of "Water Scenes," brought Nevin the greatest popularity of all, thanks largely to "Narcissus," which has been as much thrummed and whistled as any topical song.

Of the other "Water Scenes," there is a shimmering "Dragon Fly," a monody, "Ophelia," with a pedal-point of two periods on the tonic, and a fluent "Barcarolle" with a deal of high-colored virtuosity.

His book "In Arcady" (1892) contains pastoral scenes, notably an infectious romp that deserves its legend, "They danced as though they never would grow old. The next year his opus 20, "A Book of Songs," was published. It contains, among other things of merit, a lullaby, called " Sleep, Little Tulip," with a remarkably artistic and effective pedal-point on two notes (the sub-mediant and the dominant) sustained through the entire song with a fine fidelity to the words and the lullaby spirit ; a " Nocturne " in which Nevin has revealed an unsuspected voluptuousness in Mr. Aldrich' little lyric, and has written a song of irresistible climaxes. The two songs, " Dîtes-Moi " and " In der Nacht," each so completely true to the idiom of the language of its poem, are typical of Nevin's cosmopolitanism, referred to before. This same unusual ability is seen in his piano pieces as well as in his songs. He knows the difference between a *chanson* and a *Lied*, and in " Rechte Zeit " has written with truth to German soldierliness as he has been sympathetic with French nuance in "Le Vase Brisé," the effective song "Mon Desire," which in profile suggests Saint-Säens' familiar

Delilah-song, the striking " Chanson des Lavandières" and " Rapelle-Toi," one of Nevin's most elaborate works, in which Alfred De Musset's verse is splendidly set with much enharmonious color. Very Italian, too, is the " Serenade" with accompaniment à la mandolin, which is the most fetching number in the suite " Captive Memories," published in 1899.

Nevin has also put many an English song to music, notably the deeply sincere " At Twilight," the strenuous lilt " In a Bower," Bourdillon's beautiful lyric, " Before the Day-break," the smooth and unhackneyed treatment of the difficult stanza of " 'Twas April," that popular song, " One Spring Morning," which has not yet had all the charm sung out of it, and two songs with obbligati for violin and 'cello, " Deep in the Rose's Glowing Heart" and " Doris," a song with a finely studied accompaniment and an aroma of Theokritos.

A suite for the piano is "En Passant," published in 1899; it ranges from a stately old dance, "At Fontainebleau," to "Napoli," a furious tarantelle with effective *glissandi;* "In Dreamland" is a most delicious revery with an odd repetition that is not preludatory, but thematic. The suite ends with the most poetic scene of all, "At Home," which makes a tone poem of Richard Hovey's word-picture of a June night in Washington. The depicting of the Southern moonlight-balm, with its interlude of a distant and drowsy negro quartette, reminds one pleasantly of Chopin's Nocturne (op. 37, No. 1), with its intermezzo of choric monks, though the composition is Nevin's very own in spirit and treatment.

In addition to the works catalogued, Nevin has written a pantomime for piano and orchestra to the libretto of that virtuoso in English, Vance Thompson; it was called "Lady Floriane's Dream," and was given in

New York in 1898. Nevin has also a cantata in making.

It needs no very intimate acquaintance with Nevin's music to see that it is not based on an adoration for counterpoint as an end. He believes that true music must come from the emotions — the intelligent emotions — and that when it cannot appeal to the emotions it has lost its power. He says : " Above everything we need melody — melody and rhythm. Rhythm is the great thing. We have it in Nature. The trees sway, and our steps keep time, and our very souls respond." In Wagner's " Meistersinger," which he calls "a symphonic poem with action," Nevin finds his musical creed and his model.

And now, if authority is needed for all this frankly enthusiastic admiration, let it be found in and echoed from Karl Klindworth, who said of Nevin : " His talent is *ungeheures* [one of the strongest adjectives in the German language]. If he works hard and is conscien-

tious, he can say for the musical world something that no one else can say."

John Philip Sousa.

In common with most of those that pretend
to love serious music, a certain person was
for long guilty of the pitiful snobbery of
rating march-tunes as the lowest form of the
art. But one day he joined a National Guard
regiment, and his first long march was that

JOHN PHILIP SOUSA.

heart-breaking dress-parade of about fifteen miles through the wind and dust of the day Grant's monument was dedicated. Most of the music played by the band was merely rhythmical embroidery, chiefly in bugle figures, as helpful as a Clementi sonatina ; but now and then there would break forth a magic elixir of tune that fairly plucked his feet up for him, put marrow in unwilling bones, and replaced the dreary doggedness of the heart with a great zest for progress, a stout martial fire, and a fierce *esprit de corps ;* with patriotism indeed. In almost every case, that march belonged to one John Philip Sousa.

It came upon this wretch then, that, if it is a worthy ambition in a composer to give voice to passionate love-ditties, or vague contemplation, or the deep despair of a funeral cortège, it is also a very great thing to instil courage, and furnish an inspiration that will send men gladly, proudly, and gloriously through hardships into battle and death. This last has been the office of the march-tune, and it is as susceptible of structural logic or embellishments as the fugue, rondo, or what not. These architectural qualities Sousa's marches have in high degree, as any one will find that examines their scores or listens analytically. They have the further merit of distinct individuality, and the supreme merit of founding a school.

It is only the plain truth to say that Sousa's marches have founded a school; that he has indeed revolutionized march-music. His career resembles that of Johann Strauss in many ways. A certain body of old fogies has always presumed to deride the rapturous waltzes of Strauss, though they have won enthusiastic praise from even the esoteric Brahms, and gained from Wagner such words as these : "One Strauss waltz overshadows, in respect to animation, finesse, and real musical worth, most of the mechanical, borrowed, factory-made products of the present time." The same words might be applied to Sousa's marches with equal justice. They have served also for dance music, and the two-step, borne into vogue by Sousa's music, has driven the waltz almost into desuetude.

There is probably no composer in the world with a popularity equal to that of Sousa. Though he sold his "Washington Post" march outright for $35, his "Liberty Bell" march is said to have brought him $35,000. It is found that his music has been sold to eighteen thousand bands in the United States alone. The amazing thing is to learn that there are so many bands in the country. Sousa's marches have appeared on programs in all parts of the civilized world. At the Queen's Jubilee, when the Queen stepped forward to begin the grand review of the troops, the combined bands of the household brigade struck up the "Washington Post." On other important occasions it appeared constantly as the chief march of the week. General Miles heard the marches played in Turkey by the military bands in the reviews.

The reason for this overwhelming appeal to the hearts of a planet is not far to seek. The music is conceived in a spirit of high martial zest. It is proud and gay and fierce, thrilled and thrilling with triumph. Like all great music it is made up of simple elements, woven together by a strong personality. It is not difficult now to write something that sounds more or less like a Sousa march, any more than it is difficult to write parodies, serious or otherwise, on Beethoven, Mozart, or Chopin. The glory of Sousa is that he was the first to write in this style ; that he has made himself a style ; that he has so stirred the musical world that countless imitations have sprung up after him.

The individuality of the Sousa march is this, that, unlike most of the other influential marches, it is not so much a musical exhortation from without, as a distillation of the essences of soldiering from within. Sousa's marches are not based upon music-room enthusiasms, but on his own wide experiences of the feelings of men who march together in the open field.

And so his band music expresses all the nuances of the military psychology : the exhilaration of the •long unisonal stride, the grip on the musket, the pride in the regimentals and the regiment, — *esprit de corps.* He expresses the inevitable foppery of the severest soldier, the tease and the taunt of the evolutions, the fierce wish that all this ploying and deploying were in the face of an actual enemy, the mania to reek upon a tangible foe all the joyous energy, the bloodthirst of the warrior.

These things Sousa embodies in his music as no other music writer ever has. To approach Sousa's work in the right mood, the music critic must leave his stuffy concert hall and his sober black; he must flee from the press, don a uniform, and march.   After his legs and spirits have grown aweary under the metronomic tunes of others, let him note the surge of blood in his heart and the rejuvenation of all his muscles when the brasses flare into a barbaric Sousa march.   No man that marches can ever feel anything but gratitude and homage for Sousa.

Of course he is a trickster at times; admitted that he stoops to conquer at times, yet in his field he is supreme.   He is worthy of serious consideration, because his thematic material is almost always novel and forceful, and his instrumentation full of contrast and climax.   He is not to be judged by the piano versions of his works, because they are abominably thin and inadequate, and they are not *klaviermaessig.*   There should be a Liszt or a Taussig to transcribe him.

When all's said and done, Sousa is the

pulse of the nation, and in war of more inspiration and power to our armies than ten colonels with ten braw regiments behind them.

Like Strauss', Mr. Sousa's father was a musician who forbade his son to devote himself to dance music. As Strauss' mother enabled him secretly to work out his own salvation, so did Sousa's mother help him. Sousa's father was a political exile from Spain, and earned a precarious livelihood by playing a trombone in the very band at Washington which later became his son's stepping-stone to fame. Sousa was born at Washington in 1859. His mother is German, and Sousa's music shows the effect of Spanish yeast in sturdy German rye bread. Sousa's teachers were John Esputa and George Felix Benkert. The latter Mr. Sousa considers one of the most complete musicians this country has ever known. He put him through such a thorough theoretical training, that at fifteen Sousa was teaching harmony. At eight he had begun to earn his own living as a violin player at a dancing-school, and at ten he was a public soloist. At sixteen he was the conductor of an orchestra in a variety theatre. Two years later he was musical director of a travelling company in Mr. Milton Nobles' well-known play, " The Phœnix," for which he composed the incidental music. Among other incidents in a career of growing importance was a position in the orchestra with which Offenbach toured this country. At the age of twenty-six, after having played, with face blacked, as a negro minstrel, after travelling with the late Matt Morgan's Living Picture Company, and working his way through and above other such experiences in the struggle for life, Sousa became the leader of the United States Marine Band. In the twelve years of his leadership he developed this unimportant organization into one of the best military bands in the world.

In 1892 his leadership had given him such fame that he withdrew from the government service to take the leadership of the band carrying his own name.

A work of enormous industry was his collection and arrangement, by governmental order, of the national and typical tunes of all nations into one volume, an invaluable book of reference.

Out of the more than two hundred published compositions by Sousa, it is not possible to mention many here. Though some of the names are not happily chosen, they call up many episodes of parade gaiety and jauntiness, or warlike fire. The " Liberty Bell," " Directorate," " High School Cadets," "King Cotton," "Manhattan Beach," "'Sound Off!'" "Washington Post," " Picador," and others, are all stirring works ; his best, I think, is a deeply patriotic march, "The Stars and Stripes Forever." The second part of this has some brass work of particular originality and vim.

In manuscript are a few works of larger form: a symphonic poem, "The Chariot Race," an historical scene, "Sheridan's Ride," and two suites, "Three Quotations" and "The Last Days of Pompeii."

The "Three Quotations" are:

(*a*) "The King of France, with twenty thousand men,
      Marched up a hill and then marched down
      again,"

which is the motive for a delightful scherzo-march of much humor in instrumentation;

(*b*) "And I, too, was born in Arcadia,"

which is a pastorale with delicious touches of extreme delicacy;

(*c*) "In Darkest Africa,"

which has a stunning beginning and is a stirring grotesque in the negro manner Dvôràk advised Americans to cultivate. All three are well arranged for the piano.

The second suite is based on "The Last

Days of Pompeii." It opens with a drunken
revel, "In the House of Burbo and Strato-
nice;" the bulky brutishness of the gladiators
clamoring for wine, a jolly drinking-song,
and a dance by a jingling clown make up a
superbly written number. The second movement is named "Nydia," and represents the
pathetic reveries of the blind girl; it is tender
and quiet throughout.

The third movement is at once daring and
masterly. It boldly attacks "The Destruction," and attains real heights of graphic suggestion. A long, almost inaudible roll on
the drums, with occasional thuds, heralds the
coming of the earthquake; subterranean
rumblings, sharp rushes of tremor, toppling
stones, and wild panic are insinuated vividly,
with no cheap attempts at actual imitation.
The roaring of the terrified lion is heard, and,
best touch of all, under the fury of the scene
persists the calm chant of the Nazarenes,
written in one of the ancient modes. The

rout gives way to the sea-voyage of Glaucus and Ione, and Nydia's swan-song dies away in the gentle splash of ripples. The work is altogether one of superb imagination and scholarly achievement.

Sousa, appealing as he does to an audience chiefly of the popular sort, makes frequent use of devices shocking to the conventional. But even in this he is impelled by the enthusiasm of an experimenter and a developer. Almost every unconventional novelty is hooted at in the arts. But the sensationalism of to-day is the conservatism of to-morrow, and the chief difference between a touch of high art and a trick is that the former succeeds and the latter does not. Both are likely to have a common origin.

The good thing is that Sousa is actuated by the spirit of progress and experiment, and has carried on the development of the military band begun by the late Patrick S. Gilmore. Sousa's concert programs devote what is in fact the greater part of their space to music by the very best composers. These, of course, lose something in being translated over to the military band, but their effect in raising the popular standard of musical culture cannot but be immense. Through such instrumentality much of Wagner is as truly popular as any music played. The active agents of such a result should receive the heartiest support from every one sincerely interested in turning the people toward the best things in music. Incidentally, it is well to admit that while a cheap march-tune is almost as trashy as an uninspired symphony, a good march-tune is one of the best things in the best music.

Though chiefly known as a writer of marches, in which he has won glory enough for the average human ambition, Sousa has also taken a large place in American comic opera. His first piece, "The Smugglers," was produced in 1879, and scored the usual failure of a first work. His "Katherine" was never produced, his "Desirée" was brought out in 1884 by the McCaull Opera Company, and his "Queen of Hearts," a one-act piece, was given two years later. He forsook opera then for ten years; but in 1896 De Wolf Hopper produced his " El Capitan " with great success.

The chief tune of the piece was a march used with Meyerbeerian effectiveness to bring down the curtain. The stout verve of this " El Capitan " march gave it a large vogue outside the opera. Hopper next produced "The Charlatan," a work bordering upon opéra comique in its first version. Both of these works scored even larger success in London than at home.

In "The Bride Elect," Sousa wrote his own libretto, and while there was the usual stirring march as the pièce de resistance, the work as a whole was less clangorous of the cymbal than the operas of many a tamer com-

Used by permission of the John Church Company, owners of the copyright.

A PAGE FROM "EL CAPITAN," BY JOHN PHILIP SOUSA.

poser. In " Chris and the Wonderful Lamp," an extravaganza, the chief ensemble was worked up from a previous march, " Hands Across the Sea."

But Sousa can write other things than marches, and his scoring is full of variety, freedom, and contrapuntal brilliance.

Henry Schoenefeld.[1]

Long before Dvôrák discovered America, we aboriginals had been trying to invent a national musical dialect which should identify us as completely to the foreigner as our nasal intonation and our fondness for the correct and venerable use of the word "guess." But Dvôrák is to credit for taking the problem off the shelf, and persuading our composers to think. I cannot coax myself into the enthusiasm some have felt for Dvôrák's own explorations in darkest Africa. His quartette (op. 96) and his " New World " symphony are

[1] See p. 493.

HENRY SCHOENEFELD.

about as full of accent and infidelity as Mlle.
Yvette Guilbert's picturesque efforts to sing
in English. But almost anything is better
than the phlegm that says, "The old ways are
good enough for all time;" and the Bohemian
missionary must always hold a place in the
chronicle of American music.

A disciple of Dvôrák's, both in advance and
in retrospect, is Henry Schoenefeld, who
wrote a characteristic suite (op. 15) before the
Dvôrákian invasion, and an overture, "In the
Sunny South," afterward. The suite, which
has been played frequently abroad, winning
the praises of Hanslick, Nicodé, and Rubinstein, is scored for string orchestra. It opens
with an overly reminiscent waltz-tune, and
ends conventionally, but it contains a movement in negro-tone that gives it importance.
In this the strings are abetted by a tambourine, a triangle, and a gong. It is in march-
time, and, after a staccato prelude, begins
with a catchy air taken by the second violins,

while the firsts, divided, fill up the chords.
A slower theme follows in the tonic major;
it is a jollificational air, dancing from the first
violins with a bright use of harmonics. Two
periods of loud chorale appear with the gong
clanging (to hint a church-bell, perhaps). The
first two themes return and end the picture.

The overture (op. 22) has won the high
esteem of A. J. Goodrich, and it seems to
me to be one of the most important of native
works, not because of its nigrescence, but
because of its spontaneity therein. It adds
to the usual instruments only the piccolo,
the English horn, the tambourine, and triangle and cymbals. The slow introduction
gives forth an original theme in the most
approved and most fetching darky pattern.
The strings announce it, and the wood re-
plies. The flutes and clarinets toss it in a
blanket furnished by an interesting passage
in the cellos and contrabasses. There is a
choral moment from the English horn, the

bassoons, and a clarinet. This solemn thought keeps recurring parenthetically through the general gaiety. The first subject clatters in, the second is even more jubilant. In the development a dance *misterioso* is used with faithful screaming repetitions, and the work ends regularly and brilliantly. There is much syncopation, though nothing that is strictly in "rag-time;" banjo-figurations are freely and ingeniously employed, and the whole is a splendid fiction in local color. Schoenefeld's negroes do not speak Bohemian.

His determined nationalism is responsible for his festival overture, "The American Flag," based on his own setting of Rodman Drake's familiar poem. The work opens with the hymn blaring loudly from the antiphonal brass and wood. The subjects are taken from it with much thematic skill, and handled artfully, but the hymn, which appears in full force for coda, is as trite as the most of its kith.

Schoenefeld was born in Milwaukee, in 1857. His father was a musician, and his teacher for some years. At the age of seventeen Schoenefeld went to Leipzig, where he spent three years, studying under Reinecke, Coccius, Papperitz, and Grill. A large choral and orchestral work was awarded a prize over many competitors, and performed at the Gewandhaus concerts, the composer conducting. Thereafter he went to Weimar, where he studied under Edward Lassen.

In 1879 he came back to America, and took up his residence in Chicago, where he has since lived as a teacher, orchestra leader, and composer. He has for many years directed the Germania Männerchor.

Schoenefeld's "Rural Symphony" was awarded the $500 prize offered by the National Conservatory. Dvôrák was the chairman of the Committee on Award, and gave Schoenefeld hearty compliments. Later works are : "Die drei Indianer," an ode for male chorus, solo, and orchestra; a most beautiful "Air" for orchestra (the air being taken by most of the strings, — the first violins haunting the G string, — while a harp and three flutes carry the burden of the accompaniment gracefully); a pleasant "Reverie" for string orchestra, harp, and organ; and two impromptus for string orchestra, a "Meditation" representing Cordelia brooding tenderly over the slumbering King Lear, — art ministering very tenderly to the mood, — and a cleverly woven "Valse Noble."

Only a few of Schoenefeld's works are published, all of them piano pieces. It is no slur upon his orchestral glory to say that these are for the most part unimportant, except the excellent "Impromptu" and "Prelude." Of the eight numbers in "The Festival," for children, only the "Mazurka" is likely to make even the smallest child think. The "Kleine Tanz Suite" is better. The six children's pieces of opus 41, "Mysteries of the Wood," make considerable appeal to the fancy and imagination, and are highly interesting. They show Grieg's influence very plainly, and are quite worth recommending. This cannot be said of his most inelegant " Valse Élégante," or of his numerous dances, except, perhaps, his " Valse Caprice."

He won in July, 1899, the prize offered to American composers by Henri Marteau, for a sonata for violin and piano. The jury was composed of such men as Dubois, Pierné, Diemer, and Pugno. The sonata is *quasi fantasia*, and begins strongly with an evident intention to make use of negro-tone. The first subject is so vigorously declared that one is surprised to find that it is elastic enough to express a sweet pathos and a deep gloom. It is rather fully developed before the second subject enters ; this, on the other hand, is hardly insinuated ·in its relative major before the rather inelaborate elaboration begins. In the romanza, syncopation and imitation are much relied on, though the general atmosphere is that of a nocturne, a trio of dance-like manner breaking in. The final rondo combines a clog with a choral intermezzo. The work is noteworthy for its deep sincerity and great lyric beauty.

Maurice Arnold.

The plantation dances of Maurice Arnold have an intrinsic interest quite aside from their intrinsic value. Arnold, whose full name is Maurice Arnold-Strothotte, was born in St. Louis in 1865. His mother was a prominent pianist and gave him his first lessons in music. At the age of fifteen he went to Cincinnati, studying at the College of Music for three years. In 1883 he went to Germany to study counterpoint and composition with Vierling and Urban in Berlin. The latter discouraged him when he attempted to imbue a suite with a negro plantation spirit.

Arnold now went upon a tramping tour in Hungary, Bulgaria, and Turkey. Some of his compositions show the influence of his journey. He then entered the Cologne Conservatory, studying under Wuellner, Neitzel, and G. Jensen. His first piano sonata was performed there at a public concert. He next went to Breslau, where, under the instruction of Max Bruch, he wrote his cantata, "The Wild Chase," and gave public performance to other orchestral work. Returning now to St. Louis, he busied himself as solo violinist and teacher, travelling also as a conductor of opera companies. When Dvôrák came here Arnold wrote his "Plantation Dances," which were produced in a concert under the auspices of the Bohemian composer. Arnold was instructor of harmony at the National Convervatory under Dvôrák.

The "Plantation Dances" are Arnold's thirty-third opus, and they have been much played by orchestras ; they are also published as a piano duet; the second dance also as a solo. Arnold has not made direct use of Ethiopian themes, but has sought the African spirit. The first of the dances is very nigresque; the second hardly at all, though it is a delicious piece of music; the third dance uses banjo figures and realizes darky hilarity in fine style; the fourth is a cake walk and hits off the droll humor of that pompous ceremony fascinatingly.

Arnold's "Dramatic Overture" shows a fire and rush very characteristic of him and likely to be kept up without sufficient contrast. So also does his cantata, "The Wild Chase." Arnold has written two comic operas. I have heard parts of the first and noted moments of much beauty and humor. The Aragonaise, which opens the third act, is particularly delightful. The orchestration throughout displays Arnold's characteristic studiousness in picturesque effect.

For piano there is a czardas, and a "Valse

Élégante" for eight hands; it is more Viennese than Chopinesque. It might indeed be called a practicable waltz lavishly adorned. The fruits of Arnold's Oriental journey are seen in his impressionistic " Danse de la Midway Plaisance ; " a very clever reminiscence of a Turkish minstrel ; and a Turkish march, which has been played by many German orchestras. There is a " Caprice Espagnol," which is delightful, and a " Banjoënne," which treats banjo music so captivatingly that Arnold may be said to have invented a new and fertile and musical form. Besides these there are a fugue for eight hands, a " Minstrel Serenade " for violin and piano, and six duets for violin and viola.

There are also a few part songs and some solos, among which mention should be made of " Ein Mārlein," in the old German style, an exquisitely tender " Barcarolle," and a setting of the poem, " I Think of Thee in Silent Night," which makes use of a particularly beautiful phrase for pre-, inter-, and post-lude. Arnold has also written some ballet music, a tarantelle for string orchestra, and is at work upon a symphony, and a book, "Some Points in Modern Orchestration." His violin sonata (now in MS.) shows his original talent at its best. In the first movement, the first subject is a snappy and taking example of negro-tone, the second has the perfume of moonlit magnolia in its lyricism. (In the reprise this subject, which had originally appeared in the dominant major, recurs in the tonic major, the key of the sonata being E minor.) The second movement is also in the darky spirit, but full of melancholy. For finale the composer has flown to Ireland and written a bully jig full of dash and spirit.

N. Clifford Page.[1]

The influence of Japanese and Chinese art upon our world of decoration has long been

[1] See p. 493.

realized. After considering the amount of interest shown in the Celestial music by American composers, one is tempted to prophesy a decided influence in this line, and a considerable spread of Japanese influence in the world of music also. Japanese music has a decorative effect that is sometimes almost as captivating as in painting.

The city of San Francisco is the natural gateway for any such impulse, and not a little of it has already passed the custom house. In this field Edgar S. Kelley's influence is predominating, and it is not surprising that he should pass the contagion on to his pupil, Nathaniel Clifford Page, who was born in San Francisco, October 26, 1866. His ancestors were American for many years prior to the Revolution. He composed operas at the age of twelve, and has used many of these immature ideas with advantage in the later years. He began the serious study of music at the age of sixteen, Kelley being his principal teacher. His first opera, composed and orchestrated before he became of age, was entitled " The First Lieutenant." It was produced in 1889 at the Tivoli Opera House in San Francisco, where most of the critics spoke highly of its instrumental and Oriental color, some of the scenes being laid in Morocco.

In instrumentation, which is considered Page's forte, he has never had any instruction further than his own reading and investigation. He began to conduct in opera and concert early in life, and has had much experience. He has also been active as a teacher in harmony and orchestration.

An important phase of Page's writing has been incidental music for plays, his greatest success having been achieved by the music for the " Moonlight Blossom," a play based upon Japanese life and produced in London in 1898. The overture was written entirely on actual Japanese themes, including the national anthem of Japan. Page was three weeks writing these twelve measures. He had a Japanese fiddle arranged with a violin finger-board, but thanks to the highly characteristic stubbornness of orchestral players, he was compelled to have this part played by a mandolin. Two Japanese drums, a whistle used by a Japanese shampooer, and a Japanese guitar were somehow permitted to add their accent. The national air is used in augmentation later as the bass for a Japanese song called "K Honen." The fidelity of the music is proved by the fact that Sir Edwin Arnold's Japanese wife recognized the various airs and was carried away by the national anthem.

Although the play was not a success, the music was given a cordial reception, and brought Page contracts for other work in England, including a play of Indian life by Mrs. Flora Annie Steel.

Previously to the writing of the "Moonlight Blossom " music, Page had arranged the incidental music for the same author's play, " The Cat and the Cherub." Edgar S. Kelley's " Aladdin " music was the source from which most of the incidental music was drawn ; but Page added some things of his own, among them being one of the most effective and unexpected devices for producing a sense of horror and dread I have ever listened to : simply the sounding at long intervals of two gruff single tones in the extreme low register of the double basses and bassoons. The grimness of this effect is indescribable.

An unnamed Oriental opera, and an opera called " Villiers," in which old English color is employed (including a grotesque dance of the clumsy Ironsides), show the cosmopolitan restlessness of Page's muse. An appalling scheme of self-amusement is seen in his " Caprice," in which a theme of eight meas- ures' length is instrumented with almost every

contrapuntal device known, and with psycho-
logical variety that runs through five move-
ments, scherzando, vigoroso, con sentimento,
religioso, and a marcia fantastico. The suite
called "Village Fête" is an experiment in
French local color. It contains five scenes:
The Peasants Going to Chapel; The Flower
Girls; The Vagabonds; The Tryst; The
Sabot Dance, and the Entrance of the
Mayor, which is a pompous march.

On the occasion of a performance of this,
Louis Arthur Russell wrote: "His orchestra
is surely French, and as modern as you
please. The idiom is Berlioz's rather than
Wagner's."

CHAPTER III.

THE ACADEMICS.

John Knowles Paine.[1]

THERE is one thing better than modernity,
— it is immortality. So while I am a most
ardent devotee of modern movements, because they are at worst experiments, and
motion is necessary to life, I fail to see why

[1] See p. 474.

it is necessary in picking up something new always to drop something old, as if one were an awkward, butter-fingered parcel-carrier.

If a composer writes empty stuff in the latest styles, he is one degree better than the purveyor of trite stuff in the old styles; but he is nobody before the high thinker who finds himself suited by the general methods of the classic writers.

The most classic of our composers is their venerable dean, John Knowles Paine. It is an interesting proof of the youth of our native school of music, that the principal symphony, "Spring," of our first composer of importance, was written only twenty-one years ago. Before Mr. Paine there had never been an American music writer worthy of serious consideration in the larger forms.

By a mere coincidence Joachim Raff had written a symphony called "Spring" in 1878, just a year before Paine finished his in America. The first movement in both is

JOHN KNOWLES PAINE.

called " Nature's Awakening ; " such an idea
is inevitable in any spring composition, from
poetry up — or down. For a second movement Raff has a wild " Walpurgis Night
Revel," while Paine has a scherzo called
" May Night Fantasy." Where Raff is
uncanny and fiendish, Paine is cheerful
and elfin. The third movement of Raff's
symphony is called " First Blossoms of
Spring," and the last is called " The Joys
of Wandering." The latter two movements
of Mr. Paine's symphony are " A Promise of
Spring " and " The Glory of Nature." The
beginning of both symphonies is, of course,
a slow introduction representing the torpid
gloom of winter, out of which spring aspires
and ascends.

Paine's symphony, though aiming to shape
the molten gold of April fervor in the rigid
mold of the symphonic form has escaped
every appearance of mechanism and restraint.
It is program music of the most legiti-

mate sort, in full accord with Beethoven's canon, "Mehr Ausdruck der Empfindung als Malerei." It has no aim of imitating spring-time noises, but seeks to stimulate by sug-gestion the hearer's creative imagination, and provoke by a musical telepathy the emotions that swayed the nympholept composer.

The first movement of the symphony has an intro-duction containing two motives distinct from the two subjects of the movement. These motives represent Winter and the Awakening. The Winter motive may be again divided into a chill and icy motif and a rushing wind-motif. Through these the timid Awakening spirit lifts its head like the first trillium of the year. There is a silence and a stealthy flutter of the violins as if a cloud of birds were playing courier to the Spring.

Suddenly, after a little prelude, as if a bluebird were tuning his throat, we are enveloped in the key of the symphony (A major) and the Spring runs lilt-ing up the 'cellos to the violins (which are divided in the naïf archaic interval of the tenth, too much ig-nored in our over-colored harmonies). The second subject is propounded by the oboes (in the rather unusual related key of the submediant). This is a lyrical and dancing idea, and it does battle with the underground resistance of the Winter motives. There is an elaborate conclusion of fiercest joy. Its ecstasy droops, and after a little flutter as of little wings, the elaboration opens with the Spring motive in the minor. In this part, scholarship revels in its own luxury, the birds quiver about our heads again, and the reprise begins (in A major of course) with new exultance, the dancing second subject appears (in the tonic), over-whelming the failing strength of the Winter with a cascade of delight. Then the conclusion rushes in ; this I consider one of the most joyous themes ever inspired.

There is a coda of vanishing bird-wings and throats, a pizzicato chord on the strings — and Spring has had her coronation.

" The May Night Fantasy " is a moonlit revel of elves caught by a musical reporter, a surreptitious " chiel amang 'em takin' notes." A single hobgob-lin bassoon croaks ludicrously away, the pixies darkle and flirt and dance their hearts out of them.

The Romance is in rondo form with love-lorn iteration of themes and intermezzo, and deftest broidery, the whole ending, after a graceful Recollec-tion, in a bliss of harmony.

The Finale is a halleluiah. It is on the sonata formula, without introduction (the second subject being not in the dominant of A major, but in C major, that chaste, frank key which one of the popes strangely dubbed " lascivious "). The elaboration is frenetic with strife, but the reprise is a many-hued rainbow after storm, and the coda in A major (ending a symphony begun in A minor) is swift with delight.

This symphony has been played much, but not half enough. It should resist the weariness of time as immortally as Fletcher's play, " The Two Noble Kinsmen " (in which Shakespeare's hand is glorious), for it is, to quote that drama, " fresher than May, sweeter than her gold buttons on the bough, or all th'enamell'd knacks o' the mead or garden."

John Knowles Paine is a name that has been held in long and high honor among American composers. He was about the earliest of native writers to convince foreign musicians that some good could come out of Nazareth.

He was born in Portland, Me., January 9, 1839. He studied music first under a local teacher, Kotzschmar, making his début as organist at the age of eighteen. A year later he was in Berlin, where for three years he studied the organ, composition, instrumentation, and singing under Haupt, Wieprecht, and others. He gave several organ concerts in Germany, and made a tour in 1865–1866. In February, 1867, his "Mass" was given at the Berlin Singakademie, Paine conducting. Then he came back to the States, and in 1872 was appointed to an instructorship of music at Harvard, whence he was promoted in 1876 to a full professorship, a chair created for him and occupied by him ever since with distinguished success.

His first symphony was brought out by Theodore Thomas in 1876. This and his other orchestral works have been frequently performed at various places in this country and abroad.

His only oratorio, "St. Peter," was first produced at Portland in 1873, and in Boston a year later. It is a work of great power and much dramatic strength. Upton, in his valuable work, "Standard Oratorios," calls it "from the highest standpoint the only oratorio yet produced in this country."

This oratorio, while containing much of the floridity and repetition of Händel at his worst, is also marked with the erudition and largeness of Händel at his best. The aria for St. Peter, "O God, My God, Forsake Me Not," is especially fine.

A much-played symphonic poem is Paine's "The Tempest," which develops musically the chief episodes of Shakespeare's play. He has also written a valuable overture to "As You Like It;" he has set Keats' "Realm of Fancy" exquisitely, and Milton's "Nativity." And he has written a grand opera on a mediæval theme to his own libretto. This is a three-act work called "Azara;" the libretto has been published by the Riverside Press, and is to be translated into German. This has not yet been performed. Being, unfortunately, an American grand opera, it takes very little acuteness of foresight to predict a long wait before it is ever heard. In it Paine has shown himself more a romanticist than a classicist, and the work is said to be full of modernity.

Paine wrote the music for Whittier's "Hymn," used to open the Centennial Exposition at Philadelphia, and was fitly chosen to write the Columbus March and Hymn for the opening ceremonies of the World's Fair, at Chicago, October 21, 1892. This was given by several thousand performers under the direction of Theodore Thomas.

A most original and interesting work is the chorus, "Phœbus, Arise." It seems good to hark back for words to old William Drummond "of Hawthornden." The exquisite flavor of long-since that marks the poetry is conserved in the tune. While markedly original, it smacks agreeably of the music of Harry Lawes, that nightingale of the seventeenth century, whose fancies are too much neglected nowadays.

Paine's strong point is his climaxes, which are never timid, and are often positively titanic, thrilling. The climax of this chorus is notably superb, and the voices hold for two measures after the orchestra finishes. The power of this effect can be easily imagined. This work is marked, to an unusual extent, with a sensuousness of color.

The year eighteen hundred eighty-one saw the first production of what is generally considered Paine's most important composition, and by some called the best work by an American, — his setting of the choruses of the " Œdipos Tyrannos " of Sophokles. It was written for the presentation by Harvard University, and has been sung, in whole or in part, very frequently since. This masterpiece of Grecian genius is so mighty in conception and so mighty in execution that it has not lost power at all in the long centuries since it first thrilled the Greeks. To realize its possibilities musically is to give proof enough of the very highest order of genius, — a genius akin to that of Sophokles. It may be said that in general Paine has completely fulfilled his opportunities.

Mendelssohn also set two Greek tragedies to music, Sophokles' "Œdipos in Kolonos" and his "Antigone." Mendelssohn is reported to have made a first attempt at writing Grecian music, or what we suppose it to be, mainly a matter of unison and meagre instrumentation. He was soon dissuaded from such a step, however, and wisely. The Greek tragedians, really writers of grand opera, made undoubted. use of the best musical implements and knowledge they had. Creative emotion has its prosperity in the minds of its audience, not in the accuracy of its mechanism. To secure the effect on us that the Greek tragedians produced on contemporary audiences, it is necessary that our music be a sublimation along the lines we are accustomed to, as theirs was along lines familiar to them and effective with them. Otherwise, instead of being moved by the miseries of Œdipos, we should be chiefly occupied with amusement at the oddity of the music, and soon bored unendurably by its monotony and thinness.

Mendelssohn decided then to use unison frequently for suggestion's sake, but not to carry it to a fault. His experiments along these lines have been of evident advantage to Paine, who has, however, kept strictly to his own individuality, and produced a work that, at its highest, reaches a higher plane, in my opinion, than anything in Mendelssohn's noble tragedies, — and I am not, at that, one of those that affect to look down upon the achievements of the genius that built "Elijah."

Paine's prelude is an immense piece of

work, in every way larger and more elaborate than that to Mendelssohn's " Antigone "
(the " Œdipos in Kolonos" begins strongly
with only one period of thirteen measures).
The opening chorus of Paine's " Œdipos " is
the weakest thing in the work. The second
strophe has a few good moments, but soon
falls back into what is impudent enough to
be actually catchy ! — and that, too, of a
Lowell Mason, Moody and Sankey catchiness. Curiously enough, Mendelssohn's
" Antigone" begins with a chorus more
like a drinking-song than anything else, and
the first solo is pure *Volkslied;* both of them
imbued with a Teutonic flavor that could be
cut with a knife. In Mendelssohn's " Œdipos
in Kolonos," however, the music expresses
emotion rather than German emotion, and
abounds in splendors of harmony that are
strikingly Wagnerian — in advance.

Paine's second chorus describes the imaginary pursuit by Fate of the murderer of

POSTLUDE TO "ŒDIPUS TYRANNUS," BY J. K. PAINE.

Poco Adagio.
cantabile
dim. e ritard.
pp
p espressivo
p
dim.
ppp
cresc.
f
ff
dim.
p dim. e ritard.
pp morendo
ppp
a tempo
ppp
sempre

King Laius. It is full of grim fire, and the second strophe is at first simply terrible with awe. Then it degenerates somewhat into an arioso, almost Italian. The fourth chorus defends the oracles from Jocasta's incredulity. It is written almost in march measure, and is full of robor.

At this point in the tragedy, where it begins to transpire to Œdipos that he himself was the unwitting murderer and the incestuous wretch whose exile the oracle demands before dispelling the plague, — here the divine genius of Sophokles introduces a chorus of general merriment, somewhat as Shakespeare uses the maundering fool as a foil to heighten King Lear's fate. No praise can be too high for Paine's music here. Its choric structure is masterly, its spirit is running fire. Note, as an instance, the effect at the words " To save our land thou didst rise as a tower ! " where the music itself is suddenly uplift with most effective suggestion.

The sixth chorus shows the effect of
Œdipos' divulged guilt and the misery of this
fool of Fate. The music is an outburst of
sheer genius. It is overpowering, frighten-
ing. The postlude is orchestral, with the
chorus speaking above the music. Jocasta
has hanged herself, Œdipos has torn out his
own eyes with her brooch. The music is a
fitting reverie on the great play, and after a
wild tumult it subsides in a resigned quietude.

From Greek tragedy to Yankee patriotism
is a long cry, yet I think Paine has not wasted
his abilities on his " Song of Promise," written for the Cincinnati May Festival of 1888.
Though the poem by Mr. George E. Wood-
berry is the very apotheosis of American
brag, it has a redeeming technic. The music,
for soprano solo, mixed chorus, and orchestra,
reaches the very peaks of inspiration. I
doubt if any living composer or many dead
masters could grow so epic, as most of this.
In a way it is academic. It shows a little of

the influence of Wagner, — as any decent music should nowadays. But it is not Wagner's music, and it is not trite academia. There is no finicky tinsel and no cheap oddity.

Considering the heights at which both words and music aimed, it is amazing that they did not fall into utter wreck and nauseating bathos. That they have proved so effective shows the sure-footedness of genius. It is all good, especially the soprano solo.

This music is exquisite, wondrously exquisite, and it is followed by a maestoso e solenne movement of unsurpassable majesty. I have never read anything more purely what music should be for grandeur. And it praises our ain countree! It might well be taken up by some of our countless vocal societies to give a much needed respite to Händel's threadbare " Messiah."

When one considers the largeness of the works to which Paine has devoted himself chiefly, he can be excused for the meagreness and comparative unimportance of his smaller works for piano and vocal solo. The only song of his I care for particularly is " A Bird upon a Rosy Bough " (op. 40), which is old-fashioned, especially in accompaniment, yet at times delicious. The song " Early Spring-time " is most curiously original.

Of piano pieces there are a sprightly " Birthday Impromptu " and a fuga giocosa, which deals wittily with that theme known generally by the words " Over the Fence Is Out ! " The " Nocturne " begins like Schu-mann, falls into the style of his second Nov-ellette, thence to the largo of Beethoven's Sonata (op. 10, No. 3), thence to Chopinism, wherein it ends, an interesting assemblage withal !

A long " Romance " for the piano is marked by some excellent incidents and much passion, but it lacks unity. It is the last work in " An Album of Pianoforte

Pieces," which is otherwise full of rare delights. It is made up of opera 25, 26, and 39. Opus 25 contains four characteristic pieces, — a " Dance " full of dance-rapture, a most original " Impromptu," and a " Rondo Giocoso," which is just the kind of brilliantly witty scherzo whose infrequency in American music is so lamentable and so surprising. Opus 26 includes ten sketches, all good, especially " Woodnotes," a charming tone-poem, the deliciously simple " Wayside Flowers," " Under the Lindens," which is a masterpiece of beautiful syncopation, a refreshingly interesting bit in the hackneyed " Millstream " form, and a " Village Dance," which has much of that quaint flavor that makes Heller's études a perennial delight.

Besides these, there are a number of motets, organ preludes, string quartettes, concert pieces for violin, cello, piano, and the like, all contributing to the furtherance of an august fame.

Dudley Buck.

Music follows the laws of supply and demand just as the other necessities of life do. But before a demand could exist for it in its more austere and unadulterated forms, the general taste for it must be improved. For this purpose the offices of skilful compromisers were required, composers who could at the same time please the popular taste and teach it discrimination. Among these invaluable workers, a high place belongs, in point both of priority and achievement, to Dudley Buck. He has been a powerful agent, or reagent, in converting the stagnant ferment into a live and wholesome ebullition, or as the old Greek evolutionists would say, starting the first progress in the primeval ooze of American Philistinism.

A more thoroughly New England ancestry it would be hard to find. The founder of the family came over from England soon

after the *Mayflower* landed. Buck was
named after Governor Dudley of the Plymouth Colony. He was born at Hartford,
March 10, 1839. His father was a prosper-
ous shipping merchant, one of whose boats,
during the Civil War, towed the *Monitor*
from New York to Fortress Monroe on the
momentous voyage that destroyed the *Merri-
mac's* usefulness.

Buck, though intended for commercial life,
borrowed a work on thorough-bass and a flute
and proceeded to try the wings of his muse.
A melodeon supplanted the flute, and when
he was sixteen he attained the glory of a
piano, a rare possession in those times.
(Would that it were rarer now!) He
took a few lessons and played a church-
organ for a salary, — a small thing, but his
own.

After reaching the junior year in Trinity
College, he prevailed upon his parents to sur-
render him to music, an almost scandalous

career in the New England mind of that day, still unbleached of its Blue Laws.

At the age of nineteen he went to Leipzig and entered the Conservatory there, studying composition under Hauptmann and E. F. Richter, orchestration under Rietz, and the piano under Moscheles and Plaidy. Later he went to Dresden and studied the organ with Schneider.

After three years in Germany, he studied for a year in Paris, and came home, settling down in Hartford as church-organist and teacher. He began a series of organ-concert tours lasting fifteen years. He played in almost every important city and in many small towns, popularizing the best music by that happy fervor of interpretation which alone is needed to bring classical compositions home to the public heart. In 1869 he was called to the " mother-church " of Chicago In the Chicago fire he lost many valuable manuscripts, including a concert overture on

Drake's exquisite poem, "The Culprit Fay,"
which must be especially regretted. He
moved his family to Boston, assuming in ten
days the position of organist at St. Paul's ;
and later he accepted charge of "the great
organ" at Music Hall, — that organ of which
Artemus Ward wrote so deliciously.

In 1875 Theodore Thomas, whose orchestra
had performed many of Buck's compositions,
invited him to become his assistant conductor
at the Cincinnati Music Festival and at the
last series of concerts at the Central Park
Garden in New York. Buck accepted and
made his home in Brooklyn, where he has
since remained as organist of the Holy Trinity
Church, and conductor of the Apollo Club,
which he founded and brought to a high state
of efficiency, writing for it many of his numerous compositions for male voices.

Buck's close association with church work
has naturally led him chiefly into sacred
music, and in this class of composition he

is by many authorities accorded the very highest place among American composers. He has also written many organ solos, sonatas, marches, a pastorale, a rondo caprice, and many concert transcriptions, as well as a group of études for pedal phrasing, and several important treatises on various musical topics. His two "Motett Collections" were a refreshing relief and inspiration to church choirs thirsty for religious Protestant music of some depth and warmth.

In the cantata form Buck also holds a foremost place. In 1876 he was honored with a commission to set to music "The Centennial Meditation of Columbia," a poem written for the occasion by the Southern poet, Sidney Lanier. This was performed at the opening of the Philadelphia Exhibition by a chorus of one thousand voices, an organ, and an orchestra of two hundred pieces under the direction of Theodore Thomas. In 1874 he made a metrical version of "The Legend of Don

Munio " from Irving's " Alhambra," and set it to music for a small orchestra and chorus. Its adaptability to the resources of the vocal societies of smaller cities has made it one of his most popular works.

Another bit of Washington Irving is found in Buck's cantata, " The Voyage of Columbus," the libretto for which he has taken from Irving's " Life of Columbus." It consists of six night-scenes, — " The Chapel of St. George at Palos," " On the Deck of the *Santa Maria*," " The Vesper Hymn," " Mutiny," " In Distant Andalusia," and " Land and Thanksgiving." The opportunities here for Buck's skilful handling of choruses and his dramatic feeling in solos are obvious, and the work has been frequently used both in this country and in Germany with much success. Buck, in fact, made the German libretto as well as the English, and has written the words for many of his compositions. His largest work was " The Light of Asia," com-

posed in 1885 and based on Sir Edwin
Arnold's epic. It requires two and one-half
hours for performance and has met the usual
success of Buck's music; it was produced
in London with such soloists as Nordica,
Lloyd, and Santley. It has been occasionally
given here.

He has found the greater part of his texts
in American poetry, particularly in Lanier,
Stedman, and Longfellow, whose "King Olaf's
Christmas" and "Nun of Nidaros" he has
set to music, as well as his "Golden Legend,"
which won a prize of one thousand dollars at
the Cincinnati Festival in a large competition.
His work is analyzed very fully in A. J.
Goodrich' "Musical Analysis."

Here, as in his symphonic overture to
Scott's "Marmion," Buck has adopted the
Wagnerian idea of the *leit-motif* as a vivid
means of distinguishing musically the various
characters and their varying emotions. His
music is not markedly Wagnerian, however,

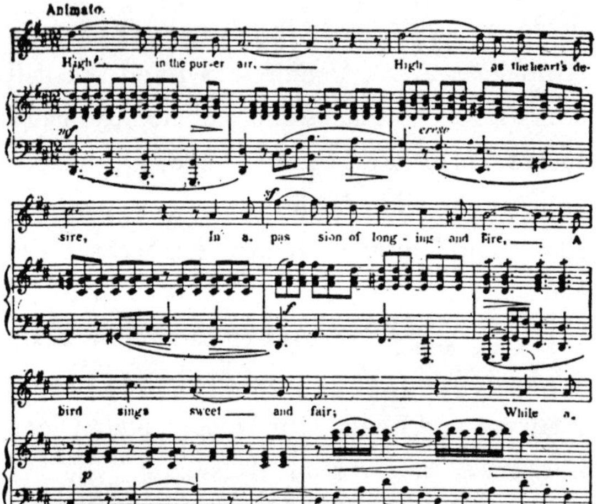

FRAGMENT FROM "SPRING'S AWAKENING," BY MR. BUCK

in other ways, but seems to show, back of his individuality, an assimilation of the good old school of canon and fugue, with an Italian tendency to the declamatory and well-rounded melodic period.

It might be wished that in his occasional secular songs Buck had followed less in the steps of the Italian aria and the English ballad and adopted more of the newer, nobler spirit of the *Lied* as Schumann and Franz represent it, and as many of our younger Americans have done with thorough success and not a little of exaltation. Note for instance the inadequacy of the old-style balladry to both its own opportunity and the otherwise-smothered fire of such a poem as Sidney Lanier's "Sunset," which is positively Shakespearean in its passionate perfection.

In religious music, however, Mr. Buck has made a niche of its own for his music, which it occupies with grace and dignity.

Horatio W. Parker.[1]

When one considers the enormous space occupied by the hymn-tune in New England musical activity, it is small wonder that most of its composers should display hymnal proclivities. Both Buck and Parker are natives of New England.

Parker was born, September 15, 1863, at Auburndale, Mass. His mother was his first teacher of music. She was an organist, and gave him a thorough technical schooling which won the highest commendation later from Rheinberger, who entrusted to him the first performance of a new organ concerto.

[1] See p. 466.

HORATIO W. PARKER.

After some study in Boston under Stephen A. Emery, John Orth, and G. W. Chadwick, Parker went to Munich at the age of eighteen, where he came under the special favor of Rheinberger, and where various compositions were performed by the Royal Music School orchestra. After three years of Europe, he returned to America and assumed the direction of the music at St. Paul's school. He has held various posts since, and has been, since 1894, the Battell Professor of Music at Yale.

His rather imposing list of works includes a symphony (1885), an operetta, a concert overture (1884), an overture, "Regulus" (1885), performed in Munich and in London, and an overture, "Count Robert of Paris" (1890), performed in New York, a ballad for chorus and orchestra, "King Trojan," presented in Munich in 1885, the Twenty-third Psalm for female chorus and orchestra (1884), an "Idylle" (1891); "The Normans," "The

Kobolds," and "Harold Harfager," all for
chorus and orchestra, and all dated 1891 ; an
oratorio, three or more cantatas, and various
bits of chamber-music. His opus number
has already reached forty-three, and it is
eked out to a very small degree by such
imponderous works as organ and piano solos,
hymns, and songs. In 1893, Parker won the
National Conservatory prize for a cantata, and
in 1898 the McCagg prize for an a capella
chorus.

Parker's piano compositions and secular
songs are not numerous. They seem rather
the incidental byplays and recreations of a
fancy chiefly turned to sacred music of the
larger forms.

Opus 19 consists of "Four Sketches," of
which the "Étude Melodieuse" is as good as
is necessary in that overworked style, wherein
a thin melody is set about with a thinner
ripple of arpeggios. The "Romanza" is
lyric and delightful, while the "Scherzino"

is delicious and crisp as celery; it is worthy of Schumann, whom it suggests, and many of whose cool tones and mannerisms it borrows.

The " 5 Morceaux Charactéristiques" are on the whole better. The "Scherzo" is shimmering with playfulness, and, in the Beethoven fashion, has a tender intermezzo amoroso. This seriousness is enforced with an ending of a most plaintive nature. The "Caprice" is brilliant and whimsical, with some odd effects in accent. The "Gavotte" makes unusual employment of triplets, but lacks the precious yeast of enthusiasm necessary to a prime gavotte.

This enthusiasm is not lacking however from his "Impromptu," and it makes his "Elégie" a masterly work, possibly his best in the smaller lines. This piece is altogether elegiac in spirit, intense in its sombrest depths, impatient with wild outcries, — like Chopin's "Funeral March," — and working up to an immense passion at the end. This subsides in ravishingly liquid arpeggios, — "melodious tears"? — which obtain the kindred effect of Chopin's tinkling "Berceuse" in a slightly different way. This notable work is marred by an interlude in which the left hand mumbles harshness in the bass, while the right hand is busy with airy fioriture. It is too close a copy of the finish of the first movement of Beethoven's "Moonlight" sonata. The lengthening skips of the left hand are also Beethovenesque trademarks.

Parker is rather old-fashioned in his forms of musical speech. That is, he has what you might call the narrative style. He follows his theme as an absorbing plot, engaging enough in itself, without gorgeous digressions and pendent pictures. His work has something of the Italian method. A melody or a theme, he seems to think, is only marred by abstruse harmony, and is endangered by diversions. One might almost say that a uniform lack of attention to color-possibilities and a monotonous fidelity to a cool, gray tone characterize him. His fondness for the plain, cold octave is notable. It is emphasized by the ill-success of his "Six Lyrics for Piano, without octaves." They are all of thin value, and the "Novelette" is dangerously Schumannesque.

The "Three Love Songs" are happy, "Love's Chase" keeping up the arch raillery and whim of Beddoe's verse. "Orsame's Song" is smooth and graceful, ending with a well-blurted, abrupt "The devil take her!" The "Night-piece to Julia" is notable. We have no poet whose lyrics are harder to set to music than good Robin Herrick's. They have a lilt of their own that is incompatible with ordinary music. Parker has, however, been completely successful in this instance. A mysterious, night-like carillon accompaniment, delicate as harebells, gives sudden way

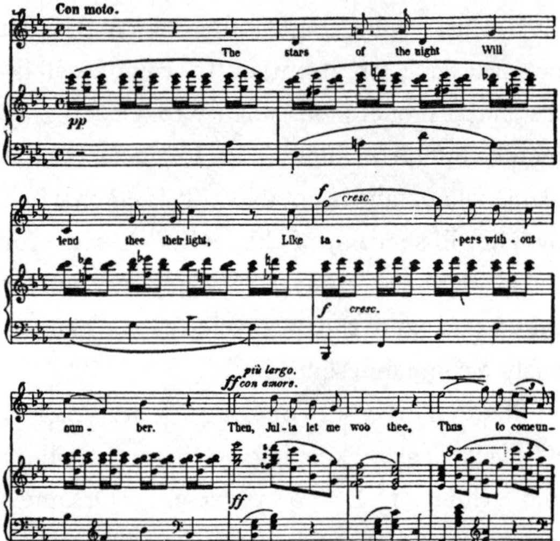

FRAGMENT OF MR. PARKER'S SONG, "NIGHT-PIECE TO JULIA."

to a superb support of a powerful outburst at the end of the song.

The " Six Songs " show not a little of that modernity and opulent color I have denied to the most of Mr. Parker's work. " Oh, Ask Me Not " is nothing less than inspiration, rapturously beautiful, with a rich use of unexpected intervals. The " Egyptian Serenade " is both novel and beautiful. The other songs are good ; even the comic-operatic flavor of the " Cavalry Song " is redeemed by its catchy sweep.

Among a large number of works for the pipe-organ, few are so marked by that purposeless rambling organists are so prone to, as the " Fantaisie." The " Melody and Intermezzo " of opus 20 makes a sprightly humoresque. The " Andante Religioso " of opus 17 has really an allegretto effect, and is much better as a gay pastorale than as a devotional exercise. It is much more shepherdly than the avowed " Pastorale " (opus 20), and almost as much so as the "Eclogue," delicious with the organ's possibilities for reed and pipe effects. The "Romanza" is a gem of the first water. A charming quaint effect is got by the accompaniment of the air, played legato on the swell, with an echo, staccato, of its own chords on the great. The interlude is a tender melody, beautifully managed. The two "Concert Pieces" are marked by a large simplicity in treatment, and have this rare merit, that they are less gymnastic exercises than expressions of feeling. A fiery "Triumphal March," a delightful "Canzonetta," and a noble "Larghetto," of sombre, yet rich and well-modulated, colors, complete the list of his works for the organ. None of these are registered with over-elaboration.

To sacred music Parker has made important contributions. Besides a dignified, yet impassioned, complete "Morning and Evening Service for the Holy Communion," he has written several single songs and anthems.

It is the masterwork, "Hora Novissima," however, which lifts him above golden mediocrity. From the three thousand lines of Bernard of Cluny's poem, "De Contemptu Mundi," famous since the twelfth century, and made music with the mellowness of its own Latin rhyme, Mrs. Isabella G. Parker, the composer's mother, has translated 210 lines. The English is hardly more than a loose paraphrase, as this random parallel proves :

Pars mea, Rex meus,	Most Mighty, most Holy,
In proprio Deus,	How great is the glory,
Ipse decore.	Thy throne enfolding.

Or this skilful evasion :

Tunc Jacob, Israel,	All the long history,
Et Lia, tunc Rachel	All the deep mystery
Efficietur.	Through ages hidden.

But it is perhaps better for avoiding the Charybdis of literalness.

Those who accuse Rossini's "Stabat

Mater" of a fervor more theatric than religious, will find the same faults in Parker's
work, along with much that is purely ecclesiastical. Though his sorrow is apt to become
petulance, there is much that is as big in
spirit as in handling. The work is frequently
Mendelssohnian in treatment. An archaism
that might have been spared, since so little
of the poem was retained, is the sad old
Händelian style of repeating the same words
indefinitely, to all neglect of emptiness of
meaning and triteness. Thus the words
"*Pars mea, Rex meus*" are repeated by the
alto exactly thirteen times! which, any one
will admit, is an unlucky number, especially
since the other voices keep tossing the same
unlucky words in a musical battledore.

The especially good numbers of the work
(which was composed in 1892, and first produced, with almost sensational success, in
1893) are: the magnificent opening chorus;
the solo for the soprano; the large and fiery

finale to Part I.; the superb tenor solo, "Golden Jerusalem," which is possibly the most original and thrilling of all the numbers, is, in every way, well varied, elaborated, and intensified, and prepares well for the massive and effective double chorus, "Stant Syon Atria," an imposing structure whose ambition found skill sufficing; an alto solo of original qualities; and a finale, tremendous, though somewhat long drawn out. Of this work, so careful a critic as W. J. Henderson was moved to write:

"His melodic ideas are not only plentiful, but they are beautiful, . . . graceful and sometimes splendidly vigorous. . . . There is an a capella chorus which is one of the finest specimens of pure church polyphony that has been produced in recent years. . . . It might have been written by Hobrecht, Brumel, or even Josquin des Pres. It is impossible to write higher praise than this. . . . The orchestration is extraordinarily . . . rich. As a whole . . . the composition . . . may be set down as one of the finest achievements of the present day."

And Philip Hale, a most discriminant musical enthusiast, described the chorus "Pars Mea" as:

"A masterpiece, true music of the church," to which "any acknowledged master of composition in Europe would gladly sign his name. . . . For the a capella chorus there is nothing but unbounded praise. . . . Weighing words as counters, I do not hesitate to say that I know of no one in the country or in England who could by nature and by student's sweat have written those eleven pages. . . . I have spoken of Mr. Parker's quasi-operatic tendency. Now he is a modern. He has shown in this very work his appreciation and his mastery of antique religious musical art. But as a modern he is compelled to feel the force of the dramatic in religious music. . . . But his most far-reaching, his most exalted and rapt conception of the bliss beyond compare is expressed in the language of Palestrina and Bach."

In September, 1899, the work was produced with decisive success in London, Parker conducting.

Besides this, there are several secular

cantatas, particularly "King Trojan," which contains a singable tune for Trojan with many delicate nuances in the accompaniment, and a harp-accompanied page's song that is simply ambrosial. Then there is Arlo Bates' poem, "The Kobolds," which Parker has blessed with music as delicate as the laces of gossamer-spiders.

His latest work is devoted to the legend of St. Christopher, and displays the same abilities for massive and complex scoring whenever the opportunity offers. On the other hand, the work discloses Parker's weaknesses as well, for the libretto drags in certain love episodes evidently thought desirable for the sake of contrast and yet manifestly unnecessary to the story. The character of the queen, for instance, is quite useless, and, in fact, disconcerting. The love scene between the king and queen reminds one uncomfortably of Tristan and Isolde, while a descending scale constantly used throughout the work in the accompaniment incessantly suggests the "Samson and Delilah" of Saint-Saëns.

In spite of flaws, however, — flaws are to be had everywhere for the looking, — Parker's work has its fine points. The struggle between the demons and the singers of the sacred Latin Hymn has made excellent use of the Tannhäuser effect. The Cathedral scene shows Parker's resources in the massive use of choruses to be very large. The barcarolling billows of the river are ravishingly written, and the voice of the child crying out is effectively introduced. The song the giant Christopher sings through the storm is particularly superb.

Frank van der Stucken.[1]

On the bead-roll of those who have had both the ability and the courage to take a stand for our music, the name of Frank van

[1] See p. 477.

FRANK VAN DER STUCKEN.

der Stucken must stand high. His Americanism is very frail, so far as birth and breeding count, but he has won his naturalization by his ardor for native music.

Van der Stucken's life has been full of labors and honors. He was born at Fredericksburg, Texas, in 1858, of a Belgian father and a German mother. After the Civil War, in which the father served in the Confederate army as a captain of the Texan cavalry, the family returned to Belgium, where, at Antwerp, Van der Stucken studied under Benoit. Here some of his music was played in the churches, and a ballet at the Royal Theatre.

In 1878 he began studies in Leipzig, making important acquaintances, such as Reinecke, Grieg, and Sinding. His first male chorus was sung there, with great success. Of his fifth opus, consisting of nine songs, Edvard Grieg wrote an enthusiastic criticism. After travelling for some time, Van der Stucken was appointed kapellmeister at the Breslau Stadt-Theatre. This was his début as conductor. Here he composed his well-known suite on Shakespeare's "Tempest," which has been performed abroad and here. Here, also, he wrote a "Festzug," an important work in Wagnerian style, and his passionate "Pagina d' Amore," which, with the published portions of his lyric drama, "Vlasda," has been performed by many great orchestras.

In 1883, Van der Stucken met Liszt, at Weimar, and under his auspices gave a concert of his own compositions, winning the congratulations of Grieg, Lassen, Liszt, and many other celebrated musicians. A prominent German critic headed his review of the performance : "A new star on the musical firmament."

Van der Stucken was now called to the directorship of the famous Arion Male Chorus in New York, a position which he held for eleven years with remarkable results. In 1892 he took his chorus on a tour in Europe and won superlative praises everywhere.

In 1885 and successive years Van der Stucken conducted orchestral " Novelty Concerts," which have an historical importance as giving the first hearing to symphonic works by American composers. In Berlin and in Paris he also gave our musicians the privilege of public performance. From 1891 to 1894 he devoted himself to reforming the Northeastern Säengerbund, achieving the enormous task of making five thousand male voices sing difficult music artistically. Since 1895 Van der Stucken has been conductor of the newly formed Cincinnati Symphony Orchestra, as well as dean of the faculty of the College of Music in that city. The influence of this man, who is certainly one of the most important musicians of his time, is bringing Cincinnati back to its old musical prestige.

As a composer, Van der Stucken shows the same orginality and power that characterize him as an organizer. His prelude to the opera "Vlasda" (op. 9) is one long rapture of passionate sweetness, superbly instrumented. An arrangement of it has been made for the piano for four hands by Horatio W. Parker.

Van der Stucken's music to "The Tempest" (op. 8) is published in three forms. Besides the orchestral score, there is an arrangement for piano solo, by A. Siloti, of the "Dance of the Gnomes," "Dance of the Nymphs," and "Dance of the Reapers," the first and third being especially well transcribed. For four hands, Hans Sitt has arranged these three dances, as well as a short but rich "Exorcism," some splendid melodramatic music, and the rattling grotesque, "The Hound-chase after Caliban." All these pieces are finely imagined and artistically handled.

For piano solo, there is a group of three Miniatures (op. 7). The first is an Albumblatt of curious dun colors; the second is a Capriccietto, a strange whim; the third is a beautiful bit called "May Blossom."

Of Van der Stucken's songs I have seen two groups, the first a setting of five love lyrics by Rückert. None of these are over two pages long, except the last. They are written in the best modern *Lied* style, and are quite unhackneyed. It is always the unexpected that happens, though this unexpected thing almost always proves to be a right thing. Without any sense of strain or bombast he reaches superb climaxes; without eccentricity he is individual; and his songs are truly interpreters of the words they express. Of these five, " Wann die Rosen aufgeblüht" is a wonderfully fine and fiery work; " Die Stunde sei gesegnet" has one of the most beautiful endings imaginable; " Mir ist, nun ich die habe " has a deep

FRAGMENT OF MR. VAN DER STUCKEN'S " DIE STUNDE SEI
GESEGNET,"

significance in much simplicity, and its ending, by breaking the rule against consecutive octaves, attains, as rule-breakings have an unpleasant habit of doing, an excellent effect. "Liebste, nur dich seh'n" is a passionate lyric; and "Wenn die Vöglein sich gepaart" is florid and trilly, but legitimately so; it should find much concert use. These songs, indeed, are all more than melodies; they are expressions.

Of the second group of eight songs for low voice, "O Jugendlust" is athrill with young ecstasy; "Einsame Thräne" has superb coloring, all sombre, and a tremendous climax; "Seeligkeit" is big with emotion and ravishing in harmony, "Ein Schäferlied" is exquisite, "Von schön Sicilien war mein Traum" begins in the style of Lassen, but ends with a strength and vigor far beyond that tender melodist. Besides these groups, there is a rich lyric "Moonlight;" and there are many part songs.

A work of considerable importance written many years before and presented by Franz Liszt at Weimar had its first American production in 1899, at Cincinnati and New York. It is a symphonic prologue to Heine's tragedy, "William Ratcliff." The different psychological phases of the tragedy are presented by characteristic motives which war among themselves. The Scottish locale is indicated vividly, and the despair of the lovers presented in one place by the distortion and rending of all the principal motives. A dirge with bells and a final musing upon, and resignation before, implacable Fate give a dignified close to a work in which passion is exploited with erudition and modernity.

W. W. Gilchrist.

The prize competition has its evils, unquestionably; and, in a place of settled status, perhaps, they outnumber its benefits.

But in American music it has been of material encouragement to the production of large works. In the first place, those who do not win have been stimulated to action, and have at least their effort for their pains. In the second place, those who manage to win are several hundred dollars the richer, and may offer the wolf at the door a more effective bribe than empty-stomached song.

In the city of Philadelphia lives a composer of unusual luck in prize-winning. That large and ancient town is not noteworthy for its activity in the manufacture of original music. In fact, some one has spoken of it as "a town where the greatest reproach to a musician is residence there." The city's one prominent music-writer is William Wallace Gilchrist; but he stands among the first of our composers. He is especially interesting as a purely native product, having never studied abroad, and yet having won among our composers a foremost place in the larger forms of composition. He was born in Jersey City, January 8, 1846; his father was a Canadian, his mother a native of this country; both were skilled in music, and his home life was full of it, especially of the old church music. After a youth of the usual school life he tried various pursuits, — photography, law, business; but music kept calling him. A good barytone voice led him to join vocal societies, and at length he made music his profession, after studying voice, organ, and composition with Dr. H. A. Clarke, of Philadelphia. He was a successful soloist in oratorio for some years, but gradually devoted himself to church work and conducting, and to composition, though none of his music was published till he was thirty-two, when he took two prizes offered by the Abt Male Singing Society of Philadelphia.

Shortly after taking the Abt Society prize, he won three offered by the Mendelssohn

Glee Club of New York, and in 1884 he took the $1,000 prize offered by the Cincinnati Festival Association.

This last was gained by his setting of the Forty-sixth Psalm for soprano solo, chorus, and orchestra. The overture opens with a noble adante contemplatif, which deserves its epithet, but falls after a time into rather uninteresting moods, whence it breaks only at the last period. The opening chorus, " God Is Our Refuge and Strength," seems to me to be built on a rather trite and empty subject, which it plays battledore and shuttlecock with in the brave old pompous and canonic style, which stands for little beyond science and labor. It is only fair to say, however, that A. J. Goodrich, in his " Musical Analysis," praises " the strength and dignity " of this chorus ; and gives a minute analysis of the whole work with liberal thematic quotation. The psalm, as a whole, though built on old lines, is built well on those lines, and the solo " God Is in the Midst of Her " is taken up with especially fine effect by the chorus. " The Heathen Raged " is a most ingeniously complicated chorus also.

The cantata, " Prayer and Praise," is similarly conventional, and suffers from the sin of repetition, but contains much that is strong.

Of the three prize male choruses written for the Mendelssohn Glee Club, the " Ode to the Sun " is the least successful. It is written to the bombast of Mrs. Hemans, and is fittingly hysterical ; occasionally it fairly shrieks itself out. " In Autumn " is quieter ; a sombre work with a fine outburst at the end. " The Journey of Life " is an andante misterioso that catches the gloom of Bryant's verse, and offers a good play for that art of interweaving voices in which Gilchrist is an adept.

" The Uplifted Gates " is a chorus for mixed voices with solos for sopranos and altos ; it is elaborate, warm, and brilliant. In lighter tone are the "Spring Song," a trio with cheap words, but bright music and a rich ending, and "The Sea Fairies," a chorus of delightful delicacy for women's voices. It has a piano accompaniment for four hands. In this same difficult medium of women's voices is "The Fountain," a surpassingly beautiful work, graceful and silvery as a cas-cade. It reminds one, not by its manner at all, but by its success, of that supreme achievement, Wagner's song of the "Rhine-maidens." The piano accompaniment to Gilchrist's chorus aids the general picture.

A thoroughly charming work is the setting of Lowell's poem, "The Rose," for solos and chorus. The dreariness of the lonely poet and the lonely maid contrasts strongly with the rapture of their meeting. As the first half of the poem is morose yet melodious, the latter is bright with ecstasy ; the ending is of the deepest tenderness.

By all odds the best of these choruses, however, is " The Legend of the Bended Bow,"
a fine war-chant by Mrs. Hemans. Tradi-
tion tells that in ancient Britain the people
were summoned to war by messengers who
carried a bended bow ; the poem tells of the
various patriots approached. The reaper is
bidden to leave his standing corn, the hunts-
man to turn from the chase ; the chieftain, the
prince, mothers, sisters, sweethearts, and the
bards are all approached and counselled to
bravery. After each episode follow the words
" And the bow passed on," but the music
has been so well managed that the danger of
such a repetition is turned into grim force.
The only prelude is five great blasts of the
horns. A brawny vigor is got by a frequent
use of imitation and unison in the voices.
The choric work is marked throughout with
the most intense and epic power, almost
savagery ; a magnificent martial zest. The
climax is big. It is certainly one of

the best things of its kind ever done over here.

Another work of fine quality throughout is "A Christmas Idyl," for solos, chorus, and orchestra. A terrible sombreness is achieved in its former half by a notable simplicity. The latter part is in brighter tone ; the solo, " And Thou, Bethlehem," is especially exultant. In manuscript is "An Easter Idyl," of large proportions, for solos, chorus, and orchestra, or organ.

In the single songs the influence of Gilchrist's early training in hymns is patent. In only a few instances do they follow the latterday methods of Schumann and Franz. "A Song of Doubt and a Song of Faith " is possibly his best vocal solo. It begins with a plaint, that is full of cynic despair ; thence it breaks suddenly into a cheerful andante. " The Two Villages " is a strong piece of work on the conventional lines of what might be called the Sunday ballad. " A Dirge for

Summer " has a marked originality, and is of that deep brooding which is particularly congenial to Gilchrist's muse. The Scotch songs are charming : " My Heart is Sair " is full of fine feeling, and must be classed among the very best of the many settings of this lyric of Burns'.

Most modern in feeling of all Gilchrist's vocal solos is the group of " Eight Songs." They interpret the text faithfully and the accompaniment is in accord with the song, but yet possessed of its own individuality. " A Love Song " is tender and has a well-woven accompaniment ; " The Voice of the Sea " is effective, but hardly attains the large simplicity of Aldrich' poem ; " Autumn " is exquisitely cheery ; " Goldenrod " is ornately graceful, while " The Dear Long Ago " is quaint ; " Lullaby " is of an exquisitely novel rhythm in this overworked form.

There is much contrast between the light

A LOVE SONG.

by Barry Cornwall. Music by W. W. Gilchrist.

Allegro appassionato. (♩=100.)

A FRAGMENT.

ness of his book, "Songs for the Children," and his ponderous setting of Kipling's "Recessional." The treatment of Paul Laurence Dunbar's "Southern Lullaby" is unusual, and the songs, "My Ladye" and "The Ideal," both in MS., are noteworthy.

Gilchrist has written a vast amount of religious music, including several "Te Deums," of which the one in C and that in A flat are the best, to my thinking. He has written little for the piano except a series of duets, of which the charming "Mélodie" and the fetching "Styrienne" are the best.

It is by his orchestral works, however, that he gains the highest consideration. These include a symphony for full orchestra, which has been frequently performed with success; a suite for orchestra; a suite for piano and orchestra; as well as a nonet, a quintet, and a trio, for strings and wind. None of these have been published, but I have had the privilege of examining some of the manuscripts.

The spirit and the treatment of these works is strongly classical. While the orchestration is scholarly and mellow, it is not in the least Wagnerian, either in manipulation or in lusciousness. The symphony is not at all programmatic. The Scherzo is of most exuberant gaiety. Its accentuation is much like that in Beethoven's piano sonata (op. 14, No. 2). Imitation is liberally used in the scoring, with a delightfully comic effect as of an altercation. The symphony ends with a dashing finale that is stormy with cheer. Gilchrist is at work upon a second symphony of more modernity.

The "Nonet" is in G minor, and begins with an Allegro in which a most original and and severe subject is developed with infinite grace and an unusually rich color. The Andante is religioso, and is fervent rather than sombre. The ending is especially beautiful. A sprightly Scherzo follows. It is most ingeniously contrived, and the effects are divided with unusual impartiality among the instruments. A curious and elaborate allegro molto furnishes the finale, and ends the "Nonet" surprisingly with an abrupt major chord.

The opening Allegro of the "Quintet" begins with a 'cello solo of scherzesque quality, but as the other voices join in, it takes on a more passionate tone, whence it works into rapturously beautiful moods and ends magnificently. The piano part has a strong value, and even where it merely ornaments the theme carried by the strings, it is fascinating. The Scherzo is again of the Beethoven order in its contagious comicality. The piano has the lion's share of it at first, but toward the last the other instruments leave off embroidery and take to cracking jokes for themselves. The Andante is a genuinely fine piece of work. It ranges from melting tenderness to impassioned rage and a purified nobility. The piano part is highly elaborated, but the other instruments have a scholarly, a vocal, individuality. I was shocked to see a cadenza for the piano just before the close, but its tender brilliance was in thorough accord with the sincerity of the movement. The "Quintet" ends with a splendid Allegro.

In MS. are three interesting works for the violin, a Rhapsody, a Perpetual Motion, and a Fantasie.

This last has a piano accompaniment of much ingenuity. The fantasial nature of the work lies principally in its development, which is remarkably lyrical, various melodies being built up beautifully on fractions of the main subjects. There is nothing perfunctory, and the work is full of art and appeal. Gilchrist is one of our most polished composers contrapuntally, but has been here in a very lyric mood.

He is the founder and conductor of the Mendelssohn Club of Philadelphia, an unusually effective organization; one of the founders of the local Manuscript Club; the conductor of a choral society of two hundred voices, at Harrisburg, and the director of two church choirs.

G. W. Chadwick.[1]

One of the most sophisticated, and, at the same time, most eclectic of native music-makers, is George W. Chadwick, to whom the general consent of authorities would grant a place among the very foremost of the foremost American composers.

His reputation rests chiefly on his two symphonies, a number of concert overtures, and many pieces of chamber-music, which

[1] See p. 477.

GEORGE WHITFIELD CHADWICK.

are much praised. Chadwick was born at Lowell, Mass., November 13, 1854. His parents were American, and it was not till 1877, after studying with Eugene Thayer in Boston, and teaching music in the college at Olivet, Mich., that Chadwick studied for two years at Leipzig, under Jadassohn and Reinecke, and later at Munich for a year under Rheinberger. In 1880 he returned to America and settled in Boston, where he has since lived, as organist, teacher, and conductor, an important figure in the town's musical life.

Among his few works for the piano, are " Six Characteristic Pieces " (op. 7). The " Reminiscence of Chopin " is an interesting and skilful chain of partial themes and suggestions from Chopin. The " Étude " is a monotonous study in a somewhat Schumannesque manner, with a graceful finish. The " Congratulation " is a cheerful bagatelle ; the " Irish Melody " is sturdy, simple, and fetching ; but the " Scherzino " is a hard bit of humor with Beethoven mannerisms lacking all the master's unction.

The opus ends with an unfortunate composition inexcusably titled " Please Do !"

There are two bright " Caprices " and three excellent waltzes, of which the third is the best. It is a dreamy, tender work on a theme by " B. J. L.," which refers, I presume, to Mr. B. J. Lang.

Chadwick has done a vast amount of part-song writing. His " Lovely Rosabelle " is for chorus and orchestra, and is marked with many original effects. His " Reiterlied " is superbly joyful. A setting of Lewis Carroll's immortal " Jabberwocky " shows much rich humor of the college glee-club sort. There is an irresistibly humorous episode where the instrument of destruction goes " snicker snack," and a fine hilarity at

> " ' O frabjous day
> Callooh, callay,'
> He chortled in his joy."

What would part-song writers do if the Vikings had never been invented? Where would they get their wild choruses for men, with a prize to the singer that makes the most noise? Chadwick falls into line with "The Viking's Last Voyage" (1881), for barytone solo, male chorus, and orchestra, which gives him a very high place among writers in this form. He has also a robustious "Song of the Viking," and an excellent Dedication Ode (1884), for solo, chorus, and orchestra, to the pregnant words of Rev. H. B. Carpenter, besides two cantatas for mixed voices, "Phœnix Expirans" and "The Pilgrims." In 1889 was published his "Lovely Rosabelle," a ballad for chorus and orchestra; it contains some interesting dissonantial work in the storm-passages. And his comic opera, "Tabasco," must be mentioned, as well as an enormous mass of sacred music, which, I confess, I had not the patience to study.

The flesh was willing, but the spirit was weak.

Among Chadwick's songs is a volume of Breton melodies harmonized with extreme simplicity. Others are " Gay Little Dande-lion," which is good enough of its everlasting flower-song sort ; " In Bygone Days " and " Request," which, aside from one or two flecks of art, are trashy ; and two childish namby-pambies, " Adelaide " and " The Mill." " A Bonny Curl " catches the Scotch-ton faithfully.

Chadwick usually succeeds, however, in catching foreign flavors. His " Song from the Persian " is one of his best works, and possibly the very best is his " Sorais' Song," to Rider Haggard's splendid words. It has an epic power and a wild despair. Up to the flippancy of its last measures, it is quite inspired, and one of the strongest of Amer-ican songs. The " Danza " is captivating and full of novelty. " Green Grows the

Willow" is a burden of charming pathos and quaintness, though principally a study in theme-management. " Allah," however, is rather Ethiopian than Mahommedan. His " Bedouin Love Song" has little Oriental color, but is full of rush and fire, with a superb ending. It is the best of the countless settings of this song. I wish I could say the same of his " Thou Art so Like a Flower," but he has missed the intense repression of Heine.

The " Serenade" displays an interesting rhythm ; " The Miller's Daughter " is tender, and " A Warning " is delightfully witty. One regrets, however, that its best points were previously used in Schumann's perfect folk-song, " Wenn ich früh in den Garten geh'." Chadwick has two folk-songs of his own, however, which are superb. " He Loves Me " is a tender, cradle-song-like bit of delicious color. The " Lullaby" is a genuinely interesting study in this over-

To Mrs. G. H. Stoddard.

TWO FOLK SONGS.

I

G. W. Chadwick.

O love and joy are for a day, Then tears and sor-row af-ter, O love is for a sum - mer day, And then fare-well to laugh ter, If

Copyright, 1892, by Arthur P. Schmidt.

cresc..
love and joy are for a day And then fare - well to
cresc.
appassionato
laugh - - - ter. To live with love give
per - - den - do
me one day Though, tears for - ev - er af - ter.
p
pp

worked form. "The Lily" has the passionate lyricism of Chaminade, and "Sweet Wind
that Blows" is a fine frenzy. The "Nocturne" is dainty and has its one good climax.
"Before the Dawn" has some of Chadwick's
best work; it is especially marked by a daring harmonic — you might say — *impasto.*

His principal works, besides those mentioned, may be catalogued (I am unable to
do more than catalogue most of them, having seen only one of them, "The Lily
Nymph," performed, and having read the
score of only the "Melpomene" overture):
Concert overtures, "Rip Van Winkle" (written in Leipzig, 1879, and played there the
same year), "Thalia" (1883), "Melpomene"
(1887), "The Miller's Daughter" (1887), and
"Adonais" (in memory of a friend, 1899);
Symphonies, in C (1882), in B (1885); an
Andante for string orchestra (1884), and
numerous pieces of chamber-music. In the
case of the cantata, "The Lily Nymph,"

Chadwick's art was quite futilized by the superb inanities of the book he used. The " Melpomene " is a work of infinitely more specific gravity. It is one of the most important of American orchestral works.

As his " Thalia " was an " overture to an imaginary comedy," so this, to an imaginary tragedy. It has been played by the Boston Symphony and many other orchestras. It has that definiteness of mood with that indefiniteness of circumstance in which music wins its most dignified prosperity.

It opens with the solitary voice of the English horn, which gives a notable pathos (read Berlioz on this despairful elegist, and remember its haunting wail in the last act of " Tristan und Isolde "). The woeful plaint of this voice breathing above a low sinister roll of the tympanum establishes at once the atmosphere of melancholy. Other instruments join the wail, which breaks out wildly from the whole orchestra. Over a waving accompaniment of clarinets, the other wood-winds strike up a more lyric and hopeful strain, and a soliloquy from the 'cello ends the slow introduction, the materials of

which are taken from the two principal subjects of
the overture, which is built on the classic sonata
formula. The first subject is announced by the
first violins against the full orchestra; the subsid-
iary theme is given to the flutes and oboes; after a
powerful climax, and a beautiful subsidence of the
storm in the lower strings, the second subject appears in the relative major with honeyed lyricism.
The conclusion, which is made rather elaborate by
the latter-day symphonists, is reduced to a brief
modulation by Mr. Chadwick, and almost before
one knows it, he is in the midst of the elaboration.
It is hard to say whether the composer's emotion
or his counterpoint is given freer rein here, for the
work is remarkable both for the display of every
technical resource and for the irresistible tempest
of its passion. In the reprise there is a climax that
thrills one even as he tamely reads the score, and
must be overpowering in actual performance: the
cheerful consolation of the second subject provokes
a cyclonic outburst of grief; there is a furious climax
of thrilling flutes and violins over a mad blare of
brass, the while the cymbals shiver beneath the blows
of the kettledrum-sticks. An abrupt silence prepares for a fierce thunderous clamor from the tympani and the great drum (beaten with the sticks of
the side-drum). This subsides to a single thud of a

kettledrum; there is another eloquent silence; the English horn returns to its first plaint; but grief has died of very exercise, and the work ends in a coda that establishes a major harmony and leaves the hearer with a heart purged white and clean.

The " Melpomene " overture is a work of such inspiration and such scholarship that it must surely find a long youth in the chronicle of our music.

Arthur   Foote.[1]

The nearest approach Americans make to the enthusiastic German *Männerchor* is in the college glee clubs.   The dignity of their selections is not always up to that of the Teutonic chorus, but they develop a salutary fondness for color and shading, exaggerating both a

[1] See p. 479.

little perhaps, yet aiming at the right warmth and variety withal. Even those elaborate paraphrases and circumlocutions of Mother Goose rhymes, to which they are so prone, show a striving after dramatic effect and richness of harmony, as well as a keen sense of wit and humor that are by no means incompatible with real value in music.

Among their other good deeds must be counted the fostering of the musical ambitions of Arthur Foote, who was for two years the leader of the Glee Club of Harvard University. Though he has by no means been content to delve no deeper into music than glee-club depths, I think the training has been of value, and its peculiar character is patent in his works. He is especially fond of writing for men's voices, and is remarkably at home in their management, and he strives rather for color-masses than for separate individualities in the voices.

Among his larger works for men's voices

ARTHUR FOOTE.

is an elaborate setting of Longfellow's poem, "The Skeleton in Armor," which is full of vigor and generally sturdy in treatment, especially in its descriptions of Viking war and seafaring. The storm-scenes, as in Mr. Foote's "Wreck of the Hesperus," seem faintly to suggest Wagnerian *Donner und Blitzen*, but in general Mr. Foote has resisted the universal tendency to copy the mannerisms so many take to be the real essence of the Bayreuthian. A pretty bit of fancy is the use of a spinning-wheel accompaniment to the love-song, although the spindle is nowhere suggested by the poem. Indeed, the spinning is treated as a characteristic motif for the Norseman's bride, somewhat as it is Senta's motif in "The Flying Dutchman."

The chief fault with the "Skeleton" chorus is that it is always choric. There are no solos, and the different registers are never used separately for more than a bar or two, before the whole mass chimes in. Even the instrumental interludes are short, and the general effect must be rather undiversified, one of sympathy, too, for the unrested chorus.

"The Wreck of the Hesperus" is an ambitious work, built on large lines, but hardly represents Mr. Foote at his best. It is for mixed voices, and is pitched in a most lugubrious key, being always either vociferous with panic or dismal with minor woe. A worse trouble yet is the attempt to make a short poem fit a long composition. The Procrustean operation strains even Longfellow sadly.

This blemish is lacking in "The Farewell of Hiawatha," which is written for men's voices. Though it, too, is of a sad tone, its sombre hues are rich and varied as a tapestry. Its effects, though potent, seem more sincere and less labored. It is altogether noble.

A larger body of sacred music for mixed voices than many other Americans can boast, also swells Foote's opus-score. Here he shows the same facility with the quartette as in his other works. In fact, I think the effect of glee-club training on his young mind has strongly influenced his whole life-work. And, by the way, the most talented of all the great Sebastian Bach's twenty-one children — every one a musical opus, too — was diverted from the philosopher's career for which he was intended, and into professional musicianship, by just such a glee-club training in the universities at Leipzig and Frankfort.

Almost all of Foote's compositions are written in the close harmony and limited range of vocal music, and he very rarely sweeps the keyboard in his piano compositions, or hunts out startling novelties in strictly pianistic effect. He is not fond of the cloudy regions of the upper notes, and though he may dart brilliantly skyward now and then just to show that his wings are good for lighter air, he is soon back again, drifting along the middle ether.

He has won his high place by faithful adherence to his own sober, serene ideals, and by his genuine culture and seriousness. He is thoroughly American by birth and training, though his direct English descent accounts for his decided leaning toward the better impulses of the English school of music. He was born at Salem, Mass., March 5, 1853, and though he played the piano a good deal as a boy, and made a beginning in the study of composition with Emery, he did not study seriously until he graduated from Harvard in 1874. He then took up the higher branches of composition under the tuition of John Knowles Paine, and obtained in 1875 the degree of A. M. in the special department of music. He also studied the organ and the piano with B. J. Lang at Boston, and has since made that city his home, teaching and playing the organ.

His overture, "In the Mountains," has been much played from the manuscript by orchestras, among them the Boston Symphony.

Besides a considerable amount of highly valuable contributions to American chamber-music, and two fine piano suites, he has written a great many piano pieces and songs which deserve even greater popularity than they have won, because, while not bristling with technical difficulties, they are yet of permanent worth.

I know of no modern composer who has come nearer to relighting the fires that beam in the old gavottes and fugues and preludes. His two gavottes are to me among the best since Bach. They are an example of what it is to be academic without being only a-rattle with dry bones. He has written a Nocturne that gets farther from being a mere imitation of Chopin than almost any night-piece written since the Pole appropriated that form bodily from John Field and made it his own.

One of his most original pieces is the Capriccio of his D minor Suite, which is also unusually brilliant in color at times ; and he has an Allegretto that is a scherzo of the good old whole-souled humor. Foote, in fact, is never sickly in sentiment.

Of his rather numerous songs, the older English poets, like Marlowe, Sidney, Shakespeare, Suckling, and Herrick, have given him much inspiration. The song " It Was a Lover and his Lass " is especially taking. His three songs, " When You Become a Nun, Dear," " The Road to Kew," and " Ho, Pretty Page ! " written by modern poets in a half-archaic way, display a most delicious fund of subtile and ironic musical humor. "The Hawthorn Wins the Damask Rose " shows how really fine a well conducted English ballad can be. Among his sadder songs, the " Irish Folksong," " I'm Wearing Awa'," and the weird " In a Bower " are heavy with deepest pathos, while " Sweet Is True Love " is as wildly intense and as haunting in its woe as the fate of the poor Elaine, whose despair it sings.

This I count one of the most appealing of modern songs.

His greatest work is undoubtedly his symphonic prologue to Dante's story of "Francesca da Rimini," for full orchestra. Without being informed upon the subject, I fancy a certain programmism in the prologue that is not indicated in the quotation at the beginning of the work:

> " Nessun maggior dolore,
> Che ricordarsi del tempo felice
> Nella miseria."

The prologue, however, seems to me to contain more than the psychological content of these lines from the fifth canto of the " Inferno."

The slow introduction in C minor begins with a long, deep sigh, followed by a downward passage in the violas and 'cellos that seems to indicate the steps that bring Dante and Vergil down to the edge of the precipice past which the cyclone of the damned rolls eternally. There is some shrieking and shuddering,

IT WAS A LOVER AND HIS LASS.

ARTHUR FOOTE, Op. 10, № 1.

Animato.
o'er the green corn - field did pass, In the spring - time, the spring - time, The
love is crown-ed with the prime, In the spring - time, the spring - time, The
cresc. poch. riten. tempo. cresc.
on - ly pret - ty ring - time, When birds do sing hey ding a ding!
colla voce
dim.
Sweet lov - ers love the spring.
2. And Spring. (Shakespeare.)
ritard.

and ominous thudding of the tympani (which are tuned to unusual notes), then follows a short recitative which might represent Dante's query to Francesca how she came to yield to love. Suddenly out of the swirling strings the first subject is caught up; it is a frenzy passionately sung by the first violins, reënforced by the flutes at the crises. The second subject appears after a sudden prelude by the brass; it is a very lyric waltz-tune in the relative major, and doubtless depicts the joy recalled in sorrow. The conclusion is quite lengthy; it is also in waltz form, and is first announced by a single flute over the violins and violas, the first violins keeping to the gloomy G string. This air is now given to a solo horn, and a fierce and irresistible dance fervor is worked up. The elaboration begins with the first subject in F sharp minor, caught up fiercely from a downward rush. The reprise is not long delayed, and the second subject appears, contrary to custom, in the tonic major instead of the tonic minor. The coda is deliciously tender and beautiful, possibly because, being a prologue, the work must prepare for a drama that begins cheerfully; possibly because after all there is comfort in bliss remembered in sorrow.

Tschaïkowski has written a symphonic poem on the same subject, which has been also the inspiration of numberless dramas, and is one of the most pathetic pages in all literature ; even the stern old Dante says that when he heard Francesca tell her story he almost died of pity, and fell to the ground as one dead.

A Serenade for string orchestra (op. 25) contains a Prelude, a tender Air, a luscious Intermezzo in the rich key of B major with soli for violin and 'cello, a Romance with a good climax, and a gallant Gavotte with special attention to the too much slighted violas.

Opus 36 is a suite for full orchestra. It has been played by the Boston Symphony, and consists of a brilliant Allegro ; an Adagio of deep sincerity and beautifully varied color, a period wherein the brass choir, heavily scored, chants alone, and the division of the theme among the wood-wind over the rushing strings is especially effective ; a very whimsical Andante with frequent changes of tempo, and

soli for the English horn in antiphony with
the first oboe ; and a madcap Presto that
whisks itself out in the first violins.

Two other published works are a string
quartette (op. 4) and a quintette for piano and
strings (op. 36). This begins in A minor with
a well woven and well derived set of themes,
and ends in a scherzo in A major with spin-
ning-song characteristics. Between these two
movements comes an intermezzo of strongly
marked Scotch tone. This has been performed by the Kneisel Quartette.

S. G. Pratt.

Almost every musician has heard of Christopher Columbus, and holds him in a certain
esteem as a man without whose push the
invention of America would have been long
deferred ; but few American musicians have
felt under a sufficient debt of gratitude to
make his troubles and triumphs the founda-

tion of an appropriate musical work. Silas G. Pratt was bold enough to undertake the monumental task; and he expended upon it large resources of scholarship, research, and enthusiasm. The work was performed at New York during the Quadricentennial of the discovery of America.

If Pratt had been born in old Egypt, he would have found his chief diversion in the building of pyramids, so undismayed is he by the size of a task. His patriotism is a sharp spur to him, and has enabled him to write an orchestral composition devoted to Paul Revere's Ride; a fantasy descriptive of a battle between the Northern and Southern armies; "The Battle of Manila;" "The Anniversary Overture," in commemoration of the centennial of American Independence, performed in Berlin twice, and in London at the Crystal Palace, during Grant's visit there; and a march called by the curious name of "Homage to Chicago." Besides these works

Pratt has written the "Magdalen's Lament," his first orchestral composition, suggested by Murillo's picture; the lyric opera, "Antonio;" a first symphony, of which the adagio was performed in Berlin, the other movements being produced in Boston and Chicago; a second symphony, "The Prodigal Son;" a romantic opera, "Zenobia," produced in Chicago; a lyric opera, "Lucille," which ran for three weeks in Chicago; a symphonic suite based on the "Tempest;" a canon for a string quartette; a serenade for string orchestra; a grotesque suite, "The Brownies," produced in New York and at Brighton Beach by Anton Seidl. Besides these works of musical composition, Pratt has delivered various musical lectures, ingeniously contrived to entertain the great public and at the same time inform it. He has been active also in the organization of various musical enterprises, among them the Apollo Club of Chicago.

Pratt was born in Addison, Vermont, August 4, 1846. At the age of twelve, he was thrown on his own resources, and connected himself with music publishing houses in Chicago. After various public performances, he went to Germany in 1868, to study the piano under Bendel and Kullak, and counterpoint under Kiel. In 1872 he returned to Chicago and gave a concert of his own works. But the phœnix city had not entirely preened its wings after the great fire of 1871, and Pratt found no support for his ambitions. After teaching and giving concerts, he returned to Germany in 1875, where he attended the rehearsals of Wagner's Trilogy at Bayreuth, met Liszt here, and gave a recital of his own compositions at Weimar. His "Anniversary Overture" was cordially received by the press of both Berlin and London. A third visit to Europe was made in 1885 for the production of the "Prodigal Son" at the Crystal Palace, on the occasion of which, Berthold Tours wrote that both the symphony and the "Anniversary Overture" were "grandly conceived works, full of striking originality, modern harmony, flowing melody, and beautiful, as well as imposing effects."

Activity along such lines has left Pratt little time for the smaller forms of composition ; a few have been published, among them the song, "Dream Vision," in which Schumann's "Träumerei" is used for violin obbligato ; and a few piano pieces, such as "Six Soliloquies," with poetic text. In these each chord shows careful effort at color, and the work is chromatic enough to convince one that he has studied his Bach thoroughly.

Among his massive compositions there are two that seem likely to win, as they surely deserve, a long life. These are the symphonic suite, "The Tempest," and the "Prodigal Son." To the latter splendid achievement, A. J. Goodrich devotes several pages of his "Musical Analysis," to which I can do no better than to refer the reader. The "Tempest" is based, of course, on Shakespeare's play, and is described as follows by the composer :

"It is intended, in the first movement, Adagio, to typify the sorrow of Prospero, and his soul's protest against the ingratitude and persecution of his enemies. His willing attendant Ariel is briefly indicated in the closing measures. The Pastoral furnishes an atmosphere or stage setting for the lovers, Miranda and Ferdinand, whose responsive love-song follows the droning of a shepherd's pipe in the distance. Prospero's interruption to their passionate assurances of devotion, and the imposition of the unpleasant task, are briefly touched upon, and the movement closes with a repeat of the pastoral, and alternate reiteration of the lover's song. The Finale, after a short introduction, in most sombre vein, indicates the flitting about of Ariel and his companion sprites as they gather for revelry. The presence of the master is soon made apparent by the recurrence, in a subdued manner, of Prospero's first theme from the Adagio, the fantastic tripping of the elves continuing, as though the controlling spirit were conjuring up the fête for the amusement of the lovers and himself.

" ' Ye elves of hills, brooks, standing lakes and
       groves ;
    And ye that on the sand, with printless foot
    Do chase the ebbing Neptune, and do fly him
    When he comes back.'

" The dance then begins, and continues in a fantastic, at times grotesque and furious manner, the
theme of the lovers being interwoven at times, in an
unobtrusive way. At length, Caliban is heard approaching, singing his drunken song.

" ' 'Ban, 'Ban, Ca-caliban
    Has a new master: get a new man.'

" Ariel and his companions flit about, ridiculing,
mocking, and laughing at him; eventually prodding
and pinching him until, shivering, with aching joints,
he staggers away. The revelry then continues, the
song of the lovers becoming more and more prominent until, somewhat broadened out, it asserts itself triumphantly above all, Ariel and his companions
flitting about, Prospero happy, and Caliban subju-
gated, all the chief themes being united to form the
climax and close of the work."

Although Pratt intentionally omitted the
English horn and the bass clarinet, the scoring is remarkable for its color and faery.

The work is highly lyrical in effect, and the woodsiness is beautifully established. The solemnity of Prospero, the adroitness of the lovers and the contrasting natures of the volatile Ariel and the sprawling Caliban, make up a cast of characters in the development of which music is peculiarly competent. The stertorous monologue of Caliban and his hobbling dance, and the taunting and pinching torment he is submitted to, make excellent humor.

Henry K. Hadley.[1]

The word symphony has a terrifying sound, particularly when it is applied to a modern work ; for latter-day music is essentially romantic in nature, and it is only a very rare composer that has the inclination or the ability to force the classic form to meet his new ideas. The result is that such a work usually lacks spontaneity, conviction. The

[1] See p. 454.

modern writer does much better with the symphonic poem.

The number of American symphonies worth listening to, could be counted on the fingers with several digits to spare. A new finger has been preëmpted by Henry K. Hadley's symphony called "Youth and Life." The title is doubly happy. Psychologically it is a study of the intense emotional life of youth, written by an American youth, — a young man who, by the way, strangely reminds one, in his appearance, of Macmonnies' American type, as represented by his ideal statue of Nathan Hale.

And musically the work is imbued with both youth and life. It has blood and heart in it. The first movement is a conflict between good and evil motives struggling like the mediæval angels for the soul of the hero. The better power wins triumphantly. The second movement, however, shows doubt and despair, remorse and deep spiritual de-

HENRY K. HADLEY.

pression. The climax of this feeling is a
death-knell, which, smitten softly, gives an
indescribably dismal effect, and thrills without starting. Angelus bells in pedal-point
continue through a period of hope and prayer ;
but remorse again takes sway. The ability
to obtain this fine solemnity, and follow it
with a scherzo of extraordinary gaiety, proves
that a genius is at large among us. The
Scherzo displays a thigh-slapping, song-sing-
ing *abandon* that typifies youthful frivolity
fascinatingly. A fugue is used incidentally
with a burlesque effect that reminds one of
Berlioz' "Amen" parody in the "Damnation of Faust." The Finale exploits motives
of ambition and heroism, with a moment of
love. The climax is vigorous. Without
being at all ariose, the symphony is full of
melody. Its melodies are not counterpoint,
but expression ; and each instrument or choir
of instruments is an individuality.

Hadley is galvanic with energy and optimism, dextrous to a remarkable degree in the mechanism of composition. His scoring is mature, fervent, and certain. His symphony is legitimately programmatic and alive with brains, biceps, and blood, — all three, — the three great B's of composition.

Hadley was born at Somerville, Mass., in 1871. His father was a teacher of music and gave him immediate advantages. He studied harmony with Stephen A. Emery, counterpoint with G. W. Chadwick, and the violin with Henry Heindl and Charles N. Allen of Boston. Before attaining his majority, he had completed a dramatic overture, a string quartette, a trio, and many songs and choruses. In 1894 he went to Vienna and studied composition with Mandyczewski. Here he composed his third suite for the orchestra. In 1896 he returned to America and took charge of the music department of St. Paul's school at Garden City, L. I. He has had some experience as a conductor and has been very prolific in composition. His first symphony was produced under the direction of Anton Seidl, in December, 1897 ; and at a concert of his own compositions, again, in January, 1900, Hadley conducted this symphony, and also two movements from his second symphony, " The Seasons." These two movements show a mellower technic, perhaps, but are less vital. He has written three ballet suites with pronounced success, the work being musical and yet full of the ecstasy of the dance. His third ballet suite, which is the best, was produced at a concert of the American Symphony Orchestra, under Sam Franko.

The existence of a festival march, a concert overture, " Hector and Andromache," two comic operas, and six songs for chorus and orchestra, besides a number of part songs and piano pieces, and over one hundred songs, forty of which are published, gives proof of the restless energy of the man. The high average of scholarship is a proof of his right to serious acceptance.

A cantata for orchestra, "Lelewala," a legend of Niagara, is published for piano accompaniment. Now, Niagara is a dangerous subject for the frail skiffs of rhyme, prose, or music to launch out upon. Barrel staves may carry one through the whirlpool, but music staves cannot stand the stress. Of all the comments upon the Falls of Niagara that I have ever read, or heard of, there has been only one that seemed anything but ridiculously inappropriate; that one was the tribute of a young boy who, on standing face to face with the falls, simply exclaimed, in an awe-smothered whisper, "Well, by gosh!" But it must be admitted that these words would baffle the music-making propensities even of the composer of Händel's "Hallelujah Chorus." That learned composer, George F. Bristow, now dead, made the mistake of attempting to compass Niagara in a work for chorus and orchestra. Hadley is not exactly guilty of the same fatal attempt in his "Lelewala," for the poem is chiefly a story of love and sacrifice; but Niagara comes in as a programmatic incident, and the author of the text has fallen lamentably short of his subject in certain instances. In other moments, he has written with genuine charm, and the music has much that is worth while.

Among his published songs are to be noted the unusually good setting of Heine's "Wenn ich in deine Augen seh'" and of his less often heard "Sapphire sind die Augen dein," and "Der Schmetterling ist in die Rose verliebt." A deservedly popular work is "I Plucked a Quill from Cupid's Wing." Among so many morose or school-bound composers, Hadley is especially important for the fact that he is thrilled with a sane and jubilant music.

Adolph M. Foerster.[1]

It has been fortunate for American song that it forsook the narrow, roystering school of English ballad and took for its national model the *Lied* of the later German school. It is true that the earlier English had its poetry-respecting music in the work of such a man as Henry Lawes, or Purcell, just as it had its composers who far preceded Bach in the key-roving idea of the " Well-tempered Clavier ; " but that spirit died out of England, and found its latest avatar in such men as Robert Franz, who confessed that he had his first and fullest recognition from this country.

A correspondence with Franz was carried on for eighteen years by one of the solidest of American composers, Adolph M. Foerster, who gives distinction to the musical life of Pittsburg. He knew Franz personally, and has written an important appreciation of him for

[1] See p. 543.

ADOLPH M. FOERSTER.

the magazine *Music.* Foerster was born at Pittsburg in 1854. After three years of commercial life, he took up music seriously, and spent the years from 1872 to 1875 at Leipzig, — studying the piano under Coccius and Wenzel, singing under Grill and Schimon, and theory under E. F. Richter and Papperitz. Returning to America, he connected himself with the Fort Wayne (Ind.) Conservatory of Music, then under the direction of the beneficent inventor of the Virgil Clavier. A year later he returned to Pittsburg, where he has since remained. For awhile he was conductor of a symphonic society and a choral union, which are no longer extant. Since, he has devoted himself to teaching and composition.

Of Foerster's piano compositions opus 11 is a "Valse Brillante," warm and melodious. Opus 13 is a "Sonnet," based, after the plan of Liszt, upon a lyric of Petrarch's, a beautiful translation from his "Gli occhi di ch'io

parlai si caldamente." It is full of passion,
and shows a fine variety in the handling of
persistent repetition. Opus 18 couples two
sonatinas. The second has the more merit,
but both, like most sonatinas, are too trivial of psychology and too formal even to
be recommended for children's exercises.
"Eros" is a fluent melody, with a scherzesque
second part.

Opus 37 contains two concert études, both
superb works. The first, "Exaltation," is
very original, though neither the beginning
nor the ending is particularly striking. The
music between, however, has a fervor that
justifies the title. This étude is, like those
of Chopin, at the same time a technical study
and a mood. The second, a "Lamentation,"
begins with a most sonorous downward harmony, with rushes up from the bass like
the lessening onsets of a retreating tide.
Throughout, the harmonies and emotions are
remarkably profound and the climaxes wild.

I should call it one of the best modern piano compositions.

Twelve " Fantasy Pieces" are included in opus 38. They are short tone-poems. The second, " Sylvan Spirits," is fascinating, and " Pretty Marie" has an irresistibly gay melody. He has dedicated the six songs of opus 6 to Robert Franz. These are written in a close unarpeggiated style chiefly, but they are very interesting in their pregnant simplicity. In two cases they are even impressive : the well-known lyric, " Im Rhein, im heiligen Strome," and "Meeresstille." Opus 12 is a notable group of three songs : "Mists" is superbly harmonious. Opus 25 includes " Ask Thou Not the Heather Gray," a rhapsody of the utmost ingenuity in melody and accompaniment. It has a catching blissfulness and a verve that make it one of the best American songs. Opus 28 is a book called "Among Flowers." The music is in every case good, and especially satisfactory in its emancipation from the Teutonism of Foerster's earlier songs. The song "Among the Roses" has a beautiful poem, which deserves the superb music. It ends hauntingly with an unre-solved major ninth chord on the dominant of the dominant. So the frenzy of "In Blossom Time" is emotion of a human, rather than a botanical sort. "The Cradle Song" adapts the Siegfried Idyl, and the "Old Proverb" is rollicking. The two songs of opus 34 are fitted with words by Byron. The three songs of opus 44 also make use of this poet, now so little in vogue with composers. There are three songs in opus 42 : a pathetic "Little Wild Rose," and "By the Seaside," which is full of solemnity. "The Shepherd's Lament" is one of his best lyrics, with a strange accompaniment containing an inverted pedal-point in octaves. There are also several part songs.

In larger forms, Mr. Foerster is even more successful. Opus 10 is a Character-piece for full orchestra, based on Karl Schäfer's poem, "Thusnelda." It is short but vigorous, and well unified. Opus 15 is a Fantasie for violin and piano, the piano having really the better of it. The treatment is very original, and the strong idea well preserved. Opus 21 is a Quartette for violin, viola, 'cello, and piano. The first movement begins solemnly, but breaks into an appassionato. All four instruments have an equal voice in the parley, and all the outbursts are emotional rather than contrapuntal. A climax of tremendous power is attained. The second movement omits the piano for a beautiful adagio. The third is an hilarious allegro, and the finale is an even gayer presto, with movements of sudden sobriety, suddenly swept away. Foerster calls this Quartette " far inferior " to a second one, opus 40. This, however, I have not seen ; but I do not hesitate to call opus 21 a masterly work.

Opus 24 is an " Albumblatt " for 'cello and

piano. It is a wonder-work of feeling and deep richness of harmony, of absolute sincerity and inspiration. Opus 29 is a Trio for violin, 'cello, and piano. The three begin in unison, andante, whence the 'cello breaks away, followed soon by the others, into the joviality of a drinking bout. There is a military moment, a lyric of more seriousness, and a finish agitato. The second movement is a larghetto highly embroidered. The third movement is a vivace with the spirit of a Beethoven presto.

Opus 36 is a suite for violin and piano, beginning with a most engaging and most skilful Novelette.

In MS. are: an elaborate ballad, "Hero and Leander," which, in spite of an unworthy postlude and certain "Tristan und Isolde" memories, is ardent and vivid with passion; "Verzweifelung," which is bitter and wild with despair; a suite for piano (op. 46) containing a waltz as ingenious as it is captivating; and a finale called "Homage to Brahms." This is a remarkably clever piece of writing, which, while it lacks the Brahmsian trade-mark of thirds in the bass, has much of that composer's best manner, less in his tricks of speech than in his tireless development and his substitution of monumental thematicism for lyric emotion. In MS. is also a prelude to Goethe's "Faust" for full orchestra. It has very definite leading motives, which include "Faust's Meditations," "Visions of Margarethe," "Evil" and "Love" (almost inversions of each other), "Mephistopheles," and the like. The strife of these elements is managed with great cleverness, ending beatifically with the motive of Gretchen dying away in the wood-wind.

An orchestral score that has been published is the Dedication March for Carnegie Hall in Pittsburg. It begins with a long fanfare of horns heard behind the scenes. Suddenly enters a jubilant theme beginning with Andrew Carnegie's initials, a worthy tribute to one to whom American music owes much.

Charles Crozat Converse.

Musicians are not, as a class, prone to a various erudition (a compliment fully returned by the learned in other directions, who are almost always profoundly ignorant of the actual art of music). One of the rule-proving exceptions is Charles Crozat Converse, who has delved into many philosophies. An example of his versatility of interest is his coining of the word "thon" (a useful substitute for the ubiquitous awkwardness of "he or she" and "his or her"), which has been adopted by the Standard Dictionary.

Converse' ancestry is American as far back as 1630. Converse was born at Warren, Mass., October 7, 1832. After being well grounded in English and the classics, he went, in 1855, to Germany. Here he

CHARLES CROZAT CONVERSE.

studied law and philosophy, and music at
the Conservatorium in Leipzig. He enjoyed
the instruction of Richter, Hauptmann,
Plaidy, and Haupt, and made the acquaintance of Liszt and Spohr. Spohr was especially interested in, and influential in, his
work, and confident of its success.

Returning to America, he graduated from
the Law Department of Albany University
in 1860, with the degree of LL.B. The B
has since been dignified into a D, as a tribute
to his unusual accomplishments. Converse
declined the honor of a Doctorship of
Music from the University of Cambridge,
offered him by its professor, the well-known
English composer, Sterndale Bennett, in recognition of his mastery of lore as evinced in
a five-voiced double fugue that ends his
Psalm-Cantata on the 126th Psalm.

This scholarly work was performed under
the direction of Theodore Thomas in 1888,
at Chicago.

A widely known contribution to religious music is Converse' hymn, "What a Friend We Have in Jesus," which has been printed, so they say, in all the tongues of Christendom, and sold to the extent of fifty millions of copies. This tune occupied a warm place in my Sunday-schoolboy heart, along with other singable airs of the Moody and Sankey type, but as I hum it over in memory now, it tastes sweetish and thin. Its popularity is appalling, musically at least. Converse has written many other hymn-tunes, which have taken their place among ecclesiastical soporifics. Besides, he has recently compiled a collection of the world's best hymns into the "Standard Hymnal." In this field Converse, though conventional, — and conventionality may be considered inevitable here, — is mellow of harmony and sincere in sentiment.

Numberless attempts are made to supply our uncomfortable lack of a distinctly national air, but few of them have that first requisite, a fiery catchiness, and most of them have been so bombastic as to pall even upon palates that can endure Fourth of July glorification. Recognizing that the trouble with "America" was not at all due to the noble words written by the man whom "fate tried to conceal by naming him Smith," Converse has written a new air to this poem. Unfortunately, however, his method of varying the much-borrowed original tune is too transparent. He has not discarded the idea at all, or changed the rhythm or the spirit. He has only taken his tune upward where "God Save the Queen" moves down, and bent his melody down where the British soars up. This, I fancy, is the chief reason why his national hymn has gone over to the great majority, and has been conspicuously absent from such public occasions as torch-light parades and ratifications.

Except the work issued under the alias

"Karl Redan," or the anagrams, "C. O. Nevers" and "C. E. Revons," his only secular musics that have been put into print are his American Overture, published in Paris, and a book of six songs, published in Germany.

Music is called the universal language, but it has strongly marked dialects, and sometimes a national flavor untranslatable to foreign peoples. So with these six songs, not the words alone are German. They are based on a Teutonic, and they modulate only from Berlin to Braunschweig and around to Leipzig. While the songs repay study, they are rather marked by a pianistic meditation than a strictly lyric emotion. "Aufmunterung zur Freude" is a tame allegretto; "Wehmuth" is better; "Täuschung" is a short elegy of passion and depth; "Ruhe in der Geliebten" is best in its middle strain where it is full of rich feeling and harmony. The ending is cheap. "Der gefangene Sänger" is only a slight variant at first on the "Adieu" credited to Schubert; it is thereafter excellent.

Converse has a large body of music in manuscript, none of which I had the pleasure of examining save a tender sacred lullaby. There are two symphonies, ten suites, and concert overture, three symphonic poems, an oratorio, "The Captivity," six string quartettes, and a mass of psalmodic and other vocal writing.

Of these works three have been produced with marked success: the "Christmas Overture," at one of the public concerts of the Manuscript Society, under the direction of Walter Damrosch; the overture "Im Frühling," at concerts in Brooklyn and New York, under the baton of Theodore Thomas; and the American overture, "Hail Columbia!" at the Boston Peace Jubilee under Patrick Gilmore, at the Columbian Exposition under Thomas, and in New York under Anton Seidl.

This last overture received the distinction of publication at Paris, by Schott et Cie. It is built on the rousing air of " Hail, Columbia ! " This is suggested in the slow minor introduction ; the air itself is indicated thematically as one of the subjects later appearing in full swing in a coda. The instrumentation is brilliant and the climax overwhelming.

Altogether the work is more than adroit musical composition. It is a prairié-fire of patriotism.

L. A. Coerne.[1]

A grand opera by an American on an American subject is an achievement to look forward to. Though I have not seen this opera, called " A Woman of Marblehead," it is safe to predict, from a study of its composer's other works, that it is a thing of merit.

Louis Adolphe Coerne, who wrote the

[1] See p. 468.

LOUIS ADOLPHE COERNE.

music for this opera, was born in **Newark,
N. J.,** in 1870, and spent the years from six
to ten in music study abroad, at Stuttgart
and Paris. Returning to America, he entered
Harvard College and studied harmony and
composition under John Knowles Paine. He
studied the violin under Kneisel. In 1890
he went to Munich, where he studied the
organ and composition at the Royal Academy
of Music, under Rheinberger, and the violin
under Hieber. He now decided to give up
the career of a violinist for that of composer,
conductor, and organist. In 1893 he returned
to Boston and acted as organist. A **year
later** he went to Buffalo, where for **three
years** he directed the Liedertafel.

While in Harvard, Coerne had composed
and produced a concerto for violin and 'cello
with string orchestra accompaniment, a fantasy for full orchestra, and a number of
anthems which were performed at the university chapel. While in Munich and Stutt-

gart he wrote and produced a string suite, an organ concerto with accompaniment of strings, horns, and harps, three choral works, and a ballet, " Evadne," on a subject of his own. His symphonic poem on Longfellow's " Hiawatha " was also produced there with much success under his personal direction, and later by the Boston Symphony Orchestra. He was invited then by Theodore Thomas to attend the World's Fair at Chicago, to give recitals on the great organ in Festival Hall.

It has been my misfortune not to have heard or seen hardly any of his writings except the published " Character Pieces " from the ballet " Evadne " (op. 155). A " Clown's Dance " in bolero rhythm is delightful. The " Introduction to Act II." contains many varied ideas and one passage of peculiar harmonic beauty. A " Valse de Salon " has its good bits, but is rather overwrought. A " Devil's Dance " introduces some excellent harmonic effects, but the " Waltz with Chorus

and Finale" is the best number of the opus.
It begins in the orchestra with a most irresistible waltz movement that is just what a
waltz should be. A chorus is then superim-
posed on this rhapsody, and a climax of superb
richness attained.

For the organ Coerne has written much
and well. There is an adaptation of three
pieces from the string quartette (op. 19) ; a
graceful Minuet, a quaint Aria, and a Fugue.
Then there are three Marches, which, like
most marches written by contemplative musicians, are rather thematic than spirited, and
marked by a restless and elaborate preparation for some great chant that is longed for,
but never comes. Besides these, there are a
very pleasant Pastoral, a good Elevation, and
a Nocturne.

Coerne's symphonic poem, "Hiawatha," has
been arranged for the piano for four hands,
and there is also an arrangement for violin or
violoncello and piano, but I have not seen

these. The thing we are all waiting for is that American grand opera, " A Woman of Marblehead." It is to be predicted that she will not receive the marble heart.

CHAPTER IV.

THE COLONISTS.

ART does not prosper as hermit. Of course, every great creator has a certain aloofness of soul, and an inner isolation; but he must at times submit his work to the comparison of his fellow artists; he must profit by their discoveries as well as their errors; he must grow overheated in those passionate musical arguments that never convince any one out of his former belief, and serve salutarily to raise the temper, cultivate caloric, and deepen convictions previously held; he must exchange criticisms and discuss standards with others, else he will be eternally making discoveries that are stale and unprofitable to the rest of the world; he will seek to reach men's souls through channels long dammed up, and his achievements will be marred by naïve triteness and primitive crudeness.

So, while the artistic tendency may be a universal nervous system, artists are inclined to ganglionate. The nerve-knots vary in size and importance, and one chief ganglion may serve as a feeding brain, but it cannot monopolize the activity. In America, particularly, these ganglia, or colonies, are an interesting and vital phase of our development. For a country in which the different federated states are, many of them, as large as old-world kingdoms, it is manifestly impossible for any one capital to dominate. Furthermore, the national spirit is too insubordinate to accept any centre as an oracle.

New York, which has certainly drawn to itself a preponderance of respectable composers, has yet been unable to gather in many of the most important, and like the

French Academy, must always suffer in prestige because of its conspicuous absentees. In the second place, New York is the least serious and most fickle city in the country, and is regarded with mingled envy and patronage by other cities.

Boston is even more unpopular with the rest of the country. And New York and other cities have enticed away so many of the leading spirits of her musical colony, that she cannot claim her once overwhelming superiority. And yet, Boston has been, and is, the highest American representative of that much abused term, culture. Of all the arts, music doubtless gets her highest favor.

The aid Boston has been to American music is vital, and far outweighs that of any other city. That so magnificent an organization as its Symphony Orchestra could be so popular, shows the solidity of its general art appreciations. The orchestra has been remarkably willing, too, to give the American composer a chance to be heard. Boston has been not only the promulgator, but in a great measure the tutor, of American music.

In Boston-town, folk take things seriously and studiously. In New York they take them fiercely, whimsically. Like most generalizations, this one has possibly more exceptions than inclusions. But it is convenient.

It is convenient, too, to group together such of the residents of these two towns, as I have not discussed elsewhere. The Chicago coterie makes another busy community; and St. Louis and Cleveland have their activities of more than intramural worth; Cincinnati, which was once as musically thriving as its strongly German qualities necessitated, but which had a swift and strange decline, seems to be plucking up heart again. For this, the energy of Frank van der Stucken is largely to credit. Aside from the foreign-born composers there, one should mention the work of Richard Kieserling, Jr., and Emil Wiegand.

The former went to Europe in 1891 and studied at the Leipzig Conservatory, under Reinecke, Homeyer, Rust, Schreck and Jadassohn. He also studied conducting under Sitt. At his graduation, he conducted a performance of his own composition, "Jeanne d'Arc." He returned to his native city, Cincinnati, in 1895, where he has since remained, teaching and conducting. Among his works, besides piano pieces and songs, are: "A May Song," for women's chorus and piano; six pieces for violin and piano; "Harold," a ballad for male chorus, barytone solo, and orchestra; "Were It Not For Love," composed for male chorus; several sets of male choruses; a motet for mixed chorus a cappella; a berceuse for string orchestra, an introduction and rondo for violin and orchestra; and a "Marche Nuptiale," for grand orchestra.

Emil Wiegand was also born in Cincinnati, and had his first tuition on the violin from his father. His theoretical studies have been received entirely in Cincinnati. He is a member of the local Symphonic Orchestra, and has composed an overture for grand orchestra, a string quartette, and various pieces for the violin, piano, and voice.

In San Francisco there is less important musical composition than there was in the days when Kelley and Page were active there. The work of H. B. Pasmore[1] is highly commended by *cognoscenti*, as are also the works of Frederick Zeck, Jr., who was born in San Francisco, studied in Germany, and has composed symphonies, a symphonic poem, " Lamia," a romantic opera, and other works ; Samuel Fleischmann, born in California and educated abroad, a concert pianist, who has written, among other things, an overture, " Hero and Leander," which was performed in New York ; and P. C. Allen, who studied in Europe, and has written well.

But the larger cities do not by any means contain all the worthy composition. In

[1] See p. 513.

many smaller cities, and in a few villages even, can be found men of high culture and earnest endeavor.

In Yonkers, New York, is Frederick R. Burton, who has written a dramatic cantata on Longfellow's "Hiawatha," which has been frequently performed. In this work use is made of an actual Indian theme, which was jotted down by H. E. Krehbiel, and is worked up delightfully in the cantata, an incessant thudding of a drum in an incommensurate rhythm giving it a decidedly barbaric tone. The cantata contains also a quaint and touching contralto aria, and a pathetic setting of the death-song of Minnehaha. Burton is a graduate of Harvard, and a writer as well as a composer. He organized, in 1896, the Yonker's Choral Society, of which he is conductor.

At Hartford, Conn., is Nathan H. Allen, who was born in Marion, Mass., in 1848. In 1867 he went to Berlin, where he was a pupil of Haupt for three years. In this country he has been active as an organist and teacher. Many of his compositions of sacred music have been published, including a cantata, "The Apotheosis of St. Dorothy."

At Providence, R. I., a prominent figure is Jules Jordan, who was born at Willimantic, Conn., November 10, 1850, of colonial ancestry. Though chiefly interested in oratorio singing, in which he has been prominent, he has written a number of songs, some of which have been very popular. The best of these are a rapturous "Love's Philosophy," a delicious "Dutch Lullaby," "An Old Song," and "Stay By and Sing." He has written some religious songs, part songs, and three works for soli, chorus, and orchestra, "Windswept Wheat," "A Night Service," and "Barbara Frietchie;" also "Joel," a dramatic scene for soprano and orchestra, sung at the Worcester Musical Festival by Mme. Nordica. This I have not seen, nor his romantic opera, " Rip Van Winkle." In June, 1895, Brown University conferred on him the degree of Doctor of Music. Two albums of his songs are published.

A writer of many religious solos and part songs is E. W. Hanscom, who lives in Auburn, Me. He was born at Durham, in the same State, December 28, 1848. He has made two extended visits to London, Berlin and Vienna, for special work under eminent teachers, but has chiefly studied in Maine. Besides his sacred songs Hanscom has published a group of six songs, all written intelligently, and an especially good lyric, " Go, Rose, and in Her Golden Hair," a very richly harmonized " Lullaby," and two " Christmas Songs," with violin obbligato.

In Delaware, Ohio, at the Ohio Wesleyan University, is a composer, Willard J. Baltzell,[1] who has found inspiration for many worthy compositions, but publishers for only two, both of these part songs, " Dreamland " and

[1] See p. 554.

" Life is a Flower," of which the latter is
very excellent writing.

Baltzell was for some years a victim of the
musical lassitude of Philadelphia. He had
his musical training there. He has written
in the large forms a suite founded on Rossetti's "Love's Nocturne," an overture,
"Three Guardsmen," a "Novelette" for orchestra, a cantata, "The Mystery of Life,"
and an unfinished setting of Psalm xvii. with
barytone solo. These are all scored for
orchestra, and the manuscript that I have
seen shows notable psychological power.
Other works are: a string quartette, a trio,
"Lilith," based on Rossetti's poem, "Eden
Bower," a nonet, and a violin sonata. He
has also written for the piano and organ
fugues and other works. These I have not
seen; but I have read many of his songs in
manuscript, and they reveal a remarkable
strenuousness, and a fine understanding of
the poetry. His song, "Desire," is full of

high-colored flecks of harmony that dance
like the golden motes in a sunbeam. His
"Madrigal" has much style and humor.
He has set to music a deal of the verse of
Langdon E. Mitchell, besides a song cycle,
"The Journey," which is an interesting failure, — a failure because it cannot interest
any public singer, and interesting because of
its artistic musical landscape suggestion ; and
there are the songs, "Fallen Leaf," which is
deeply morose, and "Loss," which has some
remarkable details and a strange, but effective, ambiguous ending. Other songs are a
superbly rapturous setting of E. C. Stedman's "Thou Art Mine," and a series of
songs to the words of Richard Watson Gilder,
a poet who is singularly interesting to composers : "Thistledown" is irresistibly volatile ; "Because the Rose Must Fade" has
a nobility of mood ; "The Winter Heart"
is a powerful short song, and "Woman's
Thought," aside from one or two dangerous

moments, is stirring and intense. Baltzell writes elaborate accompaniments, for which his skill is sufficient, and he is not afraid of his effects.

In the far Xanadu of Colorado lives Rubin Goldmark,[1] a nephew of the famous Carl Goldmark. He was born in New York in 1872. He attended the public schools and the College of the City of New York. At the age of seven he began the study of the piano with Alfred M. Livonius, with whom he went to Vienna at the age of seventeen. There he studied the piano with Anton Door, and composition with Fuchs, completing in two years a three years' course in harmony and counterpoint. Returning to New York, he studied with Rafael Joseffy and with Doctor Dvôrák for one year. In 1892 he went to Colorado Springs for his health. Having established a successful College of Music there, he has remained as its director and as a lecturer on musical topics.

[1] See p. 495.

At the age of nineteen he wrote his "Theme and Variations" for orchestra. They were performed under Mr. Seidl's leadership in 1895 with much success. Their harmonies are singularly clear and sweet, of the good old school. At the age of twenty Goldmark wrote a trio for piano, violin, and 'cello. After the first performance of this work at one of the conservatory concerts, Doctor Dvôrák exclaimed, "There are now two ·Goldmarks." The work has also had performance at the concerts of the Kaltenborn Quartette, and has been published. It begins with a tentative questioning, from which a serious allegro is led forth. It is lyrical and sane, though not particularly modern, and certainly not revolutionary in spirit. The second movement, a romanza, shows more contrapuntal resource, and is full of a deep yearning and appeal, — an extremely beautiful movement. The scherzo evinces a taking jocosity with a serious interval. The piano part is especially humorous. The finale begins with a touch of Ethiopianism that is perhaps unconscious. The whole movement is very original and quaint.

Goldmark's music shows a steady development from a conservative simplicity to a modern elaborateness, a development thoroughly to be commended if it does not lead into obscurity. This danger seems to threaten Goldmark's career, judging from his cantata for chorus and orchestra, the " Pilgrimage to Kevlaar," which, while highly interesting in places, and distinctly resourceful, is too abstruse and gloomy to stand much chance of public understanding.

Many of the works that I have had the privilege of examining in MS. have since been published ; there is much originality, much attainment, and more promise in a number of his songs. His setting of Marlowe's " Come Live with Me," in spite of a few eccentricities, shows, on the whole, a great fluency of melody over an elaborately beautiful accompaniment. His solemn and mysterious " Forest Song" could deserve the advertisement of being "drawn from the wood." "Die erste Liebe" shows a contemplative originality in harmony, and ends with a curious dissonance and resolution. "O'er the Woods' Brow" is very strange and interesting, though somewhat abstruse. Less so is a song, "An den Abendsstern;" it has a comparison-forcing name, but is a delightful song. "Es muss ein Wunderbares sein" is notable for novel effects in harmonies of crystal with light dissonances to edge the facets. A sonata for piano and violin and a romanza for 'cello have been published, and his "Hiawatha" overture has been played by the Boston Symphony Orchestra. On this occasion the always quoteworthy mezzo-tintist, James Huneker, wrote:

" The nephew of a very remarkable composer, — for Carl Goldmark outranks to-day all the Griegs,

Massenets, Mascagnis, Saint-Saëns, and Dvôráks you can gather, — he needs must fear the presence in his scores of the avuncular apparition. His ' Hiawatha ' overture was played by Mr. Gericke and the Boston Symphony Orchestra Wednesday of last week. At the first cantilena on the strings I nearly jumped out oɪ my seat. It was bewilderingly luscious and Goldmarkian, — a young Goldmark come to judgment. The family gifts are color and rhythm. This youth has them, and he also has brains. Original invention is yet to come, but I have hopes. The overture, which is not Indian, is full of good things, withal too lengthy in the free fantasia. There is life, and while there's life there's rhythm, and a nice variety there is. The allegro has one stout tune, and the rush and dynamic glow lasts. He lasts, does Rubin Goldmark, and I could have heard the piece through twice. The young American composer has not been idle lately."

The New York Colony.

In every period where art is alive there must be violent faction, and wherever there is violent faction there is sure to be a *tertium quid* that endeavors to bridge the quarrel.

The Daniel Websters call forth the Robert Haynes, and the two together evoke the compromisers, the Henry Clays.

In the struggle between modernity and classicism that always rages when music is in vitality, one always finds certain ardent spirits who endeavor to reconcile the conflicting theories of the different schools, and to materialize the reconciliation in their own work. An interesting example of this is to be found in the anatomical construction of one of the best American piano compositions, the fantasy for piano and orchestra by Arthur Whiting.[1]

The composer has aimed to pay his respects to the classic sonata formula, and at the same time to warp it to more romantic and modern usages. The result of his experiment is a form that should interest every composer. As Whiting phrases it, he has "telescoped" the sonata form. The slow introduction prepares for the first and second subjects,

[1] See p. 493.

which appear, as usual, except that they are somewhat developed as they appear. Now, in place of the regular development, the pastoral movement is brought forward. This is followed by the reprise of the first and second subjects. Then the finale appears. All these movements are performed without pause, and the result is so successful that Whiting is using the same plan for a quintette.

Handwriting experts are fond of referring to the "picture effect" of a page of writing. It is sometimes startling to see the resemblance in "picture effect" between the music pages of different composers. The handsomely abused Perosi, for instance, writes many a page, which, if held at arm's length, you would swear was one of Palestrina's. Some of Mr. Whiting's music has a decidedly Brahmsic picture effect. This feeling is emphasized when one remembers the enthusiasm shown for Brahms in Whiting's concerts,

where the works of the Ursus Minor of
Vienna hold the place of honor. The re-
semblance is only skin deep, however, and
Whiting's music has a mind of its own.

The fantasy in question (op. 11) is full of
individuality and brilliance. The first subject
is announced appassionato by the strings,
the piano joining with arabesquery that follows the general outlines. After this is
somewhat developed, the second subject
comes in whimsically in the relative major.
This is written with great chromatic lusciousness, and is quite liberally developed. It
suddenly disappears into what is ordinarily
called the second movement, a pastoral, in
which the piano is answered by the oboe,
flute, clarinet, and finally the horn. This is
gradually appassionated until it is merged
into the reprise of the first movement proper.
During this reprise little glints of reminiscence of the pastoral are seen. A coda of
great bravery leads to the last movement,

which is marked "scherzando," but is rather martial in tone. The decidedly noble composition ends with great brilliancy and strength. It is published for orchestral score and for two pianos.

Whiting was born in Cambridge, Mass., June 20, 1861. He studied the piano with William H. Sherwood, and has made a successful career in concert playing with the Boston Symphony Orchestra and the Kneisel Quartette, both of which organizations have performed works of his. In 1883 he went to Munich for two years, where he studied counterpoint and composition with Rheinberger. He is now living in New York as a concert pianist and teacher.

Four works of his for the piano are : " Six Bagatelles," of which the " Caprice " has a charming infectious coda, while the " Humoreske " is less simple, and also less amusing. The " Album Leaf " is a pleasing whimsy, and the " Idylle " is as delicate as fleece. Of

Idylle.

ARTHUR WHITING.

A FRAGMENT.

the three "Characteristic Waltzes," the "Valse Sentimentale" is by far the most interesting. It manages to develop a sort of harmonic haze that is very romantic.

For the voice, Whiting has written little. Church music interests him greatly, and he has written various anthems, a morning and evening service, which keeps largely to the traditional colors of the Episcopal ecclesiastical manner, yet manages to be fervent without being theatrical. A trio, a violin sonata, and a piano quintette, a suite for strings, and a concert overture for orchestra complete the list of his writings.

On the occasion of a performance of Whiting's "Fantasy," Philip Hale thus picturesquely summed him up :

"In times past I have been inclined to the opinion that when Mr. Whiting first pondered the question of a calling he must have hesitated between chess and music. His music seemed to me full of openings and gambits and queer things contrived as in a game.

He was the player, and the audience was his antago-
nist. Mr. Whiting was generally the easy conqueror.
The audience gave up the contest and admired the
skill of the musician.

"You respected the music of Mr. Whiting, but you
did not feel for it any personal affection. The music
lacked humanity. Mr. Whiting had, and no doubt
has, high ideals. Sensuousness in music seemed to
him as something intolerable, something against public morals, something that should be suppressed by
the selectmen. Perhaps he never went so far as to
petition for an injunction against sex in music; but
rigorous intellectuality was his one aim. He might
have written A Serious Call to Devout and Holy
Composition, or A Practical Treatise upon Musical
Perfection, to which is now added, by the same
author, The Absolute Unlawfulness of the Stage
Entertainment Fully Demonstrated.

"There was almost intolerance in Mr. Whiting's
musical attitude. He himself is a man of wit rather
than humor, a man with a very pretty knack at
sarcasm. He is industrious, fastidious, a severe judge
of his own works. As a musician he was even in his
dryest days worthy of sincere respect.

"Now this fantasia is the outward and sure expression of a change in Mr. Whiting's way of musical
thinking, and the change is decidedly for the better.

There is still a display of pure intellectuality; there is still a solving of self-imposed problems; but Mr. Whiting's musical enjoyment is no longer strictly selfish. Here is a fantasia in the true sense of the term; form is here subservient to fancy. The first movement, if you wish to observe traditional terminology, is conspicuous chiefly for the skill, yes, fancy, with which thematic material of no marked apparent inherent value is treated. The pastorale is fresh and suggestive. The ordinary pastorale is a bore. There is the familiar recipe: take an oboe the size of an egg, stir it with a flute, add a little piano, throw in a handful of muted strings, and let the whole gently simmer in a 9-8 stew-pan. But Mr. Whiting has treated his landscape and animal kingdom with rare discretion. The music gave pleasure; it soothed by its quiet untortured beauty, its simplicity, its discretion. And in like manner, without receiving or desiring to receive any definite, precise impression, the finale interested because it was not a hackneyed form of brilliant talk. The finale is something more than clever, to use a hideous term that I heard applied to it. It is individual, and this praise may be awarded the whole work. Remember, too, that although this is a fantasia, there is not merely a succession of unregulated, uncontrolled, incoherent sleep-chasings.

" In this work there is a warmer spirit than that

which animated or kept alive Mr. Whiting's former creations. There is no deep emotion, there is no sensuousness, there is no glowing color, no 'color of deciduous days.' These might be incongruous in the present scheme. But there is a more pronounced vitality, there is a more decided sympathy with the world and men and women; there is more humanity.

"The piano is here an orchestral instrument, and as such it was played admirably by Mr. Whiting. His style of playing is his own, even his tone seems peculiarly his own, with a crispness that is not metallic, with a quality that deceives at first in its carrying power. His performance was singularly clean and elastic, its personality was refreshing. He played the thoughts of Mr. Whiting in Mr. Whiting's way. And thus by piece and performance did he win a legitimate success."

Many American composers have had their first tuition from their mothers ; few from their fathers. Mr. Huss[1] is one of the latter few. The solidity of his musical foundation bespeaks a very correct beginning. He was born in Newark, N. J., June 21, 1862. His first teacher in the theory of music was

[1] See p. 493.

Otis B. Boise, who has been for the last twenty years a teacher of theory in Berlin, though he was born in this country. Huss went to Munich in 1883 and remained three years. He studied counterpoint under Rheinberger, and won public mention for proficiency. At his second examination his idyl for small orchestra, "In the Forest," was produced ; and at his graduation he performed his "Rhapsody" in C major for piano and orchestra. A year after his return to America this work was given by the Boston Symphony Orchestra. A year later Van der Stucken gave it at the first of his concerts of American compositions. The next year Huss' "Ave Maria," for women's voices, string orchestra, harp, and organ, was given a public hearing. The next year he gave a concert of his own works, and the same year, 1889, Van der Stucken produced his violin romance and polonaise for violin and orchestra at the Paris Exposition.

HENRY HOLDEN HUSS.

His piano concerto for piano and orchestra he played first with the Boston Symphony Orchestra in 1894, and has given it on numerous occasions since.

Other works, most of which have also been published, are : "The Fountain," for women's voices a cappella ; a festival "Sanctus," for chorus and orchestra ; an "Easter Theme," for chorus, organ, and orchestra ; "The Winds," for chorus and orchestra, with soprano and alto solos ; a Festival March," for organ and orchestra ; a concerto for violin, and orchestra ; a trio for piano, violin, and 'cello ; a "Prélude Appassionata," for the piano, dedicated to and played by Miss Adèle aus der Ohe, to whom the concerto is also dedicated.

This concerto, which is in D major, is a good example of the completeness of Huss' armory of resources. The first movement has the martial pomp and hauteur and the Sardanapalian opulence and color that mark a barbaric triumph. Chopin has been the evident model, and the result is always pianistic even at its most riotous point. Huss has ransacked the piano and pillaged almost every imaginable fabric of high color. The great technical difficulties of the work are entirely incidental to the desire for splendor. The result is gorgeous and purple. The andante is hardly less elaborate than the first movement, but in the finale there is some laying off of the *impedimenta* of the pageant, as if the paraders had put aside the magnificence for a period of more informal festivity. The spirit is that of the scherzo, and the main theme is the catchiest imaginable, the rhythm curious and irresistible, and the entire mood saturnalian. In the coda there is a reminder of the first movement, and the whole thing ends in a blaze of fireworks.

On the occasion of its first performance in Cincinnati, in 1889, Robert I. Carter wrote:

" It is preëminently a symphonic work, in which the piano is used as a voice in the orchestra, and used with consummate skill. The charm of the work lies in its simplicity. The pianist will tell you at once that it is essentially pianistic, a term that is much abused and means little. The traditional cadenza is there, but it is not allowed to step out of the frame, and so perfect is the relation to what precedes and follows, that the average listener might claim that it does not exist. Without wishing to venture upon any odious grounds of comparison, I want to state frankly that it is, to me, emphatically the best American concerto."

Huss is essentially a dramatic and lyric composer, though he seems to be determined to show himself also a thematic composer of the old school. In his trio, which I heard played by the Kaltenborn Quartette, both phases of his activity were seen. There was much odor of the lamp about the greater part of the trio, which seemed generally lacking that necessary capillarity of energy which sometimes saturates with life-sap the most formal and elaborate counterpoint of the pre-romantic strata. The andante of the trio, however, displayed Huss' singularly appealing gift of song. It abounded in emotion, and was — to use the impossible word Keats coined — "yearnful." Huss should write more of this sort of music. We need its rare spontaneity and truth, as we do not need the all too frequent mathematics of those who compose, as Tybalt fought, "by the book."

For the piano there are "Three Bagatelles:" an "Étude Melodique," which is rather harmonic than melodic; an "Album-blatt," a graceful movement woven like a Schumann arabesque; and a "Pastoral," in which the gracefulness of the music given to the right hand is annulled by the inexplicable harshness of that given to the left.

For the voice, there is, of course, a setting of "Du bist wie eine Blume," which, save for the fact that it looks as if the accompaniment were written first, is a very pure piece of writing. The "Song of the Syrens" is a

strong composition with a big climax, the
"Jessamine Bud" is extremely delicate, and
"They that Sow in Tears" has much dignity.
There are two songs from Tennyson, "There
is Sweet Music Here" and "Home They
Brought Her Warrior Dead," with orchestral
accompaniment.

By all odds the most important, and a
genuinely improved composition is the aria
for soprano and orchestra, "The Death of
Cleopatra." The words are taken from
Shakespeare's play and make use of the
great lines given to the dying Egypt,
"Give me my robe, put on my crown, I
have immortal longings in me," and the rest.
The music not only pays all due reverence
to the sacred text, but is inspired by it, and
reaches great heights of fervor and tragedy.
From Shakespeare, Huss drew the afflation
for another aria of great interest, a setting
for barytone voice of the "Seven Ages of
Man." The problems attending the putting

to music of Shakespeare's text are severe;
but the plays are gold mines of treasure for
the properly equipped musician.

A vivid example of the difficulties in the
way of American composers' securing an
orchestral hearing is seen in the experience
of Howard Brockway, who had a symphony
performed in 1895 by the Berlin Philharmonic Orchestra, and has been unable to
get a hearing or get the work performed in
America during the five years following, in
spite of the brilliancy of the composition.
The scoring of the work is so mature that
one can see its skill by a mere glance at the
page from a distance. When the work was
performed in Germany, it was received with
pronounced favor by the Berlin critics, who
found in it a conspicuous absence of all those
qualities which the youth of the composer
would have made natural.

Brockway was born in Brooklyn, November 22, 1870, and studied piano with H. O

C. Kortheuer from 1887 to 1889. He went to Berlin at the age of twenty and studied the piano with Barth, and composition with O. B. Boise, the transplanted American. Boise gave Brockway so thorough a training that he may be counted one of the most fluent and completely equipped American composers. At the age of twenty-four he had finished his symphony (op. 12), a ballade for orchestra (op. 11), and a violin and piano sonata (op. 9), as well as a cavatina for violin and orchestra. These, with certain piano solos, were given at a concert of Brockway's own works in February, 1895, at the Sing-Akademie. His works were accepted as singularly mature, and promising as well. A few months later, Brockway returned to New York, where he has since lived as a teacher and performer.

His symphony, which is in D major, is so ebullient with life that its dashing first subject cannot brook more than a few measures of slow introduction. The second subject is simpler, but no less joyous. The thematic work is scholarly and enthusiastic at the same time. The different movements of the symphony are, however, not thematically related, save that the coda of the last movement is a reminiscence of the auxiliary theme of the first movement. The andante, in which the 'cellos are very lyrical, is a tender and musing mood. The presto is flashing with life and has a trio of rollicking, even whooping, jubilation. The finale begins gloomily and martially, and it is succeeded by a period of beauty and grace. This movement, in fact, is a remarkable combination of the exquisitest beauty and most unrestrained prowess.

Another orchestral work of great importance in American music is the " Sylvan Suite " (op. 19), which is also arranged for the piano. In this work the composer has shown a fine discretion and conservation in

the use of the instruments, making liberal
employment of small choirs for long periods.
The work is programmatic in psychology
only. It begins with a "Midsummer Idyl,"
which embodies the drowsy petulance of hot
noon. The second number is "Will o' the
Wisps." In this a three-voiced fugue for the
strings, wood, and one horn has been used
with legitimate effect and most teasing, fleet-
ing whimsicality. The third movement is a
slow waltz, called "The Dance of the Sylphs,"
a very catchy air, swaying delicately in the bassoons and 'cello ; a short "Evening Song" is
followed by "Midnight." This is a parade
that reminds one strongly of Gottschalk's
"Marche de Nuit." The march movement
is followed by an interlude depicting the
mystery of night, as Virgil says, "*tremulo
sub lumine.*" The composer has endeavored
to indicate the chill gray of dawn by the ending of this movement : a chord taken by two
flutes and the strings shivering *sul ponticello.*

The last movement is "At Daybreak." Out of the gloom of the bassoons grows a broad and general luminous song followed by an interlude of the busy hum of life; this is succeeded by the return of the sunrise theme with a tremendously vivacious accompaniment.

Other works of Brockway's are : a cantata, a set of variations, a ballade, a nocturne, a Characterstück, a Fantasiestück, a set of four piano pieces (op. 21), and two piano pieces (op. 25). All of these, except the cantata, have been published. Two part songs and two songs with piano accompaniment have also been published ; a violin sonata, a Moment Musicale, and a romanza for violin and orchestra have been published in Berlin.

These works all show a decided tendency to write brilliant and difficult music, but the difficulties are legitimate to the effect and the occasion. The Ballade works up a very powerful climax; the Scherzino swishes fas-

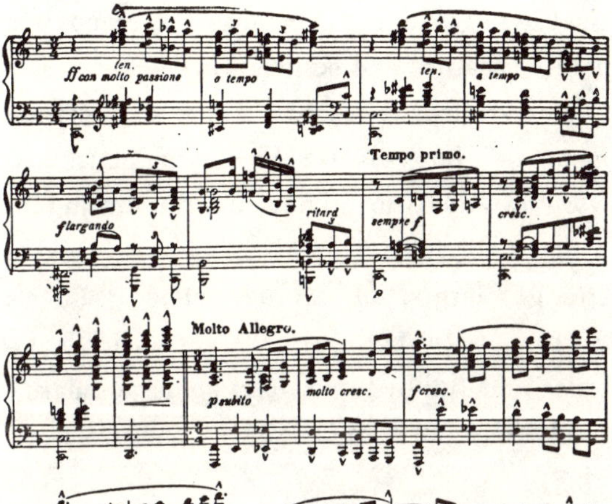

FRAGMENT OF A "BALLADE" BY HOWARD BROCKWAY.

cinatingly; and the Romanza for piano is a notably mature and serious work.

Two ballads have made the so romantic name of Harry Rowe Shelley[1] a household word in America. They are the setting of Tom Moore's fiery "Minstrel Boy," and a strange jargon of words called "Love's Sorrow." In both cases the music is intense and full of fervor, and quick popularity rarely goes out to more worthy songs.

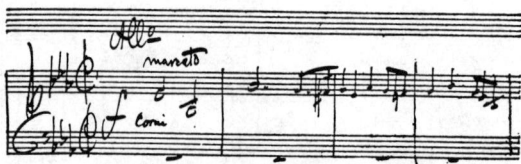

But Shelley would doubtless prefer to be judged by work to which he has given more of his art and his interest than to the many

[1] See p. 494.

HARRY ROWE SHELLEY.

songs that he has tossed off in the light name of popularity.

Shelley's life has been largely devoted to church work. Born in New Haven, Conn., June 8, 1858, and taught music by Gustav J. Stoeckel, he came under the tuition of Dudley Buck for seven years. His twentieth year found him an organist at New Haven. Three years later he went to Brooklyn in the same capacity. He was the organist at Plymouth Church for some time before Henry Ward Beecher's death. Since 1887 he has been at the Church of the Pilgrims. He visited Europe in 1887 and studied under Dvôrák when the Bohemian master was here.

Shelley's largest works have been an opera, " Leila," still in manuscript, a symphonic poem, " The Crusaders," a dramatic overture, " Francesca da Rimini," a sacred oratorio, " The Inheritance Divine," a suite for orchestra, a fantasy for piano and orchestra (written for Rafael Joseffy), a one-act musical extravaganza, a three-act lyric drama, and a virile symphony. The suite is called "Souvenir de Baden-Baden." It is a series of highly elaborated trifles of much gaiety, and includes a lively "Morning Promenade," a dreamy "Siesta," a "Conversationshaus Ball," and a quaint "Serenade Orientale" that shows the influence of Mozart's and Beethoven's marches alla turca. The orchestration of this work I have never heard nor seen. Its arrangement for four hands, however, is excellently done, with commendable attention to the interests of the *secondo* player.

The cantata is called "The Inheritance Divine," and it is much the best thing Shelley has done. It begins with a long, slow crescendo on the word "Jerusalem," which is very forceful. Shelley responds to an imaginary encore, however, and the word becomes little more than an expletive.

Page 7 — to refer more conveniently than technically — is marked by sonorous harmonies of especial nobility. Now begins a new idea worked up with increased richness and growing fervor to a sudden magnificence of climax in the second measure on page 11. The final phrase, strengthened by an organ-point on two notes, is fairly thrilling. A tenor solo follows, its introductory recitative containing many fine things, its aria being smoothly melodious. A chorus, of warm harmonies and a remarkably beautiful and unexpected ending, is next ; after which is a sombre, but impressive alto solo. The two successive choruses, the quartette, and the soprano solo catch the composer nodding. The bass solo is better ; the final chorus brings us back to the high plane. Page 62 is particularly big of spirit, and from here on the chorus climbs fiery heights. In spite of Berlioz' famous parody on the " Amen " fugues, in the " Damnation of

Faust," Shelley has used the word over a score of times in succession to finish his work. But altogether the work is one of maturity of feeling and expression, and it is a notable contribution to American sacred music.

In 1898 " Death and Life " was published. It opens with a dramatic chorus sung by the mob before the cross, and it ends daringly with a unisonal descent of the voices that carries even the sopranos down to A natural. In the duet between Christ and Mary, seeking where they have laid her Son, the librettist has given Christ a versified paraphrase which is questionable both as to taste and grammar. The final chorus, however, has a stir of spring fire that makes the work especially appropriate for Easter services.

The cantata " Vexilla Regis " is notable for its martial opening chorus, the bass solo, " Where deep for us the spear was dyed," and its scholarly and effective ending.

A lapidary's skill and delight for working
in small forms belongs to Gerrit Smith.[1] His
" Aquarelles " are a good example of his art
in bijouterie. This collection includes eight
songs and eight piano sketches. The first,
" A Lullaby," begins with the unusual skip
of a ninth for the voice. A subdued accentuation is got by the syncopation of the bass,
and the yearning tenderness of the ending
finishes an exquisite song. " Dream-wings "
is a graceful fantasy that fittingly presents
the delicate sentiment of Coleridge' lyrics.
The setting of Heine's " Fir-tree" is entirely
worthy to stand high among the numerous
settings of this lyric. Smith gets the air of
desolation of the bleak home of the fir-tree
by a cold scale of harmony, and a bold simplicity of accompaniment. The home of the
equally lonely palm-tree is strongly contrasted by a tropical luxuriance of interlude and accompaniment.

The sixth song is a delightful bit of bril·

[1] See p. 537.

liant music, but it is quite out of keeping with the poem. Thus on the words, " Margery's only three," there is a fierce climax fitting an Oriental declaration of despair. The last of these songs, "Put by the Lute," is possibly Smith's best work. It is superb from beginning to end. It opens with a most unhackneyed series of preludizing arpeggios, whence it breaks into a swinging lyric, strengthened into passion by a vigorous contra-melody in the bass. Throughout, the harmonies are most original, effective, and surprising.

Of the eight instrumental pieces in this book, the exquisite and fluent "Impromptu" is the best after the "Cradle Song," which is drowsy with luscious harmony and contains a passage come organo of such noble sonority as to put it a whit out of keeping with a child's lullaby.

Smith was born December 11, 1859, at Hagerstown, Md. His first instruction was gained in Geneva, N. Y., from a pupil of Moscheles. He began composition early, and works of his written at the age of fourteen were performed at his boarding-school. He graduated at Hobart College in 1876, whence he went to Stuttgart to study music and architecture. A year later he was in New York studying the organ with Samuel P. Warren. He was appointed organist at St. Paul's, Buffalo, and studied during the summer with Eugene Thayer, and William H. Sherwood. In 1880 he went again to Germany, and studied organ under Haupt, and theory under Rohde, at Berlin. On his return to America he took the organ at St. Peter's, in Albany. Later he came to New York, where he has since remained continuously, except for concert tours and journeys abroad. He has played the organ in the most important English and Continental towns, and must be considered one of our most prominent concert organists. He is both a Master of Arts and a Doctor of Music. As one of the founders, and for many years the president, of the Manuscript Society, he was active in obtaining a hearing for much native music otherwise mute.

In addition to a goodly number of Easter carols, Christmas anthems, Te Deums, and such smaller forms of religious music, Smith has written a sacred cantata, "King David." Aside from this work, which in orchestration and in general treatment shows undoubted skill for large effort, Doctor Smith's composition has been altogether along the smaller lines.

The five-song'd opus 14 shows well matured lyric power, and an increase in fervor of emotion. Bourdillon's "The Night Has a Thousand Eyes," which can never be too much set to music, receives here a truly superb treatment. The interlude, which also serves for finale, is especially ravishing.

"Heart Longings" is one of Mr. Smith's very best successes. It shows a free passion and a dramatic fire unusual for his rather quiet muse. The setting of Bourdillon's fine lyric is indeed so stirring that it deserves a high place among modern songs. "Melody" is a lyric not without feeling, but yet inclusive of most of Smith's faults. Thus the prelude, which is a tritely flowing allegro, serves also for interlude as well as postlude, and the air and accompaniment of both stanzas are unvaried, save at the cadence of the latter stanza. The intense poesy of Anna Reeve Aldrich, a poetess cut short at the very budding of unlimited promise, deserved better care than this from a musician. Two of Smith's works were published in Millet's "Half-hours with the Best Composers," — one of the first substantial recognitions of the American music-writer. A "Romance," however, is the best and most elaborate of his piano pieces, and is altogether

Spring.

Words by Alfred Tennyson.

GERRIT SMITH, OP. 13. No 4.

A FRAGMENT.

an exquisite fancy. His latest work, a cycle of ten pieces for the piano, "A Colorado Summer," is most interesting. The pieces are all lyrical and simple, but they are full of grace and new colors.

But Smith's most individual work is his set of songs for children, which are much compared, and favorably, with Reinecke's work along the same lines. These are veritable masterpieces of their sort, and they are mainly grouped into opus 12, called "Twenty-five Song Vignettes."

So well are they written that they are a safe guide, and worthy that supreme trust, the first formation of a child's taste. Even dissonances are used, sparingly but bravely enough to give an idea of the different elements that make music something more than a sweetish impotence, They are vastly different from the horrible trash children are usually brought up on, especially in our American schools, to the almost incurable perversion of their musical tastes. They are also so full of refinement, and of that humor without which children cannot long be held, that they are of complete interest also to "grown-ups," to whom alone the real artistic value of these songs can entirely transpire. Worthy of especial mention are the delicious "Stars and Angels;" the delightful "A Carriage to Ride In;" "Good King Arthur," a captivating melody, well built on an accompaniment of "God Save the King;" "Birdie's Burial," an elegy of the most sincere pathos, quite worthy of a larger cause, — if, indeed, any grief is greater than the first sorrows of childhood; the surprisingly droll "Barley Romance;" "The Broom and the Rod," with its programmatic *glissandos* to give things a clean sweep; and other delights like the "Rain Song," "The Tomtit Gray," "Mamma's Birthday," and "Christmas at the Door." To have given these works their present value and perfection, is to have accomplished a far greater thing than the writing of a dozen tawdry symphonies.

One of the most outrageously popular piano pieces ever published in America was Homer N. Bartlett's " Grande Polka de Concert." It was his opus 1, written years ago, and he tells me that he recently refused a lucrative commission to write fantasies on " Nearer My God to Thee " and " The Old Oaken Bucket " ! So now that he has reformed, grown wise and signed the musical pledge, one must forgive him those wild oats from which he reaped royalties, and look to the genuine and sincere work he has latterly done. Let us begin, say, with opus 38, a " Polonaise " that out-Herods Chopin in bravura, but is full of vigor and well held together. A " Dance of the Gnomes," for piano, is also arranged for a sextet, the arrangement being a development, not a bare transcription. There are two mazurkas (op. 71), the first very original and happy. "Æolian Murmurings" is a superb study in high color. A "Caprice Español" is a bravura realization of Spanish frenzy. It has also been brilliantly orchestrated. Two songs without words make up opus 96 : while "Meditation" shows too evident meditation on Wagner, "A Love Song" gets quite away from musical bourgeoisery. It is free, spirited, even daring. It is patently less devoted to theme-development than to the expression of an emotion. This "Love Song" is one of the very best of American morceaux, and is altogether commendable.

Opus 107 includes three "characteristic pieces." "The Zephyr" is dangerously like Chopin's fifteenth Prélude, with a throbbing organ-point on the same A flat. On this alien foundation, however, Bartlett has built with rich harmony. The "Harlequin" is graceful and cheery. It ends with Rubinstein's sign and seal, an arpeggio in sixths, which is as trite a musical finis as fiction's

"They lived happily ever afterward, sur-
rounded by a large circle of admiring friends."

Three mazurkas constitute opus 125. They
are closely modelled on Chopin, and naturally
lack the first-handedness of these works, in
which, almost alone, the Pole was witty.
But Bartlett has made as original an imitation as possible. The second is particularly
charming.

In manuscript is a Prélude developed
interestingly on well-understood lines. There
is a superb "Reverie Poétique." It is that
climax of success, a scholarly inspiration.
To the meagre body of American scherzos,
Bartlett's scherzo will be very welcome. It
is very festive and very original. Its richly
harmonized interlude shows a complete emancipation from the overpowering influence of
Chopin, and a great gain in strength as well
as individuality.

In his songs Bartlett attains a quality uni-
formly higher than that of his piano pieces.

" Moonbeams " has many delicacies of harmony. " Laughing Eyes " is a fitting setting of Mr. " Nym Crinkle " Wheeler's exquisite lyric. " Come to Me, Dearest," while cheap in general design, has fine details.

It makes me great dole to have to praise a song about a brooklet ; but the truth is, that Bartlett's "I Hear the Brooklet's Murmur " is superbly beautiful, wild with regret, — a noble song. It represents the late German type of *Lied*, as the earlier heavy style is exemplified in " Good Night, Dear One." Very Teutonic also is the airiness and grace of " Rosebud."

To that delightful collection of children's songs, " The St. Nicholas Song Book," Bartlett contributed largely. All of his lyrics are delicious, and " I Had a Little Pony " should become a nursery classic.

In his " Lord God, Hear My Prayer," Bartlett throws down the gauntlet to the Bach-Gounod " Ave Maria," with results rather disastrous. He chooses a Cramer étude, and adds to it parts for voice, violin, and organ. While Gounod seems passionate and unrestrained, Bartlett shows his caution and his cage at every step. A Cramer étude is among the most melancholy things of earth anyway. "Jehovah Nissi" is an excellent sacred march chorus that won a prize, and there is a cantata, "The Last Chieftain." Bartlett's cantata is without efforts at Indian color, but is a solid work with much dignity, barbaric severity, and fire.

Bartlett was born at Olive, N. Y., December 28, 1846. His ancestry runs far back into New England, his mother being a descendant of John Rogers, the martyr. Bartlett is said to have "lisped in numbers," singing correctly before he could articulate words. The violin was his first love, and at the age of eight he was playing in public. He took up the piano and organ also, and in his fourteenth year was a church organist. He studied the piano with S. B. Mills, Emil

Guyon (a pupil of Thalberg), and Alfred Pease. The organ and composition he studied with O. F. Jacobsen and Max Braun. With the exception of a musical pilgrimage in 1887, Bartlett has not come nearer the advantages of Europe than study here under men who studied there. He has resided for many years in New York as organist and teacher. As a composer he has been one of our most prolific music-makers. His work shows a steady development in value, and the best is doubtless yet to come.

He finds a congenial field in the orchestra. Seidl played his instrumentation of Chopin's "Military Polonaise" several times. As the work seemed to need a finale in its larger form, Bartlett took a liberty whose success was its justification, and added a finish made up of the three principal themes interwoven. A recent work is his "Concertstück," for violin and orchestra. It is not pianistic in instrumentation, and will appeal to violinists.

While not marked with *récherchés* violin tricks, or violent attempts at bravura, it has both brilliance and solidity, and is delightfully colored in orchestration. There are no pauses between the movements, but they are well varied in their unity.

There is an unfinished oratorio, " Samuel," an incomplete opera, " Hinotito," and a cantata of which only the tenor solo, " Khamsin," is done. This is by far the best work Bartlett has written, and displays unexpected dramatic powers. The variation of the episodes of the various phases of the awful drought to the climax in " The Plague," make up a piece of most impressive strength. The orchestration is remarkably fine with effect, color, and variety. If the cantata is finished on this scale, its production will be a national event.

The New England farmer is usually taken as a type of sturdy Philistinism in artistic matters. It was a most exceptional good fortune that gave C. B. Hawley a father who added to the dignity of being a tiller of the soil the refinements of great musical taste and skill. His house at Brookfield, Conn., contained not only a grand piano, but a pipe organ as well; and Hawley's mother was blessed with a beautiful and cultivated voice.

At the age of thirteen (he was born St. Valentine's Day, 1858) Hawley was a church organist and the conductor of musical affairs in the Cheshire Military Academy, from which he graduated. He went to New York at the age of seventeen, studying the voice with George James Webb, Rivarde, Foeder-lein, and others, and composition with Dudley Buck, Joseph Mosenthal, and Rutenber.

His voice brought him the position of solo-ist at the Calvary Episcopal Church, at the age of eighteen. Later he became assistant organist at St. Thomas' Episcopal Church, under George William Warren. For the last fourteen years he has had charge of the sum-mer music at St. James Chapel, in Elberon,

the chapel attended by Presidents Grant and
Garfield. For seventeen years he has been
one of the leading spirits of the Mendelssohn
Glee Club, and for ten years a member of the
Mendelssohn Quartet Club. Most of his
part songs were written for the club and first
sung at its concerts. He is also a successful
teacher of the voice, and has been too busy
to write a very large volume of compositions.
But those published show the authentic fire.

Notable features of Hawley's compositions are the taking quality of the melody, its
warm sincerity, and the unobtrusive opulence
in color of the accompaniment. This is
less like an answering, independent voice
than like a many-hued, velvety tapestry, back-
grounding a beautiful statue. It is only on
second thought and closer study that one
sees how well concealed is the careful and
laborious polish *ad unguem* of every chord.
This is the true art of song, where the lyrics
should seem to gush spontaneously forth

from a full heart and yet repay the closer
dissection that shows the intellect perfecting
the voice of emotion.

Take, for example, his " Lady Mine," a
brilliant rhapsody, full of the spring, and enriched with a wealth of color in the accompaniment till the melody is half hidden in a
shower of roses. It required courage to
make a setting of " Ah, 'Tis a Dream ! " so
famous through Lassen's melody ; but Hawley has said it in his own way in an air
thrilled with longing and an accompaniment
as full of shifting colors as one of the native
sunsets. I can't forbear one obiter dictum
on this poem. It has never been so translated as to reproduce its neatest bit of fancy.
In the original the poet speaks of meeting
in dreams a fair-eyed maiden who greeted
him " auf Deutsch " and kissed him " auf
Deutsch," but the translations all evade the
kiss in German.

" The Ring," bounding with the glad

frenzy of a betrothed lover, has a soaring finale, and is better endowed with a well polished accompaniment than the song, " Because I Love You, Dear," which is not without its good points in spite of its manifest appeal to a more popular taste. " My Little Love," " An Echo," " Spring's Awakening," and " Where Love Doth Build His Nest," are conceived in Hawley's own vein.

The song, "Oh, Haste Thee, Sweet," has some moments of banality, but more of novelty ; the harmonic work being unusual at times, especially in the rich garb of the words, " It groweth late." In " I Only Can Love Thee," Hawley has succeeded in conquering the incommensurateness of Mrs. Browning's sonnet by alternating 6-8 and 9-8 rhythms. His " Were I a Star," is quite a perfect lyric.

Of his part songs, all are good, some are masterly. Here he colors with the same lavish but softly blending touch as in his solos. "My Luve's Like a Red, Red Rose" is altogether delightful, containing as it does a suggestion of the old formalities and courtly graces of the music of Lawes, whose songs Milton sonneted. I had always thought that no musician could do other than paint the lily in attempting to add music to the music of Tennyson's "Bugle Song," but Hawley has come dangerously near satisfaction in the elfland faintness and dying clearness of his voices.

He has written two comic glees, one of which, "They Kissed! I Saw Them Do It," has put thousands of people into the keenest mirth. It is a vocal scherzo for men's voices. It begins with a criminally lugubrious and thin colloquy, in which the bass dolefully informs the others: "Beneath a shady tree they sat," to which the rest agree; "He held her hand, she held his hat," which meets with general consent. Now we are told in stealthy gasps, "I held my breath and lay right flat." Suddenly out of this thinness bursts a peal of richest harmony: "They kissed! I saw them do it." It is repeated more lusciously still, and then the basses and barytones mouth the gossip disapprovingly, and the poem continues with delicious raillery till it ends abruptly and archly: "And they thought no one knew it!"

Besides these scherzos, Hawley has written a few religious part songs of a high order, particularly the noble "Trisagion and Sanctus," with its "Holy, Holy!" now hushed in reverential awe and now pealing in exultant worship. But of all his songs, I like best his "When Love is Gone," fraught with calm intensity, and closing in beauty as ineffable as a last glimmer of dying day.

To the stencil-plate chivalry of the lyrics of the ubiquitous F. E. Weatherby and John Oxenford, the song-status of England can blame a deal of its stagnation. It is not often that these word-wringers have enticed Ameri-

When Love is gone.

(Soprano, or Tenor.)

C. B. HAWLEY.

can composers. One of the few victims is John Hyatt Brewer,[1] who was born in Brooklyn, in 1856, and has lived there ever since.

Brewer made his début as a six-year-old singer, and sang till his fourteenth year. A year later he was an organist in Brooklyn, where he has held various positions in the same capacity ever since, additionally busying himself as a teacher of voice, piano, organ, and harmony. His studies in piano and harmony were pursued under Rafael Navarro. Counterpoint, fugue, and composition he studied under Dudley Buck.

In 1878 Brewer became the second tenor and accompanist of the Apollo Club, of which Mr. Buck is the director. He has conducted numerous vocal societies and an amateur orchestra.

Of his cantatas, " Hesperus " is a work of the greatest promise and large performance.

For male voices Brewer has written a cantata called " The Birth of Love." Its fiery

[1] See p. 534.

ending is uncharacteristic, but the beautiful tenor solo and an excellent bass song prove his forte to lie in the realm of tenderness. Brewer's music has little fondness for climaxes, but in a tender pathos that is not tragedy, but a sort of lotos-eater's dreaminess and regret, he is congenially placed. Smoothness is one of his best qualities.

Out of a number of part songs for men, one should mark a vigorous " Fisher's Song," a " May Song," which has an effective " barber's chord," and " The Katydid," a witty realization of Oliver Wendell Holmes' captivating poem. His " Sensible Serenade " has also an excellent flow of wit. Both these songs should please glee clubs and their audiences.

For women's voices Brewer has written not a little. The best of these are " Sea Shine," which is particularly mellow, and " Treachery," a love-scherzo.

For the violin there are two pieces : one,

in the key of D, is a duet between the violin
and the soprano voice of the piano. It is
full of characteristic tenderness, full even of
tears. It should find a good place among
those violin ballads of which Raff's Cavatina
is the best-known example. Another violin
solo in A is more florid, but is well managed.
The two show a natural aptitude for composition for this favorite of all instruments.

For full orchestra there is a suite, " The
Lady of the Lake," also arranged for piano
and organ. It is smooth and well-tinted. A
sextet for strings and flute has been played
with favor.

Brewer's chief success lies along lines of
least resistance, one might say. His Album
of Songs (op. 27) is a case in point. Of the
subtle and inevitable " Du bist wie eine
Blume," he makes nothing, and " The Vio-
let " forces an unfortunate contrast with
Mozart's idyl to the same words. But
" Meadow Sweet " is simply iridescent with

cheer, a most unusually sweet song, and "The Heart's Rest" is of equal perfection.

The best-abused composer in America is doubtless Reginald de Koven.[1] His great popularity has attracted the search-light of minute criticism to him, and his accomplishments are such as do not well endure the fierce white light that beats upon the throne. The sin of over-vivid reminiscence is the one most persistently imputed to him, and not without cause. While I see no reason to accuse him of deliberate imitation, I think he is a little too loth to excise from his music those things of his that prove on consideration to have been said or sung before him. Instead of crying, "*Pereant qui ante nos nostra cantaverunt*," he believes in a live-and-let-live policy. But ah, if De Koven were the only composer whose eraser does not evict all that his memory installs!

De Koven was born at Middletown, Conn., in 1859, and enjoyed unusual advantages for

[1] See p. 475.

musical study abroad. At the age of eleven, he was taken to Europe, where he lived for twelve years. At Oxford he earned a degree with honors. His musical instructors include Speidel, Lebert, and Pruckner, at Stuttgart, Huff the contrapuntist at Frankfort, and Vannucini, who taught him singing, at Florence. He made also a special study of light opera under Genée and Von Suppé. He made Chicago his home in 1882, afterward moving to New York, where he served as a musical critic on one of the daily papers for many years.

De Koven has been chief purveyor of comic opera to his generation, and for so ideal a work as "Robin Hood," and such pleasing constructions as parts of his other operas ("Don Quixote," "The Fencing Master," "The Highwayman," for instance), one ought to be grateful, especially as his music has always a certain elegance and freedom from vulgarity.

Of his ballads, " Oh, Promise Me " has a few opening notes that remind one of " Musica Proibita," but it was a taking lyric that stuck in the public heart. His setting of Eugene Field's " Little Boy Blue " is a work of purest pathos and directness. His version of " My Love is Like a Red, Red Rose " is among the best of its countless settings, and " The Fool of Pamperlune," the " Indian Love Song," " In June," and a few others, are excellent balladwriting.

Victor Harris[1] is one of the few that selected New York for a birthplace. He was born here April 27, 1869, and attended the College of the City of New York, class of 1888. For several of his early years he was well known as a boy-soprano, whence he graduated into what he calls the " usual career " of organist, pianist, and teacher of the voice. In 1895 and 1896 he acted as the assistant conductor to Anton Seidl in the Brighton

[1] See p. 568.

Beach summer concerts. He learned harmony of Frederick Schilling.

Harris is most widely known as an accompanist, and is one of the best in the country. But while the accompaniments he writes to his own songs are carefully polished and well colored, they lack the show of independence that one might expect from so unusual a master of their execution.

Except for an unpublished one-act operetta, "Mlle. Maie et M. de Sembre," and a few piano pieces, Harris has confined himself to the writing of short songs. In his twenty-first year two of unequal merits were published, "The Fountains Mingle with the River" being a taking melody, but without distinction or originality, while "Sweetheart" has much more freedom from conventionality and inevitableness.

A later song, "My Guest," shows an increase in elaboration, but follows the florid school of Harrison Millard's once so popular rhapsody, "Waiting." Five songs are grouped into opus 12, and they reach a much higher finish and a better tendency to make excursions into other keys. They also show two of Harris' mannerisms, a constant repetition of verbal phrases and a fondness for writing close, unbroken chords, in triplets or quartoles. "A Melody" is beautiful; "Butterflies and Buttercups" is the perfection of grace; "I Know not if Moonlight or Starlight" is a fine rapture, and "A Disappointment" is a dire tragedy, all about some young toadstools that thought they were going to be mushrooms. For postlude two measures from the cantabile of Chopin's "Funeral March" are used with droll effect. "Love, Hallo!" is a headlong springtime passion. Two of his latest songs are "Forever and a Day," with many original touches, and a "Song from Omar Khayyám," which is made of some of the most cynical of the tentmaker's quatrains. Harris has given them

To N. N. H.

Song from Omar Khayyam.

VICTOR HARRIS Op. 10, No. 3

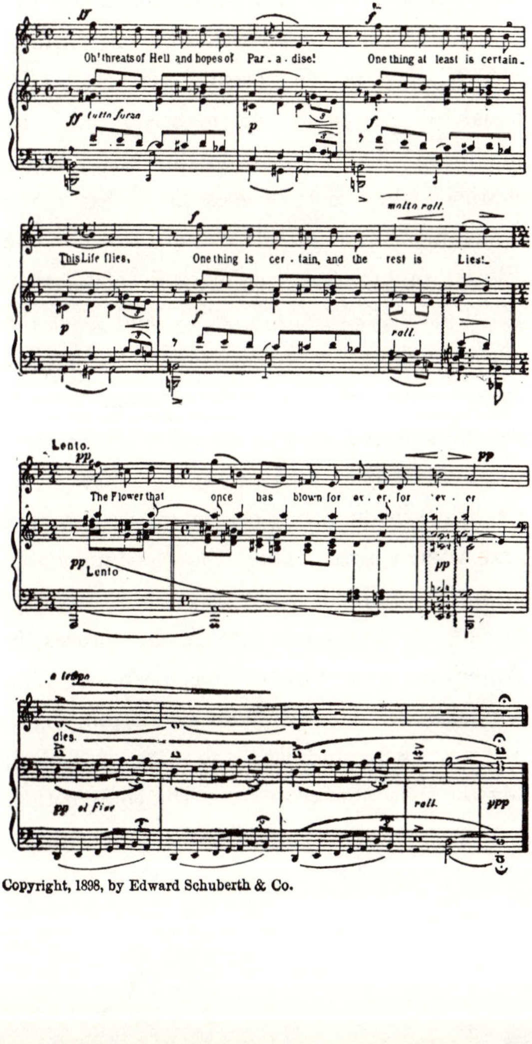

all their power and bitterness till the last line, "The flower that once has blown forever dies," which is written with rare beauty. "A Night-song" is possibly his best work; it is full of colors, originalities, and lyric qualities. Opus 13 contains six songs: "Music when Soft Voices Die" has many uncommon and effective intervals; "The Flower of Oblivion" is more dramatic than usual, employs discords boldly, and gives the accompaniment more individuality than before; "A Song of Four Seasons" is a delicious morsel of gaiety, and "Love within the Lover's Breast" is a superb song. Harris has written some choric works for men and women also. They show commendable attention to all the voice parts.

One of the most prominent figures in American musical history has been Dr. William Mason. He was born in Boston, January 24, 1829, and was the son of Lowell Mason, that pioneer in American composition.

Dr. William Mason studied in Boston, and in Germany under Moscheles, Hauptmann, Richter, and Liszt. His success in concerts abroad and here gave prestige to his philosophy of technic, and his books on method have taken the very highest rank.

His pedagogical attainments have overshadowed his composition, but he has written some excellent music. As he has been an educational force in classical music, so his compositions show the severe pursuit of classic forms and ideas. His work is, therefore, rather ingenious than inspired, and intellectual rather than emotional. Yale made him Doctor of Music in 1872.

Another composer whose studies in technic have left him only a little inclination for creation is Albert Ross Parsons, who was born at Sandusky, O., September 16, 1847. He studied in Buffalo, and in New York under Ritter. Then he went to Germany, where he had a remarkably thorough schooling under Moscheles, Reinecke, Richter, Paul, Taussig, Kullak, and others. Returning to this country, he has busied himself as organist, teacher, and an editor of musical works. What little music he has composed shows the fruit of his erudition in its correctness.

Such men as Doctor Mason and Mr. Parsons, though they add little to the volume of composition, — a thing for which any one should be thanked on some considerations, — yet add great dignity to their profession in this country.

Arthur,[1] a younger brother of Ethelbert Nevin, shows many of the Nevinian traits of lyric energy and harmonic color in his songs. He was born at Sewickley, Pa., in 1871. Until he was eighteen he had neither interest nor knowledge in music. In 1891 he began a four years' course in Boston, going thence to Berlin, where his masters were Klindworth and Boise. A book of four graceful "May Sketches" has been published, "Pierrot's

[1] See p. 474.

Guitar" being especially ingenious. There are two published songs, "Were I a Tone" and "In Dreams," both emotionally rich. In manuscript are a fine song, "Free as the Tossing Sea," and a well-devised trio.

A successful writer of songs is C. Whitney Coombs.[1] He was born in Maine, in 1864, and went abroad at the age of fourteen. He studied the piano with Speidel, and composition with Seiffritz, in Stuttgart, for five years, and pursued his studies later in Dresden under Draessecke, Janssen, and John. In 1887 he became organist at the American Church in that city, returning to America in 1891, since which time he has been an organist in New York.

In 1891 his publication begins with "My Love," an excellent lilt on lines from the Arabian. Among his many songs a few should be noted: the "Song of a Summer Night" is brilliant and poetic, and "Alone" is marked by some beautiful contramelodic

[1] See p. 536.

effects; his "Indian Serenade" is a gracious work.

J. Remington Fairlamb has been a prolific composer. He was born at Philadelphia, and at fourteen was a church organist. He studied at the Paris Conservatoire and in Italy; was appointed consul at Zurich by President Lincoln, and while in Stuttgart was decorated by the King of Wurtemburg with the "Great Gold Medal of Art and Science" for a Te Deum for double chorus and orchestra. Of Fairlamb's compositions, some two hundred have been published, including much sacred music and parts of two operas. A grand opera, "Leonello," in five acts, and a mass are in manuscript.

Frank Seymour Hastings has found in music a pleasant avocation from finance, and written various graceful songs. He has been active, too, in the effort to secure a proper production of grand opera in English.

Dr. John M. Loretz, of Brooklyn, is a

veteran composer, and has passed his opus 200. He has written much sacred music and several comic operas.

A prominent figure in New York music, though only an occasional composer, is Louis Raphael Dressler, one of the six charter members of the Manuscript Society, and long its treasurer. His father was William Dressler, one of the leading musicians of the earlier New York, where Mr. Dressler was born, in 1861. Dressler studied with his father, and inherited his ability as a professional accompanist and conductor. He was the first to produce amateur performances of opera in New York. His songs are marked with sincerity and spontaneity.

Richard Henry Warren has been the organist at St. Bartholomew's since 1886, and the composer of much religious music in which both skill and feeling are present. Among his more important works are two complete services, a scene for barytone

solo, male chorus, and orchestra, called " Ti-
conderoga," and a powerful Christmas anthem.
Warren has written also various operettas, in
which he shows a particular grasp of instrumentation, and an ability to give new turns
of expression to his songs, while keeping
them smooth and singable. An unpublished
short song of his, "When the Birds Go North,"
is a remarkably beautiful work, showing an
aptitude that should be more cultivated.

Warren was born at Albany, September
17, 1859. He is a son and pupil of George
W. Warren, the distinguished organist. He
went to Europe in 1880, and again in 1886,
for study and observation. He was the organizer and conductor of the Church Choral
Society, which gave various important religious works their first production in New
York, and, in some cases, their first hearing
in America, notably, Dvôrák's Requiem Mass,
Gounod's "Mors et Vita," Liszt's Thirteenth
Psalm, Saint-Säens' "The Heavens Declare,"

Villiers Stanford's "God is Our Hope and Strength," and Mackenzie's "Veni, Creator Spiritus." Horatio Parker's "Horạ Novissima" was composed for this society, and Chadwick's "Phœnix Expirans" given its first New York performance.

A prominent organist and teacher is Smith N. Penfield, who has also found time for the composition of numerous scholarly works, notably, an overture for full orchestra, an orchestral setting of the eighteenth psalm, a string quartette, and many pieces for the organ, voice, and piano. His tuition has been remarkably thorough. Born in Oberlin, Ohio, April 4, 1837, he studied the piano in Germany with Moscheles, Papperitz, and Reinecke, the organ with Richter, composition, counterpoint, and fugue with Reinecke and Hauptmann. He had also a period of study in Paris.

Another organist of distinction is Frank Taft, who is also a conductor and a composer.

His most important work is a "Marche Sym
phonique," which was performed by the Boston Symphony Orchestra. He was born in
East Bloomfield, New York, and had his
education entirely in this country, studying
the organ with Clarence Eddy, and theory
with Frederick Grant Gleason.

A young composer of many graceful songs
is Charles Fonteyn Manney,[1] who was born
in Brooklyn in 1872, and studied theory with
William Arms Fisher in New York, and later
with J. Wallace Goodrich at Boston. His
most original song is "Orpheus with His
Lute," which reproduces the quaint and fascinating gaucheries of the text with singular
charm. He has also set various songs of
Heine's to music, and a short cantata for
Easter, "The Resurrection."

An ability that is strongly individual is
that of Arthur Farwell,[2] whose first teacher
in theory was Homer A. Norris, and who
later studied under Humperdinck in Ger-

[1] See p. 558.   [2] See p. 508.

many. Among his works are an elaborate
ballade for piano and violin, a setting of
Shelley's "Indian Serenade," and four folk-
songs to words by Johanna Ambrosius, the
peasant genius of Germany. Among others
of his published songs is "Strow Poppy
Buds," a strikingly original composition.

A writer of numerous elegant trifles and
of a serious symphony is Harry Patterson
Hopkins, who was born in Baltimore, and
graduated at the Peabody Institute in 1896,
receiving the diploma for distinguished musicianship. The same year he went to
Bohemia, and studied with Dvôrák. He
returned to America to assist in the production of one of his compositions by Anton
Seidl.

Very thorough was the foreign training of
Carl V. Lachmund, whose "Japanese Overture" has been produced under the direction
of Thomas and Seidl, in the former case at a
concert of that society at which many impor-

tant native works have had their only hearing, the Music Teachers' National Association. Lachmund was born at Booneville, Mo., in 1854. At the age of thirteen he began his tuition at Cologne, under Heller, Jensen, and Seiss ; later he went to Berlin to study with the Scharwenkas, Kiel, and Moskowski. He had also four years of Liszt's training at Weimar. A trio for harp, violin, and 'cello was played by the Berlin Philharmonic Orchestra, and a concert prelude for the piano was much played in concerts in Germany. Before returning to America, Lachmund was for a time connected with the opera at Cologne.

The Boston Colony.

To the composer potentially a writer of grand operas, but barred out by the absolute lack of opening here, the dramatic ballad should offer an attractive form. Such works as Schubert's " Erl-King" show what can be done. Henry Holden Huss has made some interesting experiments, and Fred. Field Bullard has tried the field.

Bullard's setting of Tennyson's almost lurid melodrama in six stanzas, " The Sisters," has caught the bitter mixture of love and hate, and avoided claptrap climaxes most impressively.

" In the Greenwood " (op. 14) is graceful, and " A June Lullaby " has a charming accompaniment of humming rain. Bullard has set some of Shelley's lyrics for voice and harp or piano, in opus 17. " From Dreams of Thee " gets a delicious quaintness of accompaniment, while the " Hymn of Pan " shows a tremendous savagery and uncouthness, with strange and stubborn harmonies. Full of the same roborific virility are his settings to the songs of Richard Hovey's writing, " Here's a Health to Thee, Roberts," " Barney McGee," and the " Stein Song." These songs have an exuberance of the roistering spirit, along

HYMN OF PAN.

Words by
PERCY BYSSHE SHELLEY.

Music by
FRED. FIELD BULLARD,
Op. 17, No. 4.

Allegro giojoso.

HARP
or
PIANO-
FORTE.*

From the for-ests and high - lands I come,—— I come;——

From the riv-er-girt is - lands, Where waves—— are dumb;——

From the for-ests and high lands, From the riv-er-girt is - lands,——

Pianoforte sempre con pedale.

Copyright, 1894, by Miles & Thompson.

A FRAGMENT.

I come,____ I come,____ I come.____ The

wind____ in the reeds,____ and the rush - es,____ The

bees____ in the bells, of thyme,____ The

birds____ in the myr - tle bush - es,____ The

with a competence of musicianship that lifts them above any comparison with the average balladry. Similarly "The Sword of Ferrara," with its hidalgic pride, and "The Indifferent Mariner," and the drinking-song, "The Best of All Good Company," are all what Horace Greeley would have called "mighty interesting." Not long ago I would have wagered my head against a hand-saw, that no writer of this time could write a canon with spontaneity. But then I had not seen Bullard's three duets in canon form. He has chosen his words so happily and expressed them so easily, and with such arch raillery, that the duets are delicious. Of equal gaiety is "The Lass of Norwich Town," which, with its violin obbligato, won a prize in the *Musical Record* competition of 1899.

Bullard was born at Boston, in 1864. He studied chemistry at first, but the claims of music on his interest were too great, and in 1888 he went to Munich, where he studied

FREDERICK FIELD BULLARD.

with Josef Rheinberger. After four years of
European life he returned to Boston, where
he has taught harmony and counterpoint
along rather original lines. He is a writer
with ideas and resources that give promise
of a large future. His scholarship has not
led him away from individuality. He is
especially likely to give unexpected turns
of expression, little bits of programmism
rather incompatible with the ballad form
most of his songs take. The chief fault with
his work is the prevailing dun-ness of his
harmonies. They have not felt the impressionistic revolt from the old bituminous school.
But in partial compensation for this bleak-
ness is a fine ruggedness.

Of his other published songs, "At Day-
break" shows a beautiful fervor of repression. "On the Way" is redeemed by a
particularly stirring finish. In opus 8, "A
Prayer" is begun in D minor and ended
in D major, with a strong effect of sudden

exaltation from gloom. "The Singer" begins also in sombre style with unusual
and abrupt modulations, and ends in a bright
major. "The Hermit" is likewise grim,
but is broad and deep. It uses a hint of
"Old Hundred" in the accompaniment.

Opus 11 couples two dramatic ballads.
In this form of condensed drama is a too-
little occupied field of composition, and Bullard
has written some part songs, of which "In
the Merry Month of May," "Her Scuttle
Hat," and "The Water Song" are worth
mentioning. "O Stern Old Land" is a rather
bathetic candidate for the national hymnship.
But his "War Song of Gamelbar," for male
voices, is really a masterwork. Harmonists
insist on so much closer compliance with
rules for smoothness in vocal compositions
than in instrumental work, that the usual
composer gives himself very little liberty
here. Bullard, however, has found the right
occasion for wild dissonances, and has dared

to use them. The effect is one of terrific power. This, his "Song of Pan" and "The Sisters" give him a place apart from the rest of native song-writers.

With all reverence for German music, it has been too much inclined of late to domineer the rest of the world, especially America. A useful counter-influence is that of Homer A. Norris, who has stepped out of the crowd flying to Munich and neighboring places, and profited by Parisian harmonic methods.

His book, "Practical Harmony," imparts a, to us, novel method of disarming the bugaboo of altered chords of many of its notorious terrors. He also attacks the pedantry of music "so constructed that it appeals to the eye rather than the ear, — paper-work," a most praiseworthy assault on what is possibly the heaviest incubus on inspiration. In a later work on "Counterpoint" he used for chapter headings Greek vases and other decorative designs, to stimulate the ideal of counterpoint as a unified complexity of graceful contours.

Norris was born in Wayne, Me., and became an organist at an early age. His chief interest has been, however, in the theory of music, and he studied with G. W. Marston, F. W. Hale, and G. W. Chadwick, as well as Emery. In deciding upon foreign study he was inspired to choose France instead of Germany. This has given him a distinct place.

After studying in Paris for four years under Dubois, Godard, Guilmant, and Gigout, he made his home in Boston, where he has since confined himself to the teaching of composition.

As yet Mr. Norris has composed little, and that little is done on simple lines, but the simplicity is deep, and the harmonies, without being bizarre, are wonderfully mellow.

His first song, " Rock-a-bye, Baby," he sold for twelve printed copies, and it is said to

HOMER A. NORRIS.

have had a larger sale than any cradle-song ever published in this country.. His song, "Protestations," is tender, and has a violin obbligato that is really more important than the voice part. The song, " Parting," is wild with passion, and bases a superb melody on a fitting harmonic structure. I consider "Twilight " one of the best American songs. It gets some unusual effects with intervals of tenths and ninths, and shows a remarkable depth of emotion.

In the larger forms he has done a concert overture, "Zoroaster" (which, judging from an outline, promises many striking effects), and a cantata, " Nain," which has the sin of over-repetition of words, but is otherwise marked with telling pathos and occasional outbursts of intensely dramatic feeling.

Perhaps his most original work is seen in his book of "Four Songs for Mezzo-Voice." The first is Kipling's "O Mother Mine," with harshnesses followed by tenderest musings;

the second is a noble song, "Peace," with an accompaniment consisting entirely of the slowly descending scale of C major; a high-colored lilt, "The World and a Day," is followed by a Maeterlinckian recitative of the most melting pathos. This book is another substantiation of my belief that America is writing the best of the songs of to-day.

One of the best-esteemed musicians in Boston, G. E. Whiting has devoted more of his interest to his career as virtuoso on the organ than to composition. Not many of such works as he has found time to write have been printed. These include an organ sonata, a number of organ pieces, a book of studies for the organ, six songs, and three cantatas for solos, chorus, and orchestra, "A Tale of the Viking," "Dream Pictures," and "A Midnight Cantata."

Whiting was born at Holliston, Mass., September 14, 1842. At the age of five, he began the study of music with his brother.

At the age of fifteen, he moved to Hartford, Conn., where he succeeded Dudley Buck as organist of one of the churches. Here he founded the Beethoven Society. At the age of twenty he went to Boston, and after studying with Morgan, went to Liverpool, and studied the organ under William Thomas Best. Later he made a second pilgrimage to Europe, and studied under Radeck.

For many years he has lived in Boston as a teacher of music and performer upon the organ. In manuscript are a number of works which I have not had the privilege of seeing : two masses for chorus, orchestra, and organ, a concert overture, a concerto, a sonata, a fantasy and fugue, a fantasy and three études, a suite for 'cello and piano, and a setting of Longfellow's " Golden Legend," which won two votes out of five in the thousand dollar musical festival of 1897, the prize being awarded to Dudley Buck.

Of his compositions H. E. Krehbiel in

Peace.

EDWARD ROWLAND SILL.

HOMER A. NORRIS.

'Tis not in seek-ing, 'Tis not in end-less striv-ing, Thy quest is found:___ Thy quest is found. Be still and lis-ten; Be still and drink the qui-et of all a - round. Not for thy cry - ing, Not for thy

loud be - seech - ing, Will peace draw near: Will peace draw near:

Quietly Rest with palms fold - ed; *more quietly* Rest with thine eye - lids fal - len

Lo! peace is here.

1892 recorded the opinion that they "entitled him to a position among the foremost musicians in this country." He is an uncle of Arthur Whiting.

G. W. Marston's setting of the omnipresent "Du bist wie eine Blume" is really one of the very best Heine's poem has ever had. Possibly it is the best of all the American settings. His "There Was an Aged Monarch" is seriously deserving of the frankest comparison with Grieg's treatment of the same *Lied*. It is interesting to note the radical difference of their attitudes toward it. Grieg writes in a folk-tone that is severe to the point of grimness. He is right because it is *ein altes Liedchen*, and Heine's handling of it is also kept outwardly cold. But Marston has rendered the song into music of the richest harmony and fullest pathos. He is right, also, because he has interpreted the undercurrent of the story.

Bodenstedt's ubiquitous lyric, "Wenn der

Frühling auf die Berge steigt," which rivals
" Du bist wie eine Blume " in the favor of
composers, has gathered Marston also into
its net. He gives it a climax that fairly
sweeps one off his feet, though one might
wish that the following and final phrase had
not forsaken the rich harmonies of the climax
so completely.

This song is the first of a " Song Album "
for sopranos, published in 1890. In this
group the accompaniments all receive an
attention that gives them meaning without
obtrusiveness. " The Duet " is a delicious
marriage of the song of a girl and the accompanying rapture of a bird.

A captivating little florid figure in the
accompaniment of a setting of " Im wunder-
schönen Monat Mai " gives the song worth.
" On the Water " is profound with sombreness and big simplicity. " The Boat of My
Lover " is quaintly delightful.

Marston was born in Massachusetts, at the

little town of Sandwich, in 1840. He studied there, and later at Portland, Me., with John W. Tufts, and has made two pilgrimages to Europe for instruction. He played the organ in his native town at the age of fifteen, and since finishing his studies has lived at Portland, teaching the piano, organ, and harmony. From the start his songs caught popularity, and were much sung in concert.

Marston has written a sacred dramatic cantata, "David," and a large amount of church music that is very widely used. He has written also a set of quartettes and trios for women's voices, and quartettes for men's voices.

Possibly his best-known song has been his "Could Ye Come Back to Me, Douglas," which Mrs. Craik called the best of all her poem's many settings.

Only Marston's later piano pieces are really *klaviermässig*. So fine a work as his "Gavotte in B Minor" has no need to consider the resources of the modern instrument. It has a color scheme of much originality, though it is marred by over-repetition. "A Night in Spain" is a dashing reminiscence, not without Spanish spirit, and an "Album Leaf" is a divertissement of contagious enthusiasm.

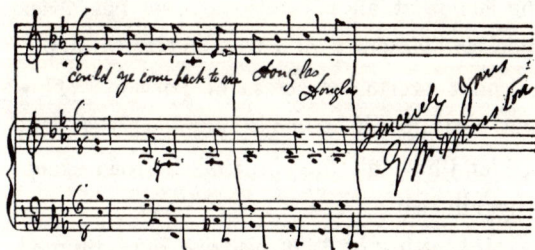

Ariel's songs, from "The Tempest," are given a piano interpretation that reaches a high plane. There is a storm prologue which suggests, in excellent harmonies, the distant mutter of the storm rather than a piano-gutting tornado. "Full Fathoms Five Thy Father Lies" is a reverie of wonderful depth and originality, with a delicious variation on the good old-fashioned cadence. Thence it works up into an immensely powerful close. A dance, "Foot it Featly," follows. It is sprightly, and contains a fetching cadenza.

One of the most prolific writers of American song is Clayton Johns.[1] He is almost always pleasing and polished. While he is not at all revolutionary, he has a certain individuality of ease, and lyric quality without storm or stress of passion. Thus his settings of seven "Wanderlieder" by Uhland have all the spirit of the road except ruggedness.

His setting of "Du bist wie eine Blume" is extremely tender and sweet.

Two of Johns' best successes have been settings of Egyptian subjects: "Were I a Prince Egyptian" and Arlo Bates' fine lyric, "No Lotus Flower on Ganges Borne." The latter is a superb song of unusual fire, with a strong effect at the end, the voice ceasing at a deceptive cadence, while the accompani-

[1] See p. 551.

ment sweeps on to its destiny in the original
key. He has also found a congenial subject
in Austin Dobson's "The Rose and the Gar-
dener." He gets for a moment far from its
florid grace in "I Looked within My Soul,"
which has an unwonted bigness, and is a
genuine *Lied*.

In later years Johns' songs have been
brought out in little albums, very artistically
got up, especially for music (which has been
heinously printed, as a rule, in this country).
These albums include three skilfully written "English Songs," and three "French
Songs," "Soupir" taking the form of melodic
recitative. Opus 19 is a group of "Wonder
Songs," which interpret Oliver Herford's
quaint conceits capitally.

Opus 26 collects nine songs, of which
"Princess Pretty Eyes" is fascinatingly archaic. It is good to see him setting two
such remotely kindred spirits as Herrick and
Emily Dickinson. The latter has hardly been

discovered by composers, and the former is too much neglected.

Johns has also written a few part songs and some instrumental works, which maintain his characteristics. A delightful "Canzone," a happy "Promenade," and "Mazurka" are to be mentioned, and a number of pieces for violin and piano, among them a finely built intermezzo, a berceuse, a romanza that should be highly effective, and a witty scherzino. He has written for strings a berceuse and a scherzino, which have been played by the Boston Symphony Orchestra, and certain part songs, as well as a chorus for female voices and string orchestra, have been sung in London.

Johns was born at New Castle, Del., November 24, 1857, of American parents. Though at first a student of architecture, he gave this up for music, and studied at Boston under Wm. F. Apthorp, J. K. Paine, and W. H. Sherwood, after which he went to Berlin, where he studied under Kiel, Grabau, Raif, and Franz Rummel. In 1884 he made Boston his home.

If San Francisco had found some way of retaining the composers she has produced, she would have a very respectable colony. Among the others who have come east to grow up with music is William Arms Fisher,[1] who was born in San Francisco, April 27, 1861. The two composers from whom he derives his name, Joshua Fisher and William Arms, settled in Massachusetts colony in the seventeenth century. He studied harmony, organ, and piano with John P. Morgan. After devoting some years to business, he committed his life to music, and in 1890 came to New York, where he studied singing. Later he went to London to continue his vocal studies. Returning to New York, he took up counterpoint and fugue with Horatio W. Parker, and composition and instrumentation with Dvôrák. After teaching harmony for several years, he

[1] See p. 568.

went to Boston, where he now lives. His work has been almost altogether the composition of songs. A notable feature of his numerous publications is their agreeable diversion from the usual practice of composers, which is to write lyrics of wide range and high pitch. Nearly all his songs are written for the average voice.

His first opus contains a setting of "Nur wer die Sehnsucht kennt," which I like better than the banal version Tschaïkowski made of the same words. The third opus contains three songs to Shelley's words. They show something of the intellectual emotion of the poet. The first work, " A Widow Bird Sate Mourning," is hardly lyrical ; " My Coursers Are Fed with the Lightning " is a stout piece of writing, but the inspired highfalutin of the words would be trying upon one who arose to sing the song before an audience. This, by the way, is a point rarely considered by the unsuccessful composers, and the words which

the singer is expected to declare to an ordinary audience are sometimes astounding. The
third Shelley setting, "The World's Wanderer," is more congenial to song.

Opus 5 is entitled "Songs without Tears."
These are for a bass voice, and by all odds the
best of his songs. An appropriate setting
is Edmund Clarence Stedman's "Falstaff's
Song," a noteworthy lyric of toss-pot moraliza-
tion on death. His song of "Joy" is exuberant with spring gaiety, and some of his best
manner is seen in his "Elégie," for violin and
piano. He has also written a deal of church
song.

A venerable and distinguished teacher and
composer is James C. D. Parker, who was
born at Boston, in 1828, and graduated from
Harvard in 1848. He at first studied law,
but was soon turned to music, and studied
for three years in Europe under Richter,
Plaidy, Hauptmann, Moscheles, Rietz, and
Becker. He graduated from the conserva-

tory at Leipzig, and returned to Boston in 1845.

His "Redemption Hymn" is one of his most important works, and was produced in Boston by the Handel and Haydn Society in 1877. He also composed other works for orchestra and chorus, and many brilliant piano compositions.

An interesting method of writing duets is that employed in the "Children's Festival," by Charles Dennée.[1] The pupil plays in some places the primo, and in others the secondo, his part being written very simply, while the part to be played by the teacher is written with considerable elaboration, so that the general effect is not so narcotic as usual with duets for children. Dennée has written, among many works of little specific gravity, a "Suite Moderne" of much skill, a suite for string orchestra, an overture and sonatas for the piano and for the violin and piano, as well as various comic operas. He was

[1] See p. 476.

FREDERICK GRANT GLEASON.

born in Oswego, N. Y., September 1, 1863, and studied composition with Stephen A. Emery.

A composer of a genial gaiety, one who has written a good minuet and an "Evening Song" that is not morose, is Benjamin Lincoln Whelpley,[1] who was born at Eastport, Me., October 23, 1863, and studied the piano at Boston with B. J. Lang, and composition with Sidney Homer and others. He also studied in Paris for a time in 1890. He has written a "Dance of the Gnomes," that is characteristic and brilliantly droll, and a piano piece, called "Under Bright Skies," which has the panoply and progress of a sunlit cavalcade.

Ernest Osgood Hiler has written some good music for the violin, a book of songs for children, "Cloud, Field, and Flower," and some sacred music. He studied in Germany for two years.

[1] See p. 556.

The Chicago Colony.

Most prominent among Chicago's composers is doubtless Frederick Grant Gleason, who has written in the large forms with distinguished success. The Thomas Orchestra has performed a number of his works, which is an excellent praise, because Thomas, who has done so much for American audiences, has worried himself little about the American composer. At the World's Fair, which was, in some ways, the artistic birthday of Chicago, and possibly the most important artistic event in our national history, some of Gleason's works were performed by Thomas' organization, among them the *Vorspiel* to an opera, "Otho Visconti" (op. 7), for which Gleason wrote both words and music.

This *Vorspiel*, like that to "Lohengrin," is short and delicate. It begins ravishingly with flutes and clarinets and four violins, pianissimo, followed by a blare of brass. After this introductory period the work runs through tenderly contemplative musing to the end, in which, again, the only strings are the four violins, though here they are accompanied by the brass and wood-winds and tympani, the cymbals being gently tapped with drumsticks. The introduction to the third act of the opera is more lyrical, but not so fine. Another opera is "Montezuma" (op. 16). Gleason is again his own librettist. Of this opera I have been privileged to see the complete piano score, and much of the orchestral.

In the first act Guatemozin, who has been exiled by Montezuma, appears disguised as an ancient minstrel and sings prophetically of the coming of a god of peace and love to supplant the terrible idol that demands human sacrifice. This superbly written aria provokes from the terrified idolaters a chorus of fear and reproach that is strongly effective. The next act begins with an elaborate aria followed by a love duet

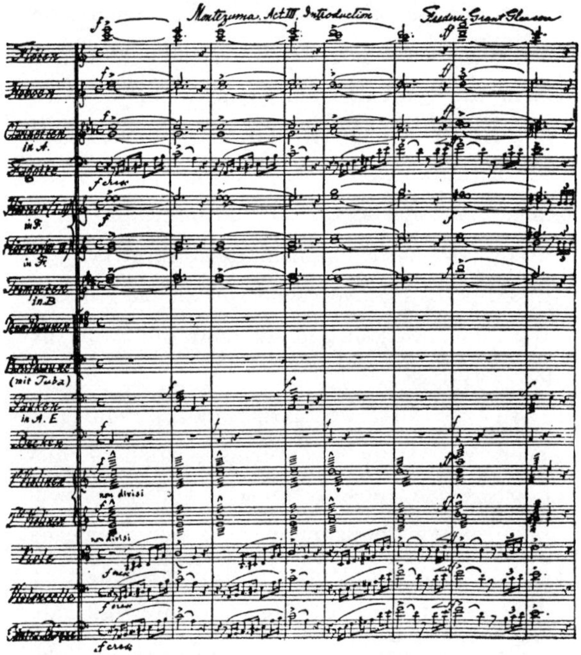

EXCERPT FROM AN ORCHESTRAL SCORE BY MR. GLEASON.

of much beauty. A heavily scored priests' march is one of the chief numbers, and like most marches written by the unco' learned, it is a grain of martial melody in a bushel of trumpet figures and preparation. The Wagnerian *leit-motif* idea is adopted in this and other works of his, and the chief objection to his writing is its too great fidelity to the Wagnerian manner, — notably in the use of suspensions and passing-notes, — otherwise he is a very powerful harmonist and an instrumenter of rare sophistication. A soprano aria with orchestral accompaniment has been taken from the opera and sung in concert with strong effect.

Another work played at the World's Fair by Thomas, is a "Processional of the Holy Grail." It is scored elaborately, but is rather brilliant than large. It complimentarily introduces a hint or two of Wagner's **Grail** motif.

The symphonic poem, "Edris," was also

performed by the Thomas Orchestra. It is based upon Marie Corelli's novel, " Ardath," which gives opportunity for much programmism, but of a mystical highly colored sort for which music is especially competent. It makes use of a number of remarkably beautiful motives. One effect much commented upon was a succession of fifths in the bass, used legitimately enough to express a dreariness of earth.

This provoked from that conservative of conservatives, the music copyist, a patronizing annotation, " Quinten !" to which Gleason added " Gewiss !" A series of augmented triads, smoothly manipulated, was another curiosity of the score.

Possibly Gleason's happiest work is his exquisite music for that most exquisite of American poems, " The Culprit Fay." It is described in detail in Upton's " Standard Cantatas," and liberally quoted from in Goodrich' " Musical Analysis." While I have seen both the piano and orchestral scores of this work (op. 15), and have seen much beauty in them, my space compels me to refer the curious reader to either of these most recommendable books.

Gleason has had an unusual schooling. He was born in Middletown, Conn., in 1848. His parents were musical, and when at sixteen he wrote a small matter of two oratorios without previous instruction, they put him to study under Dudley Buck. From his tuition he graduated to Germany, and to such teachers as Moscheles, Richter, Plaidy, Lobe, Raif, Taussig, and Weitzmann. He studied in England after that, and returned again to Germany. When he re-appeared in America he remained a while at Hartford, Conn., whence he went to Chicago in 1876. He has lived there since, working at teaching and composition, and acting as musical critic of the Chicago *Tribune*. An unusually gifted body of critics, dramatic, musical, and literary, has worked upon the Chicago newspapers, and Gleason has been prominent among them.

Among other important compositions of his are a symphonic cantata, " The Auditorium Festival Ode," sung at the dedication of the Chicago Auditorium by a chorus of five hundred ; sketches for orchestra, a piano concerto, organ music, and songs.

As is shown by the two or three vocal works of his that I have seen, Gleason is less successful as a melodist than as a harmonist. But in this latter capacity he is gifted indeed, and is peculiarly fitted to furnish forth with music Ebling's "Lobgesang auf die Harmonie." In his setting of this poem he has used a soprano and a barytone solo with male chorus and orchestra. The harmonic structure throughout is superb in all the various virtues ascribed to harmony. The ending is magnificent.

A work completed December, 1899, for

production by the Thomas Orchestra, is a symphonic poem called " The Song of Life," with this motto from Swinbourne :

" They have the night, who had, like us, the day ;
We whom the day binds shall have night as they;
We, from the fetters of the light unbound,
Healed of our wound of living, shall sleep sound."

The first prominent musician to give a certain portion of his program regularly to the American composer, was William H. Sherwood. This recognition from so distinguished a performer could not but interest many who had previously turned a deaf ear to all the musical efforts of the Eagle. In addition to playing their piano works, he has transcribed numerous of their orchestral works to the piano, and played them. In short, he has been so indefatigable a laborer for the cause of other American composers, that he has found little time to write his own ideas.

Sherwood will be chiefly remembered as a pianist, but he has written a certain amount of music of an excellent quality. Opera 1–4 were published abroad. Opus 5 is a suite, the second number of which is an "Idylle" that deserves its name. It is as blissfully clear and ringing as anything could well be, and drips with a Theokritan honey. The third number of the suite is called "Greetings." It has only one or two unusual touches. Number 4 bears the suggestive title, "Regrets for the Pianoforte." It was possibly written after some of his less promising pupils had finished a lesson. The last number of the suite is a quaint Novelette.

Sherwood's sixth opus is made up of a brace of mazurkas. The former, in C minor, contains some of his best work. It is original and moody, and ends strongly. The second, in A major, is still better. It not only keeps up a high standard throughout,

WILLIAM H. SHERWOOD.

IDYLLE.

Allegretto moderato. M. M. ♩. 60 – 69 Wm H. SHERWOOD, Op. 5 No. 2

A FRAGMENT.

but shows occasional touches of the most fascinating art.

A scherzo (op. 7) cracks a few good jokes, but is mostly elaboration. Opus 8 is a fiery romanza appassionata. Opus 9 is a Scherzo-Caprice. This is probably his best work. It is dedicated to Liszt, and though extremely brilliant, is full of meaning. It has an interlude of tender romance. " Coy Maiden " is a graceful thing, but hardly deserves the punishment of so horrible a name. " A Gypsy Dance " is too long, but it is of good material. It has an interesting metre, three-quarter time with the first note dotted. There is a good effect gained by sustaining certain notes over several measures, though few pianists get a real sostenuto. An " Allegro Patetico " (op. 12), " Medea " (op. 13), and a set of small pieces (one of them a burlesque called " A Caudle Lecture," with a garrulous " said she " and a somnolent " said he ") make up his rather short list of compositions.

Sherwood was born at Lyons, New York, of good American stock. His father was his teacher until the age of seventeen, when he studied with Heimberger, Pychowski, and Dr. William Mason. He studied in Europe with Kullak and Deppe, Scotson Clark, Weitzmann, Doppler, Wuerst, and Richter. He was for a time organist in Stuttgart and later in Berlin. He was one of those favorite pupils of Liszt, and played in concerts abroad with remarkable success, winning at the age of eighteen high critical enthusiasm. He has been more cordially recognized abroad than here, but is assuredly one of the greatest living pianists. It is fortunate that his patriotism keeps him at home, where he is needed in the constant battle against the indecencies of apathy and Philistinism.

The Yankee spirit of constructive irreverence extends to music, and in recent years a number of unusually modern-minded theorists have worked at the very foundations: Dr.

Percy Goetschius (born here, and for long a teacher at Stuttgart) ; O. B. Boise (born here, and teaching now in Berlin) ; Edwin Bruce, the author of a very radical work ; Homer A. Norris ; and last, and first, A. J. Goodrich, who has made himself one of the most advanced of living writers on the theory of music, and has made so large a contribution to the solidity of our attainments, that he is recognized among scholars abroad as one of the leading spirits of his time. His success is the more pleasing since he was not only born but educated in this country.

The town of Chilo, Ohio, was Goodrich' birthplace. He was born there in 1847, of American parentage. His father taught him the rudiments of music and the piano for one year, after which he became his own teacher. He has had both a thorough and an independent instructor. The fact that he has been enabled to follow his own conscience without danger of being convinced into error

A. J. GOODRICH.

by the prestige of some influential master, is doubtless to be credited with much of the novelty and courage of his work.

His most important book is undoubtedly his "Analytical Harmony," though his "Musical Analysis" and other works are serious and important. This is not the place to discuss his technicalities, but one must mention the real bravery it took to discard the old practice of a figured bass, and to attack many of the theoretical fetiches without hesitation. Almost all of the old theorists have confessed, usually in a foot-note to the preface or in modest disclaimer lost somewhere in the book, that the great masters would occasionally be found violating certain of their rules. But this did not lead them to deducing their rules from the great masters. Goodrich, however, has, in this matter, begun where Marx ended, and has gone further even than Prout. He has gone to melody as the groundwork of his harmonic system, and to the practice of great masters, old and new, for the tests of all his theories. The result is a book which can be unreservedly commended for self-instruction to the ignorant and to the too learned. It is to be followed by a book on " Synthetic Counterpoint," of which Goodrich says, " It is almost totally at variance with the standard books in counterpoint."

In his " Musical Analysis " he quoted freely from American composers, and analyzed many important native works. He has carried out this plan also in his book on " Interpretation," a work aiming to bring more definiteness into the fields of performance and terminology.

Goodrich' composition is "a thing of the past," he says. In his youth he wrote a score or more of fugues, two string quartettes, a trio that was played in New York and Chicago, a sonata, two concert overtures, a hymn for soprano (in English), invisible chorus (in Latin), and orchestra, a volume of songs, and numerous piano pieces. He writes : " In truth, I believed at one time that I was a real composer, but after listening to Tschaïkowski's Fifth Symphony that illusion was dispelled. Had not Mrs. Goodrich rescued from the flames a few MSS. I would have destroyed every note."

Only a piano suite is left, and this leads one to regret that Tschaïkowski should have served as a deterrent instead of an inspiration. The suite has an inelaborate prelude, which begins strongly and ends gracefully, showing unusual handling throughout. A minuet, taken scherzando, is also most original and happy. There is a quaint sarabande, and a gavotte written on simple lines, but superbly. Its musette is simply captivating. All these little pieces indeed show sterling originality and unusual resources in a small compass.

W. H. Neidlinger's first three songs were kept in his desk for a year and then kept by a publisher for a year longer, and finally brought out in 1889. To his great surprise, the "Serenade," which he calls "just a little bit of commonplace melody," had an immense sale and created a demand for more of his work. The absolute simplicity of this exquisite gem is misleading. It is not cheap in its lack of ornament, but it eminently deserves that high-praising epithet (so pitilessly abused), "chaste." It has the daintiness and minute completeness of a Tanagra figurine.

Mr. Neidlinger was born in Brooklyn, N. Y., in 1863, and was compelled to earn the money for his own education and for his musical studies. From Dudley Buck and, later, C. C. Muller, of New York, he has had his only musical instruction. He lived abroad for some time, teaching the voice in Paris, then returned to live in Chicago. He has written two operas, one of them having been produced by the Bostonians.

Mr. Neidlinger builds his songs upon one

guiding principle, that is, faithfulness to elo-
cutionary accent and intonation. As he neatly
phrases it, his songs are "colored sketches
on a poet's engravings."

The usual simplicity of Mr. Neidlinger's
songs does not forbid a dramatic outburst at
the proper time, as in the fine mood, "A
Leaf;" or the sombre depth of "Night,"
"Nocturne," and "Solitude;" or yet the
sustainedly poignant anguish of "The Pine-
tree." Occasionally the accompaniment is
developed with elaborateness, as in the bird-
flutings of "The Robin," and "Memories,"
an extremely rich work, with its mellow
brook-music and a hint of nightingale complaint in the minor. "Evening Song," a bit
of inspired tenderness, is one of Mr. Neidlinger's best works. Almost better is "Sun-
shine," a streak of brilliant fire quenched
with a sudden cloud at the end. Other
valuable works are "Messages," the happy
little Scotch song, "Laddie," and "Dream-

ing," which is now sombre, now fierce with outbursts of agony, but always a melody, always ariose.

Mr. Neidlinger has made a special study of music for children, his book, "Small Songs for Small Children," being much used in kindergarten work. A book of his, devoted to a synthetic philosophy of song, is completed for publication ; he calls it "Spenser, Darwin, Tyndall, etc., in sugar-coated pills ; geography, electricity, and hundreds of other things in song."

The Cleveland Colony.

The city of Cleveland contains a musical colony which is certainly more important than that of any town of its size. About the tenth of our cities in population, it is at least fourth, and possibly third, in productiveness in valuable composition.

The most widely known of Cleveland com-

posers is Wilson G. Smith.[1] He has been
especially fortunate in hitting the golden
mean between forbidding abstruseness and
trivial popularity, and consequently enjoys
the esteem of those learned in music as well
as of those merely happy in it.

Papillons (Butterflies)
(Étude-Caprice)

His erudition has persuaded him to a large
simplicity; his nature turns him to a musical
optimism that gives many of his works a
Mozartian cheer. Graciousness is his key.

He was born in Elyria, O., and educated
in the public schools of Cleveland, where he
graduated. Prevented by delicate health
from a college education, he has nevertheless,

[1] See p. 552.

by wide reading, broadened himself into culture, and is an essayist of much skill. His musical education began in 1876, at Cincinnati, where his teacher, Otto Singer, encouraged him to make music his profession. In 1880 he was in Berlin, where he studied for several years under Kiel, Scharwenka, Moskowski, and Oscar Raif. He then returned to Cleveland, where he took up the teaching of organ, piano, voice, and composition.

The most important of Smith's earlier works was a series of five pieces called "Hommage à Edvard Grieg," which brought warmest commendation from the Scandinavian master. One of the most striking characteristics of Smith's genius is his ability to catch the exact spirit of other composers. He has paid "homage" to Schumann, Chopin, Schubert, and Grieg, and in all he has achieved remarkable success, for he has done more than copy their little tricks of expression, oddities of manner, and pet weaknesses.

He has caught the individuality and the spirit of each man.

In his compositions in Grieg-ton Smith has seized the fascinating looseness of the Griegorian tonality and its whimsicality. The " Humoresque " is a bit of titanic merriment ; the " Mazurka " is most deftly built and is full of dance-fire ; the " Arietta " is highly original, and the " Capricietto " shows such ingenious management of triplets, and has altogether such a crisp, brisk flavor, that it reminds one of Lamb's rhapsody on roast pig, where he exclaims, " I tasted *crackling !* " The " Romance," superb in gloom and largeness of treatment, is worthy of the composer of " The Death of Asra." A later work, " Caprice Norwegienne," is also a strong brew of Scandinavian essence.

A " Schumannesque " is written closely on the lines of Schumann's " Arabesque." A later " Hommage à Schumann " is equally faithful to another style of the master, and dashes forth with characteristic and un-naïve gaiety and challenging thinness of harmony, occasionally bursting out into great rare chords, just to show what can be done when one tries.

The man that could write both this work and the highly faithful " Hommage à Schubert," and then whirl forth the rich-colored, sensuous fall and purr of the " Hommage à Chopin," must be granted at least an unusual command over pianistic materials, and a most unusual acuteness of observation.

He can write *à la* Smith, too, and has a vein quite his own, even though he prefers to build his work on well-established lines, and fit his palette with colors well tempered and toned by the masters.

In this line is opus 21, a group of four pieces called " Echoes of Ye Olden Time." The " Pastorale " is rather Smithian than olden, with its mellow harmony, but the " Minuetto " is the perfection of chivalric foppery and pompous gaiety. The "Gavotte" suggests the contagious good humor of Bach, and the "Minuetto Grazioso," the best of the series, has a touch of the goodly old intervals, tenths and sixths, that taste like a draught of spring water in the midst of our modern liqueurs.

The musical world in convention assembled has covenanted that certain harmonies shall be set apart for pasturage. Just why these arbitrary pastorales should suggest meads and syrinxes, and dancing shepherds, it would be hard to tell. But this effect they certainly have, and a good pastorale is a better antidote for the blues and other civic ills than anything I know, except the actual green and blue of fields and skies. Among the best of the best pastoral music, I should place Smith's "Gavotte Pastorale." It is one of the five pieces in his book of "Romantic Studies" (op. 57).

This same volume contains a "Scherzo

alla Tarantella," which is full of reckless wit. But the *abandon* is so happy as to seem misplaced in a tarantella, that dance whose traditional origin is the maniacal frenzy produced by the bite of the tarantula. An earlier Tarantella (op. 34) is far truer to the meaning of the dance, and fairly raves with shrieking fury and shuddering horror. This is better, to me, than Heller's familiar piece.

The "Second Gavotte" is a noble work, the naïve gaiety of classicism being enriched with many of the great, pealing chords the modern piano is so fertile in. I count it as one of the most spontaneous gavottes of modern times, one that is buoyant with the afflation of the olden days. It carries a musette of which old Father Bach need not have felt ashamed, — one of the most ingenious examples of a drone-bass ever written.

The "Menuet Moderne" is musical champagne. A very neat series of little variations is sheafed together, and called

"Mosaics." Mr. Smith has written two pieces well styled "Mazurka Poétique;" the later (opus 48) is the more original, but the sweet geniality and rapturously beautiful ending of opus 38 is purer music. "Les Papillons" is marked with a strange touch of negro color; it is, as it were, an Ethiopiano piece. Its best point is its cadenza. Smith has a great fondness for these brilliant pre-cipitations. They not only give further evidence of his fondness for older schools, but they also partially explain the fondness of concert performers for his works. His fervid "Love Sonnet," his "Polonaise de Concert," full of virility as well as virtuosity, and his delicious "Mill-wheel Song," and a late composition, a brilliant "Papillon," rich as a butterfly's wing, are notable among his numerous works. Possibly his largest achieve-ment is the three concert-transcriptions for two pianos. He has taken pieces by Grieg, Raff, and Bachmann, and enlarged, enforced, decorated, and in every way ennobled them. But to me his most fascinatingly original work is his " Arabesque," an entirely unhackneyed and memorable composition.

Smith's experience in teaching has crystallized into several pedagogic works. His " Scale Playing with particular reference to the development of the third, fourth, and fifth fingers of each hand;" his " Eight Measure," " Octave," and " Five Minute " studies, have brought the most unreserved commendation from the most important of our teachers. A late and most happy scheme has been the use of a set of variations for technical and interpretative instruction. For this purpose he wrote his " Thèmes Arabesques," of which numbers one and eighteen not only have emotional and artistic interest, but lie in the fingers in a strangely tickling way.

What might be called a professorial simplicity is seen in many of Smith's songs.

The almost unadorned, strictly essential beauty of his melodies and accompaniments is neither neglect nor cheapness; it is restraint to the point of classicism, and romanticism all the intenser for repression. Take, for example, that perfect song, "If I but Knew," which would be one of a score of the world's best short songs, to my thinking. Note the open fifths, horrifying if you thump them academically, but very brave and straightforward, fitly touched.

There is something of Haydn at his best in this and in the fluty "Shadow Song," in "The Kiss in the Rain," and "A Sailor's Lassie," for they are as crystalline and direct as "Papa's" own immortal "Schäferlied."

Smith has gone over to the great majority, — the composers who have set "Du bist wie eine Blume;" but he has joined those at the top. Two of Smith's songs have a quality of their own, an appeal that is bewitching: "Entreaty," a perfect melody, and "The

ARABESQUE.

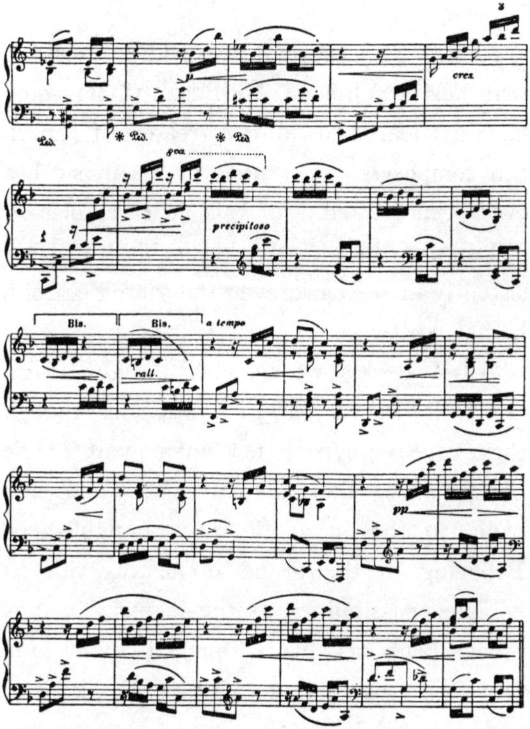
Ped.
p
cres.
8va
precipitoso
Bis.
Bis.
rall.
a tempo
pp

Dimple in Her Cheek," which is fairly peachy in color and flavor.

A strange place in the world of music is that held by Johann H. Beck, whom some have not feared to call the greatest of American composers. Yet none of his music has ever been printed. In this he resembles B. J. Lang, of Boston, who keeps his work persistently in the dark, even the sacred oratorio he has written.

All of Beck's works, except eight songs, are built on very large lines, and though they have enjoyed a not infrequent public performance, their dimensions would add panic to the usual timidity of publishers. Believing in the grand orchestra, with its complex possibilities, as the logical climax of music, Beck has devoted himself chiefly to it. He feels that the activity of the modern artist should lie in the line of " amplifying, illustrating, dissecting, and filling in the outlines left by the great creators of music and

the drama." He foresees that the most complicated scores of to-day will be Haydnesque
in simplicity to the beginning of the next
century, and he is willing to elaborate his
best and deepest learning as far as in him
lies, and wait till the popular audience grows
up to him, rather than write down to the
level of the present appreciation.

The resolve and the patient isolation of
such a devotee is nothing short of heroic;
but I doubt that the truest mission of the
artist is to consider the future too closely.
Even the dictionaries and encyclopædias of
one decade, are of small use to the next.
The tiny lyrics of Herrick, though, have no
quarrel with time, nor has time any grudge
against the intimate figurines of Tanagra.
The burdened trellises of Richard Strauss
may feel the frost long before the slender ivy
of Boccherini's minuet.

Science falls speedily out of date, and
philosophy is soon out of fashion. Art that

A FRAGMENT OF THE SCORE OF "SALAMMBÔ," BY
JOHANN H. BECK.

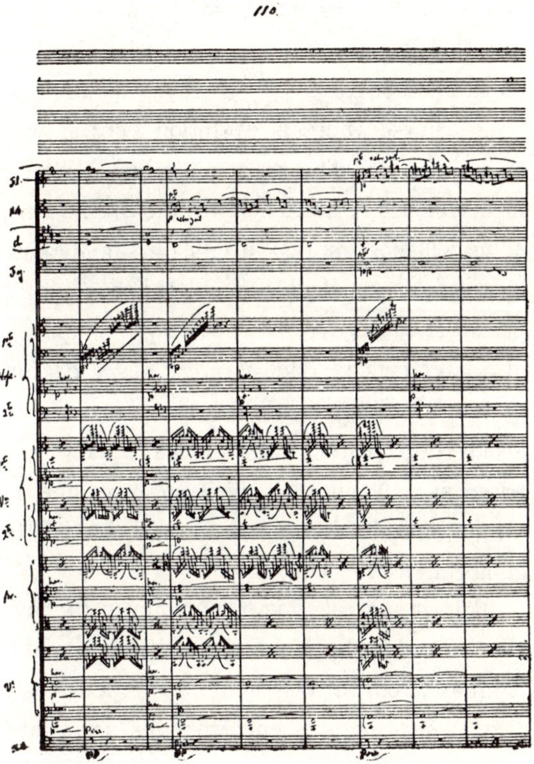
110.

uses both, is neither. When it makes crutches of them and leans its whole weight on them, it will fall with them in the period of their inevitable decay.

Of course, there is evolution here as well as in science. The artist must hunt out new forms of expressing his world-old emotions, or he will not impress his hearers, and there is no gainsaying Beck's thesis that the Chinese puzzle of to-day will be the antique simplicity of a later epoch. But it must never be forgotten, that art should be complex only to avoid the greater evils of inadequacy and triteness. A high simplicity of plan and an ultimate popularity of appeal are essentials to immortal art.

It is my great misfortune never to have heard one of Beck's works performed, but, judging from a fragment of a deliciously dreamy moonlight scene from his unfinished music drama, "Salammbô," which he kindly sent me, and from the enthusiasm of the

severest critics, he must be granted a most
unusual poetic gift, solidity and whimsicality,
and a hardly excelled erudition. His orchestration shows a hand lavish with color and
cunning in novel effects. Several of his
works have been performed with great applause in Germany, where Beck spent many
years in study. He was born at Cleveland,
in 1856, and is a graduate of the Leipzig
Conservatorium.

In art, quality is everything; quantity is
only a secondary consideration. It is on
account of the quality of his work that James
H. Rogers must be placed among the very
best of modern song-writers, though his published works are not many. When one considers his tuition, it is small wonder that his
music should show the finish of long mastery.
Born in 1857, at Fair Haven, Conn., he took
up the study of the piano at the age of twelve,
and at eighteen was in Berlin, studying there
for more than two years with Löschorn,

Rohde, Haupt, and Ehrlich, and then in Paris for two years under Guilmant, Fissot, and Widor. Since then he has been in Cleveland as organist, concert pianist, and teacher.

His songs are written usually in a charac teristic form of dramatic, yet lyric recitative. His " Album of Five Songs " contains notable examples of this style, particularly the " Good-Night," " Come to Me in My Dreams," and the supremely tragic climax of " Jealousy." The song, " Evening," with its bell-like ac-companiment, is more purely lyric, like the

enchanting " At Parting," which was too
delicately and fragrantly perfect to escape
the wide popularity it has had. His " Declaration " is ravishingly exquisite, and offers a
strange contrast to the " Requiescat," which
is a dirge of the utmost largeness and grandeur. His graceful " Fly, White Butterflies,"
and " In Harbor," and the dramatic setting
of " The Loreley," the jovial " Gather Ye
Rosebuds " of jaunty Rob Herrick, the fop-
pish tragedy of " La Vie est Vaine " (in
which the composer's French prosody is a
whit askew), that gallant, sweet song, " My
True Love Hath My Heart," and a gracious
setting of Heine's flower-song, are all noteworthy lyrics. He has set some of Tolstoï's
words to music, the sinister love of " Doubt
Not, O Friend," and the hurry and glow of
" The First Spring Days," making unusually
powerful songs. In the " Look Off, Dear
Love," he did not catch up with Lanier's
great lyric, but he handled his material most

effectively in Aldrich' " Song from the Persian," with its Oriental wail followed by a
martial joy. The high verve that marks his
work lifts his " Sing, O Heavens," out of the
rut of Christmas anthems.

Of instrumental work, there is only one
small book, " Scènes du Bal," a series of nine
pieces with lyric characterization in the spirit,
but not the manner of Schumann's " Carné-
val." The most striking numbers are " Les
Bavardes," " Blonde et Brune," and a fire-
eating polonaise.

These close the lamentably small number
of manifestations of a most decisive ability.

Another Cleveland composer well spoken
of is Charles Sommer.

A young woman of genuine ability, who
has been too busy with teaching and concert
pianism to find as much leisure as she
deserves for composition, is Patty Stair, a
prominent musical figure in Cleveland. Her
theoretical studies were received entirely at

Cleveland, under F. Bassett. Her published works include a book of " Six Songs," all of them interesting and artistic, and the " Madrigal" particularly ingenious ; and a comic glee of the most irresistible humor, called " An Interrupted Serenade ; " in manuscript are a most original song, " Flirtation," a jovial part song for male voices, " Jenny Kissed Me," a berceuse for violin and piano, a graceful song, " Were I a Brook," a setting of Thomas Campion's " Petition," and another deeply stirring religious song for contralto, " O Lamb of God."

The St. Louis Colony.

The most original and important contribution to American music that St. Louis has made, is, to my mind, the book of songs written by William Schuyler. The words were chosen from Stephen Crane's book of poems, "The Black Riders." The genius of Crane, concomitant with eccentricity as

III.

WILLIAM SCHUYLER.

Words used by permission of Copeland and Day.
Copyright, 1897, by Wm. Schuyler.

FROM WM. SCHUYLER'S "BLACK RIDERS."

All was lost But this place of beau . ty and her......

When I gazed, And in my gaz . ing, de . sired...... Then came a . gain......

Mile up . on mile, Of snow, ice, burn . ing sand, burn . . ing

sand.

it was, is one of the most distinctive among American writers. The book called " The Black Riders " contains a number of moods that are unique in their suggestiveness and originality. Being without rime or meter, the lines oppose almost as many difficulties to a musician as the works of Walt Whitman ; and yet, as Alfred Bruneau has set Zola's prose to music, so some brave American composer will find inspiration abundant in the works of Walt Whitman and Emily Dickinson.

Schuyler was born in St. Louis, May 4, 1855, and music has been his livelihood. He is largely self-taught, and has composed some fifty pieces for the piano, a hundred and fifty songs, a few works for violin, viola, and 'cello, and two short trios.

In his setting of these lines of Crane's, Schuyler has attacked a difficult problem in an ideal manner. To three of the short poems he has given a sense of epic vastitude, and to two of them he has given a tantalizing mysticism. The songs, which have been published privately, should be reproduced for the wide circulation they deserve.

Another writer of small songs displaying unusual individuality is George Clifford Vieh, who was born in St. Louis and studied there under Victor Ehling. In 1889, he went to Vienna for three years, studying under Bruckner, Robert Fuchs, and Dachs. He graduated with the silver medal there, and returned to St. Louis, where he has since lived as a teacher and pianist.

Alfred George Robyn is the most popular composer St. Louis has developed. He was born in 1860, his father being William Robyn, who organized the first symphonic orchestra west of Pittsburg. Robyn was a youthful prodigy as a pianist; and, at the age of ten, he succeeded his father as organist at St. John's Church, then equipped with the best choir in the city. It was necessary for the pedals of the organ to be raised to his feet. At the age of sixteen he became solo pianist with Emma Abbott's company. As a composer Robyn has written some three hundred compositions, some of them reaching a tremendous sale. A few of them have been serious and worth while, notably a piano concerto, a quintette, four string quartettes, a mass, and several orchestral suites.

There are not many American composers that have had a fugue published, or have written fugues that deserve publication. It is the distinction of Ernest Richard Kroeger[1] that he has written one that deserved, and secured, publication. This was his 41st opus. It is preceded by a prelude which, curiously enough, is thoroughly Cuban in spirit and is a downright Habanera, though not so announced. This fiery composition is followed by a four-voiced "real" fugue. The subject is genuinely interesting, though the counter-subject is as perfunctory as most

[1] See p. 492.

counter-subjects. The middle-section, the stretto-work, and the powerful ending, give the fugue the right to exist.

Among other publications are a suite for piano (op. 33), in which a scherzo has life, and a sonata for violin and piano, in which, curiously enough, the violin has not one instance of double-stopping, and the elaborating begins, not with the first subject taken vigorously, but with the second subject sung out softly. The last movement is the best, a quaint and lively rondo. A set of twelve concert études show the influence of Chopin upon a composer who writes with a strong German accent. The étude called "Castor and Pollux" is a vigorous number with the chords of the left hand exactly doubled in the right; another étude, "A Romanze," is noteworthy for the practice it gives in a point which is too much ignored even by the best pianists; that is, the distinction between the importance of the tones of the same chord struck by the same hand. A work of broad scholarship, which shows the combined influence of Beethoven and Chopin, who have chiefly affected Kroeger, is his sonata (op. 40). A dominant pedal-point of fifty-eight measures, in the last movement, is worth mentioning. In a "Danse Négre" and a "Caprice Négre," he has evidently gone, for his Ethiopian color, not to the actual negro music, but to the similar compositions of Gottschalk. Kroeger was born in St. Louis, August 10, 1862. At the age of five he took up the study of the piano and violin. His theoretical tuition was all had in this country. He has written many songs, a piano concerto, sonatas for piano and viola, and piano and 'cello, two trios, a quintette, and three string quartettes, as well as a symphony, a suite, and overtures based on "Edymion," "Thanatopsis," "Sardanapalus" (produced by Anton Seidl, in New York), "Hiawatha," and "Atala."

CHAPTER V.

THE WOMEN COMPOSERS.

THIS is not the place to take up cudgels for a contest on the problem of woman's right to respect in the creative arts. There are some, it is true, who deny fervently that the feminine half of mankind ever has or can or ever will do original and important work there. If you press them too hard they will take refuge up this tree, that all women who ever have had success have been actually mannish of mind, — a dodge in question-begging that is one of the most ingenious ever devised ; a piece of masculine logic that puts to shame all historic examples of womanly fallacy and sophistry. It seems to me that the question is easily settled on this wise : it is impossible for a rational mind to deny that the best work done in the arts by women is of better quality than the average work done by men. This lets the cat's head out of the bag, and her whole body follows pell-mell.

In a few instances it seems to me that the best things done by women equal the best things done by men in those lines. The best verses of Sappho, the best sonnets of Mrs. Browning, the best chapters of George Eliot, the best animal paintings of Rosa Bonheur, do not seem to me surpassed by their rivals in masculine work. If anything in verse of its sort is nobler than Mrs. Howe's "Battle Hymn of the Republic," it is still in manuscript. If there is any poet of more complete individuality than Emily Dickinson, I have not run across his books. In music I place two or three of Miss Lang's small songs among the chief of their manner.

All over the world the woman-mind is taking up music. The ban that led Fanny Mendelssohn to publish her music under her brother's name, has gone where the puritanic theory of the disgracefulness of the musical profession now twineth its choking coils. A publisher informs me that where compositions by women were only one-tenth of his manuscripts a few years ago, they now form more than two-thirds. From such activity, much that is worth while is bound to spring. Art knows no sex, and even what the women write in man-tone is often surprisingly strong, though it is wrongly aimed. But this effort is like the bombast of a young people or a juvenile literature; the directness and repose of fidelity to nature come later. The American woman is in the habit of getting what she sets her heart on. She has determined to write music.

With an ardor that was ominous of success, Miss Amy Marcy Cheney, after a short preliminary course in harmony, resolved to finish her tuition independently. As an example of the thoroughness that has given her such unimpeachable knowledge of her subject, may be mentioned the fact that she made her own translation of Berlioz and Gavaërt. She was born in New Hampshire, of descent American back to colonial times. At the age of four she wrote her opus 1. She is a concert pianist as well as a frequent composer in the largest forms. She is now Mrs. H. H. A. Beach.[1]

Not many living men can point to a composition of more maturity and more dignity than Mrs. Beach' "Jubilate," for the dedication of the Woman's Building at the Columbian Exposition. The work is as big as its name ; it is the best possible answer to skeptics of woman's musical ability. It may be too sustainedly loud, and the infrequent and short passages piano are rather breathing-spells than contrasting awe, but frequently this work

[1] See p. 519.

MRS. H. H. A. BEACH.

shows a very magnificence of power and exaltation. And the ending is simply superb, though I could wish that some of the terrific dissonances in the accompaniment had been put into the unisonal voices to widen the effect and strengthen the final grandeur. But as it is, it rings like a clarion of triumph, — the cry of a Balboa discovering a new sea of opportunity and emotion.

Another work of force and daring is the mass in E flat (op. 5), for organ and small orchestra. It is conventionally ecclesiastic as a rule, and suffers from Mrs. Beach' besetting sin of over-elaboration, but it proclaims a great ripeness of technic. The "Qui Tollis" is especially perfect in its sombre depth and richness. The "Credo" works up the cry of "crucifixus" with a thrilling rage of grief and a dramatic feeling rare in Mrs. Beach' work. This work was begun at the age of nineteen and finished three years later. It was given with notable effect in

1892 by the Handel and Haydn Society of Boston.

Mrs. Beach' "Valse Caprice" has just one motive, — to reach the maximum of technical trickiness and difficulty. There is such a thing as hiding one's light under a bushel, and there is such a thing as emptying a bushel of chaff upon it.

"Fireflies" is a shimmering and flitting caprice of much ingenuity, but it keeps in the field of dissonance almost interminably, and clear harmony is not so much the homing-place of its dissonance, as an infrequent glint through an inadvertent chink. This neat composition is one of four "Sketches for the Piano," of which "Phantoms" is delightful with ghostliness. "In Autumn" is a most excellent tone-poem, and "Dreaming" is a well-varied lyric. As a colorist Mrs. Beach is most original and studious. Her tireless hunt for new tints often diverts her indeed from the direct forthright of her meaning,

PHANTOMS.

("Toutes fragiles fleurs, sitôt mortes que nées.")
Victor Hugo.

A FRAGMENT.

but the "Danse des Fleurs" is rich in its gorgeousness. The flowing grace of the "Menuet Italien" makes it an uncharacteristic but charming work.

Horace, you know, promises to write so that any one will think him easy to equal, though much sweat will be shed in the effort. It is the transparency of her studiousness, and the conspicuous labor in polishing off effects and mining opportunity to the core, that chiefly mars the work of Mrs. Beach, in my opinion. One or two of the little pieces that make up the half-dozen of the "Children's Carnival" are among her best work, for the very cheery ease of their look. "Pantalon," "Harlequin," "Columbine," and "Secrets" are infinitely better art than a dozen valse-caprices.

Both the defects and effects of her qualities haunt Mrs. Beach' songs. When she is sparing in her erudition she is delightful. Fourteen of her songs are gathered into a

"Cyclus." The first is an "Ariette," with an accompaniment imitating the guitar. It is both tender and graceful. Probably her best song is the setting of W. E. Henley's fine poem, "Dark is the Night." It is of the "Erl-King" style, but highly original and tremendously fierce and eerie. The same poet's "Western Wind" is given a setting contrastingly dainty and serene. "The Blackbird" is delicious and quite unhackneyed. "A Secret" is bizarre, and "Empress of the Night" is brilliant. With the exception of a certain excess of dissonance for a love-song, "Wilt Thou Be My Dearie?" is perfect with amorous tenderness. "Just for This!" is a delightful vocal scherzo of complete originality and entire success. "A Song of Love" is passionate and yet lyric, ornamented but not fettered. "Across the World" has been one of Mrs. Beach' most popular songs; it is intense and singable. "My Star" is tender, and the accompaniment is richly worked out

on simple lines.   Three Vocal Duets are well·
handled, but the long " Eilende Wolken " has
a jerky recitative of Händelian *naïveté*, to
which the aria is a welcome relief.   Her
sonata for piano and violin has been played
here by Mr. Kneisel, and in Berlin by Mme.
Carreño and Carl Halir.

Besides these, Mrs. Beach has done not a
little for the orchestra.   Her " Gaelic Sym·
phony " is her largest work, and it has been
often played by the Boston Symphony, the
Thomas, and other orchestras.   It is char·
acterized by all her exuberant scholarship
and unwearying energy.

Margaret Ruthven Lang,[1] the daughter of
B. J. Lang, is American by birth and training.   She was born in Boston, November 27,
1867.   She has written large works, such as
three concert overtures, two of which have
been performed by the Thomas and the Boston Symphony Orchestras, though none of
them are published.   Other unpublished

[1] See p. 520.

works are a cantata, two arias with orchestral accompaniment, and a rhapsody for the piano. One rhapsody has been published, that in E minor ; in spite of its good details, it is curiously unsatisfying, — it seems all prelude, interlude, and postlude, with the actual rhapsody accidentally overlooked. A " Meditation " is bleak, with a strong, free use of dissonance.

" The Jumblies " is a setting of Edward Lear's elusive nonsense, as full of the flavor of subtile humor as its original. It is for male chorus, with an accompaniment for two pianos, well individualized and erudite. It is in her solo songs, however, that her best success is reaped.

When I say that Mrs. Beach' work is markedly virile, I do not mean it as compliment unalloyed ; when I find Miss Lang's work supremely womanly, I would not deny it great strength, any more than I would deny that quality to the sex of which Joan of Arc and Jael were not uncharacteristic members.

Such a work as the "Maiden and the Butterfly" is as fragile and rich as a butterfly's wing. "My Lady Jacqueminot" is exquisitely, delicately passionate. "Eros" is frail, rare, ecstatic. "Ghosts" is elfin and dainty as snowflakes. The "Spinning Song" is inexpressibly sad, and such music as women best understand, and therefore ought to make best. But womanliness equally marks "The Grief of Love," which is in every sense big in quality; marks the bitterness of "Oh, What Comes over the Sea," the wailing Gaelic sweetness of the "Irish Love Song," and the fiery passion of "Betrayed," highly dramatic until its rather trite ending. "Nameless Pain" is superb. Her "Lament" I consider one of the greatest of songs, and proof positive of woman's high capabilities for composition. Miss Lang has a harmonic individuality, too, and finds out new effects that are strange without strain.

"My Turtle Dove," among the "Five

Norman Songs," in fearlessness and harmonic exploration shows two of the strongest of Miss Lang's traits. Her *récherchés* harmonies are no pale lunar reflection of masculine work. Better yet, they have the appearance of spontaneous ease, and the elaborateness never obtrudes itself upon the coherence of the work, except in a few such rare cases as " My Native Land," " Christmas Lullaby," and " Before My Lady's Window." They are singable to a degree unusual in scholarly compositions. To perfect the result Miss Lang chooses her poems with taste all too rare among musicians, who seem usually to rate gush as feeling and gilt as gold. Her " Oriental Serenade " is an example of weird and original intervals, and " A Spring Song," by Charlotte Pendleton, a proof of her taste in choosing words.

Her opus 32 is made up of two songs, both full of fire and originality. Opus 33 is a cap-

GHOSTS.

Words by Munkittrick.

MARGARET RUTHVEN LANG.

Out in the mis-ty moon-light, the first snow flakes I see,___ As they fro-lie a-mong the leaf-less boughs of the ap-ple-tree.___

Copyright, 1889, by Arthur P. Schmidt & Co.

pp
Faint - ly they seem to
whis - per, as round the boughs they wing; "We are the ghosts of the
flow - ers who died in the ear - ly spring, Who died in the
pp rit. e dim.
ear - ly spring."
ppp

tivating "Spring Idyl" for the piano, for
which she has also written a "Revery," of
which the exquisiteness of sleep is the theme.
The music is delicious, and the ending is a
rare proof of the beautiful possibilities of
dissonance.

Personally, I see in Miss Lang's compositions such a depth of psychology that I place
the general quality of her work above that of
any other woman composer. It is devoid
of meretriciousness and of any suspicion of
seeking after virility; it is so sincere, so true
to the underlying thought, that it seems to
me to have an unusual chance of interesting
attention and stirring emotions increasingly
with the years.

An interesting and genuine individuality
will transpire through the most limited
amount of creative art. This has been the
case with the few published works of a
writer, whose compositions, though unpretentious in size and sentiment, yet reveal a

graceful fancy, and a marked contemplation upon the details of the moods.

Irene Baumgras was born at Syracuse, New York, and studied the piano at the Cincinnati Conservatory of Music, where she took the Springer gold medal in 1881. She studied in Berlin with Moszkowski and Oscar Raif. She was married in Berlin, in 1884, to Philip Hale, the distinguished Boston musical critic.

Her devotion to her art was so great that her health broke down from overwork, and she was compelled to give up piano playing. Some of her compositions have been published under the name of "Victor René." Her 15th opus is made up of three "Morceaux de Genre," of which the "Pantomime" is a most volatile harlequinade, with moods as changeful as the key; a remarkably interesting composition. Four "Pensées Poétiques" make up opus 16. They include a blithe "Chansonette" and a "Valse Impromptu," which, unlike the usual impromptu, has the *ex tempore* spirit. Of her songs, " Mystery " is a charming lyric ; " Maisie " is faithful to the ghoulish merriment of the words ; and " An Opal Heart " is striking for interesting dissonances that do not mar the fluency of the lyric.

Of much refinement are the fluent lyrics of Mrs. Mary Knight Wood. They show a breadth in little, and a fondness for unexpected harmonies that do not disturb the coherence of her songs. They possess also a marked spontaneity. An unexpected effect is gained by the brave E flat in her " Serenade." Her popular " Ashes of Roses" also has a rich harmonic structure. Among other songs, one with an effective obbligato for the violoncello deserves special praise. She has written also for the violin and piano, and trios for 'cello, violin, and piano.

Other women who have written certain works of serious intention and worthy art, are

Mrs. Clara A. Korn, Laura Sedgwick Collins, the composer of an ingenious male quartette, " Love is a Sickness," and many excellent songs, among them, " Be Like That Bird," which is ideally graceful ; Fanny M. Spencer, who has written a collection of thirty-two original hymn tunes, a good anthem, and a Magnificat and Nunc Dimittis of real strength; Julie Rivé-King, the author of many concert pieces ; Patty Stair, of Cleveland ; Harriet P. Sawyer, Mrs. Jessie L. Gaynor, Constance Maud, Jenny Prince Black, Charlotte M. Crane, and Helen Hood.

CHAPTER VI.

OURS is so young, and so cosmopolite, a country, that our art shows the same brevity of lineage as our society. Immigration has played a large part in the musical life of the United States, as it has in the make-up of the population; and yet for all the multi-plexity of his ancestry, the American citizen has been assimilated into a distinctive indi-viduality that has all the traits of his different forbears, and is yet not closely like any of them. So, American music, taking its scale and most of its forms from the old country, is yet developing an integrity that the future will make much of. As with the federation

442

of the States, so will one great music ascend polyphonically, — *e pluribus unum.*

In compiling this directory of American composers, it has been necessary to discuss the works only of the composers who were born in this country. It is interesting to see how few of these names are un-American, how few of them are Germanic (though so many of them have studied in Germany). Comment has often been made upon the Teutonic nature of the make-up of our orchestras. It is pleasant to find that a very respectable list of composers can be made up without a preponderance of German names.

The music life of our country, however, has been so strongly influenced and enlivened and corrected by the presence of men who were born abroad that some recognition of their importance should somewhere be found. Many of them have become **naturalized** and have brought with them so much enthusiasm for our institutions that they are actually more American than many of the Americans; than those, particularly, who, having had a little study abroad, have gone quite mad upon the superstition of "atmosphere," and have brought home nothing but foreign mannerisms and discontent.

Among the foreign born who have made their home in America, I must mention with respect, and without attempting to suggest order of precedence, the following names:

C. M. Loeffler,[1] Bruno Oscar Klein, Leopold Godowski, Victor Herbert,[2] Walter Damrosch,[3] Julius Eichberg, Dr. Hugh A. Clarke, Louis V. Saar, Asgar Hamerik, Otto Singer, August Hyllested, Xavier Scharwenka, Rafael Joseffy, Constantin von Sternberg, Adolph Koelling, August Spanuth, Aimé Lachaume, Max Vogrich, W. C. Seeboeck, Julian Edwards, Robert Coverley, William Furst, Gustave Kerker, Henry Waller,

[1] See p. 481.　　[2] See p. 463.　　[3] See p. 468.

P. A. Schnecker, Clement R. Gale, Edmund Severn, Platon Brounoff, Richard Burmeister, Augusto Rotoli, Emil Liebling, Carl Busch,[1] John Orth, Ernst Perabo, Ferdinand Dunkley, Mrs. Clara Kathleen Rogers, Miss Adele Lewing, Mrs. Elisa Mazzucato Young.

It is perhaps quibbling to rule out some of these names from Americanism, and include certain of those whom I have counted American because they were born here, in spite of the fact that their whole tuition and tendency is alien. But the line must be drawn somewhere. The problem is still more trying in the case of certain composers who, having been born here, have expatriated themselves, and joined that small colony of notables whom America has given to Europe as a first instalment in payment of the numerous loans we have borrowed from the old country.

For the sake of formally acknowledging this debt, I will not endeavor to discuss here the careers of George Templeton Strong, Arthur

[1] See p. 522.

Bird, or O. B. Boise, all three of whom were born in this country, but have elected to live in Berlin. Their distinction in that city at least palely reflects some credit upon the country that gave them birth.

POSTLUDE.

In the ninth century Iceland was the musical center of the world; students went there from all Europe as to an artistic Mecca. Iceland has long lost her musical crown. And Welsh music in its turn has ceased to be the chief on earth. Russia is sending up a strong and growing harmony marred with much discord. Some visionaries look to her for the new song. But I do not hesitate to match against the serfs of the steppes the high-hearted, electric-minded free people of our prairies; and to prophesy that in the coming century the musical supremacy and inspiration of the world will rest here overseas, in America.

PART II.
AMERICAN COMPOSERS SINCE
1900
BY ARTHUR ELSON

TO THE READER.

MR. RUPERT HUGHES wrote the main body of this work in 1900; and as much has happened since then, it has been deemed advisable to bring the book down to a more recent date; but nothing has been changed in the original work, as it covered its ground thoroughly, except that, wherever material about the earlier composers has been added in later pages, the requisite references have been given.

Mr. Hughes himself was so busy in other fields that he did not feel able to give his time to the preparation of this work; but he had collected much material, upon which the following chapters are based in large part, and for which thanks are due to him.

ARTHUR ELSON.

PART II.

AMERICAN COMPOSERS SINCE
1900

CHAPTER I.

THE ORCHESTRAL MASTERS.

FOURTEEN years have passed since Mr. Hughes wrote his able and comprehensive work on American composers. Within this period many of those mentioned have continued their activity, while others have jumped from obscurity to importance, and still others have passed away from our mundane sphere of activity. Among the most important whom death has claimed are Edward MacDowell, John K. Paine, and the veteran Dudley Buck.

Of those who are working in the orchestral field, one of the most important, if not the leader, is Henry Kimball Hadley. His earlier works have been described in some detail by Mr. Hughes.[1] His " Youth and Life " symphony has won recent attention in New York and elsewhere, while " The Four Seasons " took two prizes in 1901, and soon made its way into the orchestral repertoire. In addition to the " Hector and Andromache " overture, he has composed two others, " In Bohemia," and " Herod," the latter for Stephen Phillips' tragedy. A cantata, " In Music's Praise," continued its composer's prize-winning career. Six Ballades with orchestra belong among the larger works; also three comic operas. Abroad, Hadley brought out the one-act opera " Safie," a short but exciting affair. His " Atonement of Pan," written for the open-air " high jinks " of the San Francisco " Bohemians," is practically an-

[1] See p. 241.

other opera. Among what are called lesser works (which are sometimes of paramount importance) Hadley numbers a string quartet and trio, a piano quintet, a violin sonata, piano pieces, and songs. But he seems to delight in continuing in the larger forms. His " Merlin and Vivian " is a lyric drama for solo voices, chorus, and orchestra. " The Fate of Princess Kiyo " is an orchestral cantata for women's voices. But perhaps his most radical compositions are his symphonic poems, " Salome " and " The Culprit Fay." The former is a strong work, in which the orchestra is handled with Strauss-like ease and power. The latter is based on Joseph Rodman Drake's poem of the same name, written to show that American scenes and rivers, as well as those of the Old World, could be made romantic. The culprit fay, who has been disgraced through the glance of a mortal maiden's eye, must make himself pure by finding and bringing back the glistening drop

of water from the leaping sturgeon, and the
spark from a falling star.   In a mussel-shell

How do I love Thee? [1]

Sonnet from the Portuguese, No XLIII

Elizabeth Barrett Browning   Henry K. Hadley
                                                     Op. 20, No 2

boat he wins both prizes, and with them he

[1] Copyright, MCM, by Oliver Ditson Company.

returns into his rights, and joins the fairy dance that lasts till cock-crow. In this work the composer has given a number of delightful tone-pictures, — the fairies, the troubles of the culprit, the immensity of sea and sky, the final welcome, and many other dainty bits. It is little wonder that this composition, too, won a prize. A still later work is the symphony "North, East, South and West," in which the compass is boxed in most inspired fashion. The Oriental mystery of the East, the lively merriment of the South, the energy of the golden West, and the rugged spirit of the North, all are contrasted here in most excellent fashion, and made to form still another important work.

Frederick Shepherd Converse, whose activity is of more recent date, is another orchestral leader, somewhat contemplative in style, but with that same style very well suited to his subjects. Thus his symphonic poem "The Festival of Pan," based on a scene from the "Endymion" of Keats, is a most excellent reflection of the poet's own delicacy of style. There is revelry enough in the music, but it is of an ethereal kind. The revels of the mythical satyr-king are mirrored in a medium as translucent as that of the poet himself. The same is true of a second symphonic poem on the same general subject, entitled "Endymion's Narrative." This depicts the scene where Endymion, drawn apart by his solicitous sister Peona, confesses that he cherishes ideals beyond the common view, but is yet bound by affection and devotion to conditions which confine and stifle his higher aspirations. To use the composer's words more directly, "The piece begins with despondency and indecision. The hero is harassed by alluring glimpses of the ideal, and soothed by simple affection and love. There is a sort of dramatic growth of the various elements, until finally the idea comes victorious out of the struggle, and the

ungovernable impulse rushes exultantly on
with the mad joy of determination." Still
another symphonic poem, of even more dramatic force, is " Ormazd." That gentleman
is the good member of the pair of old Persian gods, while Ahriman is the evil one.
The former is constructive, the latter de-
structive. They are always in conflict,
though finally Ormazd will purge his wicked
rival of sin. The composition begins with
Ormazd assembling his heavenly host, and
trumpet-calls, vague at first, lead into a
strong martial passage. The moans of
Ahriman and his followers are then heard
ascending from the pit of Dusakh. At length
there is revolt and conflict, ending in the
victory of Ormazd, to whom the blessed
Fravashis sing hymns of praise. This work
shows Mr. Converse at his best. It has been
called " decorative and imaginative," " showing dignity and musicianly skill," and " more
luminous, more amply sonorous without

being blatant," than any of his other works.

Converse was born at Newton, Mass., in 1871. His study was carried on under Paine, Chadwick, Baermann, and, later, with Rheinberger at Munich. His early works included a violin sonata, a string quartet, a concert overture " Youth," and a symphony in D minor, given at Munich. After returning to teach, he soon gave up that work and devoted himself to composition. At this time the symphonic poems were created, and other works of large dimensions. There were the poems " Night " and " Day," on words of Whitman, and a work inspired by the same poet's " Mystic Trumpeter; " there was the baritone ballad " La Belle Dame sans Merci; " the oratorio (or dramatic poem) " Job; " a violin concerto; a second string quartet; and incidental music to Percy Mackaye's " Joan of Arc."

But perhaps the composer is more widely

known for his connection with that much-
discussed subject, American opera. His one-

Suite.[1]

I. Prelude.

[1] Copyright, 1899, by G. Schirmer, Jr. — By permission
of The Boston Music Company.

act " Pipe of Desire " was the first native work in this form to be given at the Metropolitan Opera House. Its allegorical subject rendered it somewhat undramatic, but this fault was absent from the composer's next opera, the three-act " Sacrifice." The sacrifice is made by an American captain, who loves a Spanish girl during the taking of California by the United States, but finds that she loves one of her own compatriots devotedly. The plot is based on a story written by Lieutenant H. A. Wise, but with altered names. Chonita is the girl who receives Captain Burton's devotion in the first act, though all the while she loves Bernal. In this act are an impressive Indian prophecy, a captivating song by Chonita, and a fervid love-duet at the close. The second act, in one of the old missions, begins in spirited fashion, with a red-blooded soldiers' chorus and a rhythmic dance of Gypsy and Mexican girls. There is also a melodious prayer when the chapel is left empty and Chonita appears; and a dramatic finale when Bernal, discovered in disguise, tries to kill Burton, but only succeeds in wounding Chonita, who throws herself between the men. The third act shows Chonita recovering, and Burton anxious to free Bernal for her. When the Mexicans arrange a surprise, Burton solves the tangle by allowing them to kill him. Except for the climax, the third act drags a little; but the second act, with its strong and well-contrasted scenes, is about the best thing yet done in American opera. Mr. Converse is at work on another stage piece, a Mackaye affair, and the result will be a " Fantastic Opera," entitled " Beauty and the Beast."

Victor Herbert, although originally placed among the foreigners by Mr. Hughes,[1] is another who has made an earnest effort to help found an American school of opera. Known by his many musical comedies, he has also

[1] See p. 444.

written serious music, — a symphonic poem, 'cello works, and so on. His grand opera " Natoma " is based on an Indian subject, the heroine having the title role. Natoma is an Indian maiden who serves and loves Barbara, the daughter of a Spanish gentleman. Barbara is loved by Alvarado, a young Spaniard, and by Paul Merrill, a United States naval officer. Natoma is admired by the half-breed Castro. The unwelcome Spanish and half-breed suitors are repulsed, whereupon Castro forms a plot for Alvarado to kidnap Barbara, who, in common with Natoma, loves Merrill. The second act portrays a festival, under cover of which Alvarado is to act; but Natoma, doing the " dagger dance " with Castro, rushes past him and stabs Alvarado fatally, after which she seeks sanctuary in a church. Here, in the third act, Natoma is meditating vengeance of various sorts; but the priest calms her anger, and she finally becomes one of the

VICTOR HERBERT.

nuns. The libretto is in rather weak prose, but the composer devoted serious work to it. The score contains Indian melodies, used in very rhythmic fashion. They are pushed forward rather noticeably, and the ear sometimes grows tired of them; but there is no doubt of the composer's skill in many instances. There are Spanish passages, also, such as the festival dance in the second act. Here the auditors are given examples of Bizet-like strength. There are pretty choruses, and a charming minuet. The dagger dance is made most impressive by strangely intense effects on the brasses. The third act is made into a coherent and impressive whole in the score. The orchestration is brilliant, varied, and effective, and with a good libretto the work would have shown much vitality. A shorter opera by Herbert is " Madeleine." This is a one-act lyric work, based on the French play which was anglicized into " I Dine with My Mother."

If poetic librettos, however, were the only necessity for success, then Horatio Parker's [1] " Mona " would have a strong claim to fame. The book is by Brian Hooker, and deals with the time of Roman rule in Britain. Quintus, son of the Roman Governor by a British captive, has been brought up by Britons as Gwynn, and has won some power as a bard. He wishes to wed Mona, foster-child of Eyna and Arth, and last descendant of Boadicea. Caradoc, the chief bard, is urging rebellion, aided by Gloom, Mona's foster-brother. By birthright and prophecies she is chosen as leader, and has been brought up to hate Rome. Gwynn, whose Roman origin is unknown to his associates, works for peace. He must join the conspiracy to keep Mona's good will, but even so is practically cast off. Yet he follows her as she travels to raise revolt, even saving her from the Romans many times. He

[1] See p. 174.

is blamed by his father, but tells the latter
that he will yet avert the war. If he does
this, the Governor agrees to pardon the con-
spirators. Gwynn then declares his love to
Mona, and wins hers in return. But when
he suggests peace, she distrusts him, and
calls in her Britons. They keep him
prisoner while the attack is made. The
Britons are routed, and Gloom wounded in
saving Mona against her will. Gwynn tells
Mona of his parentage, and wishes to save her;
but she disbelieves him, and kills him with
her own hand. Taken captive, she finds
with vain regrets that Gwynn told the truth.

The score of this opera is scholarly, musicianly, and masterful in its orchestration
and handling of choral work with contrapuntal skill. But it is not a melodic work.
It sometimes lacks the warmly insistent glow
of rich harmonic progressions, and is devoted
too largely to declamatory effects. Prof.
Parker is a great musician, as Mr. Hughes'

description of the masterly " Hora Novissima " shows; [1] but opera needs a certain
dramatic fluency that does not always go
with greatness. If the next generation should
prefer declamatory effects, then " Mona "
will come into its own.

Walter Damrosch, too, though formerly
classed with the foreigners, [2] has entered the
field of serious American opera. Those who
heard his ill-fated " Scarlet Letter " remember learned music not well suited to its subject. In " Cyrano," however, he has found
a text capable of more lively treatment than
the austere severity of the Puritans. This
he has handled with sure touch, and skilful
use of variety and contrast.

Louis Adolphe Coerne, whose early work
came to Mr. Hughes' notice, [3] is another who
has won success abroad. Born in 1870 at Newark, he studied in this country and Munich,
returning to become organist, musical direc-

[1] See p. 183.   [2] See p. 444.   [3] See p. 262.

tor, teacher in various colleges (now the University of Wisconsin), and an important composer. His first opera, " A Woman of Marblehead," won favorable mention in America, while his more recent and larger " Zenobia " was accorded a welcome reception in Germany. In 1912 his works had reached the respectable opus number of 70, and contained many examples of the large forms. Thus op. 5 is an orchestral Fantasie; op. 7 is a concert overture; op. 15 is a fairy ballet, " Evadne," a work of rare beauty; op. 18 is a symphonic poem on the favorite subject of " Hiawatha; " op. 30 is an orchestral Requiem; op. 36 is another overture; op. 39 is a tone-picture, " Liebesfruehling; " op. 59 is a large tone-poem entitled " George Washington; " and there are other works in cantata form that are nearly as large. In addition to these are many compositions for voice, piano, violin, organ, and other instruments. His music is decidedly modern, and replete with harmonic individuality. Those who wish to know his style will find it clearly marked even in the smaller works, such as the song " The Sea." There is here a broad melody, supported by harmonies that change and flash with kaleidoscopic beauty.

Most interesting among native operas should be the forthcoming Indian work by Charles Wakefield Cadman. This will be called " Daoma." The story is a true Ponka tale, set in shape by Francis La Flesche and put into very poetic libretto form by Nelle Richmond Eberhart. The last-named has written the poems for a number of Cadman's songs, and has put into them the utmost expressive beauty. The music of the opera will be based on forty or more Indian melodies, mostly Omaha, but some from the Iroquois and Pawnee music.

Charles Wakefield Cadman is an American product, too recent to have been treated in the earlier text. Born at Johnstown, Pa., in

CHARLES WAKEFIELD CADMAN.

1881, he showed an early aptitude for music, and began to study piano at the age of thirteen. Some years later he composed music for a Pittsburg comic opera, but he did not take up composition seriously until about twenty years old. His first compositions were published in 1904, and consisted of ballads, organ works, and teaching pieces. He, himself, states that his serious works began when he took up the Indian music. In the last few years he has made great use of the native tunes. His " Four American Indian Songs " are remarkable alike in their beauty and in their fidelity to the Indian melodies used. The latter are kept with all their repetitions and syncopations, but are harmonized by the composer into the most artistic and beautiful lyrics. Best among the four is perhaps " From the Land of the Sky-Blue Water," with its minor plaint of captivity. Infinitely sweet, too, is the third of the group, " Far Off I Heard a Lover's

From the Land of the Sky-blue Water

Omaha Tribal Melodies
collected by Alice C. Fletcher
Poem by Nelle Richmond Eberhart

Charles Wakefield Cadman
Opus 45, No.1

Flute." The question of Indian music will be discussed in connection with Arthur Farwell's· work. Cadman, too, has used the Indian melodies in piano works, but his chief employment of them has been in song, where the voice keeps the melody intact and the words heighten the aboriginal effect.

Of the other veins adopted by this composer, not the least successful has been the " Three Songs to Odysseus," dedicated to and sung by Nordica. These consist of Circe's welcome, Calypso's pleading for the hero to remain, and Nausicaa's lament at his departure. They show the composer's art at its best. There are broad sweeps of melody and declamation; bold changes; and a strange abruptness of modulation that seems odd at first, but grows into wonderful beauty upon closer acquaintance. The same is true of many of his single lyrics, such as the Persian " Groves of Shiraz," " The Sea hath a Hundred Moods," " As in a Rose

Jar," and others. Another cycle is the Japanese Romance " Sayonara," and a still more recent one is a set of South Sea Island songs. With Cadman as composer, it is safe to say that the latter will be truly exotic and original.

Less successful than the work of Cadman, but still distinctively Indian, has been the work of Arthur Nevin, a younger brother of Ethelbert. His shorter pieces are described by Mr. Hughes,[1] but his chief work has been the Indian opera " Poia," which was given abroad, and the suites " Lorna Doone " and " Love Dreams."

John K. Paine did not live long after composing his opera " Azara." His other works, as described by Mr. Hughes,[2] are mostly well known; but it is possible that he escaped the disappointment of finding his cherished opera either shelved or unsuccessful. It is based on the legendary story of " Aucassin and Nicolette," and has both Provençal

[1] See p. 342.   [2] See p. 145.

and Saracen episodes. While the music is dignified and worthy, it lacks the easy flow and the pronounced (sometimes even tawdry) flavor that constitute dramatic style and make for operatic popularity. It is no disgrace to fail in opera. Schubert, Schumann, and Mendelssohn did so, and even Beethoven seemed most at home upon the concert stage. Opera demands a special faculty, and its absence does not prevent a composer from being great in other fields.

Paul Allen has composed several operas for Italy, — a fair revenge for the invasion of America by Italian opera.

Many American composers have operas in manuscript. Of these, Arthur Bird, Alexander Hull, Harvey Worthington Loomis, Gaston Borch, J. Remington Fairlamb, and W. Franke-Harling, are perhaps the most prominent. It is a healthy sign, and one that portends an early florescence of the school.

In the field of light opera, Herbert and De

Koven naturally stand at the head. The former seems usually to put some serious work even into his comedies, such as the Angelus in " The Serenade," the Bridal Chorus in " The Red Mill," and so on. These bits are comparable with the Kreutzer or Lortzing school, and are simply but fluently melodious, even if far less impressive than the work in " Natoma." De Koven [1] has kept up a constant stream of light operas, including " Maid Marian," which showed more than passing value. He has composed many songs, and if none of them has equalled " Promise Me " in popular favor, they are still graceful and melodious. Among light operas, Charles Dennée's music to " The Defender " is also worthy of mention.[2]

Returning to orchestral music, we find many more names to be added to the roll of honor and the scroll of originality.

[1] For his earlier work, see p. 334.
[2] For his earlier work, see p. 374.

REGINALD DE KOVEN.

Franz van der Stucken is one of those who has grown to handle the full modern orchestra with the utmost ease. He has long been known by " William Ratcliff " and other works.[1] His " Pax Triumphans " is a fairly recent example of this, and peace triumphs grandly, but with almost as much noise as we are accustomed to expect for war.

Of those who continue careers already famous, George W. Chadwick, described in detail in the earlier text,[2] has perhaps been most active in the large forms. His two classical overtures, to Melpomene and Thalia, have found a companion in the more recent " Euterpe " Overture. This is a work of bright and pleasing style, not striking the deeper note of the " Melpomene " Overture, but evidently not intended to do so. A more pathetic threnody is the " Adonais " Overture, brought out in 1900, and endowed with the adjective " Elegiac." The composer's

[1] See p. 188.   [2] See p. 210.

" Noel " is a spirited and successful cantata. The Symphonic Sketches date back some sixteen years, but an interesting Symphonietta is six years younger. This work is in four movements, all effective and well contrasted. A resolute first movement is full of vigor and spirit, with an Oriental flavor in its side-theme. A Canzonetta follows, with lyrical themes and a march-like suggestion. The light and bright Scherzino is very dainty, while the animated Finale, with its well-contrasted side episodes in slow tempo, makes an effective close for the work. Another orchestral work is the Suite Symphonique. More sensuous in style is the symphonic poem " Cleopatra," brought out in 1906. A still later work in this free form, and one that has proved most attractive, is the composer's " Aphrodite." The idea of the work was suggested by a beautiful head of the goddess, found on the island of Cnidos, and now in the Boston Art Museum. The composition endeavors to portray the scenes that might have taken place before such a statue when worshipped in its temple by the sea. There are festal dances; a storm at sea; the thanks of rescued mariners to their patron goddess; religious services in the temple; and other similar suggestions of suitable nature. All these are woven into the score with a skill and musicianship that obtain beautiful effects and bear full witness to the composer's gifts.

Another composer who uses the classical forces with most admirable ease and fluency is Arthur Foote, who is duly described in the earlier text.[1] His orchestral suites show a dignity, an ease of expression, and an earnestness of material that place them among the best American compositions. He has continued in this field by orchestrating some of his piano thoughts into the Four Character Pieces, Op. 48. The original set was entitled

[1] See p. 221.

" Five Poems after Omar Khayyam." Four of these have been worked up into orchestral form. Each is given for motto a quatrain of the lyrical tent-maker. First is that one regretting Iram, but taking consolation in the ruby of the vine. Next comes the lament over Jamshyd's emptied court. The third piece illustrates the famous " Jug of wine, loaf of bread, — and Thou." Last comes again the idea

> " Better be jocund with the fruitful grape
>   Than sadden after none, or bitter, fruit."

The work is unusually interesting, and un-expectedly poetic in a composer who has hitherto avoided the free forms. Foote has also written a string suite, chamber works, and many new songs.

In the main body of this book, Mr. Hughes did not have space to treat the foreign-born composers with any detail.[1] But at pres-

[1] See p. 444.

ent a few deserve more extended mention, through having become more definitely identified with our country.

Of these, Charles Martin Loeffler is a leader. Born in Alsace in 1861, he has now for many years made Boston and its environs his home. His works, especially the larger orchestral compositions, show a grasp of tone-color, an ability to handle the large orchestra, and an originality of harmonic effects that unite to make this composer one of the foremost of the modernists. There is a rapidity of chordal change in his works that makes them very hard for the simplicity-loving old-timers to follow. But the compositions are built on broad lines, and the mosaic effects of theme and harmony are blended always into an impressive whole. Modernism has certainly come to stay, and Mr. Loeffler is one of its best exponents. His style is his own, — sonorous, rich, and in no way a slavish imitation of anything made in France. Of his works, four at least deserve especial mention. " The Death of Tintagiles " is based on Maeterlinck's play of that name, and is a wellwrought and dramatic representation of the vague fears and unseen tragedy of the play. " La Villanelle du Diable," based on a Verlaine poem with the wild refrain " Le Diable rôde et circule," is an effective picture of infernal revelry. In the strongest contrast is " La Bonne Chanson," illustrating another Verlaine poem, this time a tender love-passage; the music is of ideal and ineffable beauty, carrying its message to radical and conservative alike. Last of the four works is " A Pagan Poem," a pleasing affair based on the eighth Eclogue of Virgil, which depicts a girl trying to charm her lover home from the city. The mysterious rites and the final triumph form a most admirable contrast in the score.

Gustav Strube, whose chief work has been done in the present century, was born at

GUSTAV STRUBE.

Ballenstedt, in Anhalt, in 1867. After studying at Leipsic, and teaching at Mannheim,
Mr. Strube came to Boston, where for over
twenty years he was a violinist with the
Symphony Orchestra. He became well known
also as a conductor. His chief works consist
of an overture, " The Maid of Orleans," two
symphonies, a " Hymn to Eros," an Orchestral Rhapsody, the overture " Puck," two
violin concertos, a 'cello concerto, several
chamber works, and the symphonic poems
" Longing," " Fantastic Dance," " Echo and
Narcissus," and " Die Lorelei." The last
two are poetic enough, but the second symphony, in B minor, is a more important work.
It shows the composer as a forceful, virile
personality. There is enough of modernism
in the work; it has its bits of augmented
triad effects and whole-tone scales; but it
does not run these to death at the expense
of other interesting styles. The composer's
work is radical without being extreme, mod-

ern without growing decadent, and at the same time beautiful enough to appeal to the conservative faction as well. Rhythm, variety, skill in figure treatment and development, all play their part, and Strube's compositions do not depend upon exotic flavor alone for their popularity.

Another gifted composer in the Boston Symphony Orchestra is its admirable first flutist, André Maquarre. He, too, has entered the operatic field; but Boston has experienced only his orchestral prowess, in the shape of the overture " On the Sea Cliff."

Still another composer in the same organization is Otto Urack, the new 'cellist and conductor. A symphony of his, given recently, proved shapely in design and attractive in material. His orchestra is large, but his material noticeably conservative. More than one of his audience has spoken of him as a modern Mendelssohn.

The New York Philharmonic Orchestra

numbers among its violinists the composer
Fritz Stahlberg. In 1909 he brought out a
symphonic poem in memory of Abraham
Lincoln, and three years later came his two
symphonic sketches, " In the Highlands."
Still more recent is his Symphonic Scherzo.
The main body of this work is a rather in-
volved echo of modern Germanism, with
slight traces of Debussy added. The trio
is more melodic, and most suitably orchestral
in style, and the work as a whole shows
real musicianship and sufficient imaginative
power.

One of the foremost of the native Americans
treated by Mr. Hughes is Edgar Stillman
Kelley,[1] who has continued his activity in
many fields. For some years he has been
abroad, living and working in Berlin at the
advice of Xaver Scharwenka. Recently he
came back to his native land, to hold a col-
legiate fellowship for composition at Oxford,

[1] See p. 57.

Ohio, and to take charge of the composition in the famous Cincinnati College of Music.

Among Kelley's Berlin successes were a piano quintet in F-sharp minor, op. 20, and a string quartet, op. 25. The former, brought out in 1906, made a strong impression. The opening Allegro Risoluto is marked by an effective chief theme and a well-contrasted lyrical side theme. Piano and strings alternate and modulate in a most interesting manner. The movement is a trifle long, but the Lento Sostenuto e Misterioso that follows it becomes very impressive with its bell-like effects and broad melodic sweep. A dainty Allegretto Scherzando and a rhythmic Finale bring the work to a strong close. The quartet makes the interesting experiment of developing all four movements from a single theme. At first it becomes a theme with variations; the second movement brings the theme as Toccatina and Fugue; an Adagio-Intermezzo then leads into the

Finale, which suggests the sonata form and brings three new variations in its course. Both of these works show Mr. Kelley at his best. He writes clearly and logically, and at the same time has valuable musical ideas and real inspiration. To quote Arthur Farwell, Kelley has " been a leader in the movement to gain mastery over the unbridled and rampant forces of modern harmony, and is one of the first composers to have attained a lucid and well-ordered harmonic character in the midst of the post-Wagnerian harmonic chaos. His work is poetic, original, and beautiful in a high degree, exquisite in its formal proportions, and colored with rare art in its rich harmonies."

Among Kelley's larger works are " Two Moods of Nature," for mixed chorus; music for the play " The Jury of Fate; " a Suite of " Macbeth " music; and still more ambitious, his recent New England Symphony, which was successful in Germany. The Macbeth

Suite has been remodeled into something very striking. The symphony, in the unusual key of B-flat minor, aims to reflect the mental and spiritual life of New England. The first movement, Lento, Allegro Appasionata, bears the motto " All great and honorable actions are accompanied with great difficulties; and must be both enterprised and overcome with answerable courages." The music shows a contrast between two strong themes representing duty and love of life; and these themes are effectively developed. The second movement, Andante Pastorale, is almost a scherzo, its motto being " Warm and fair the weather, the birds sang in the woods most pleasantly." The music is evolved largely from actual New England bird calls. The third movement, with the words " Great lamentations and heaviness," is based partly on Timothy Swan's old hymn tune " Why do we mourn departed friends," and becomes a species of dirge. The final motto is " The fit way to honor and lament the departed is to be true to one another and to work together bravely for the cause to which living and dead have consecrated themselves." The music here is strongly rhythmic and full of conflict, though ending devotionally. The words are in every case quotations from the Log of the Mayflower. Still another orchestral work by this composer is the set of pictures entitled " Christmas Eve with Alice." Here we are taken to Wonderland again, and meet with such familiar subjects as the white rabbit, the caucus race, the Cheshire cat, the magic draught, and the forest of forgetfulness. In the smaller forms, too, the composer is still active. His settings of Poe's ballads " Eldorado " and " Israfel " literally glow with harmonic color.

Ernest Schelling has attained twentieth-century fame as a pianist and a pupil of Paderewski. Schelling was born at Philadelphia in 1876. At an early age he entered the Paris Conservatoire as a pupil of Mathias, and was playing in concerts when only eight years old. At sixteen he was forced by neuritis to give up music, and for four years after that he earned a very precarious living in America. When Paderewski came to Philadelphia, Schelling broke into the green-room — literally broke in, as he had to pass an obdurate guard — and recalled himself to the great Pole. Paderewski then insisted on having the young man come to his Swiss home for aid, comfort, and renewed musical work. In Switzerland, too, he had to fight for admission, for the servants had had no word of his coming, and set the dogs on him when he appeared. But all's well that ends well, and Schelling soon became a performer of international repute.

Among Schelling's works, perhaps the most interesting to Americans is the Suite Fantastique for piano and orchestra. This

ERNEST SCHELLING.

is because that composition contains some well-known American songs as themes, although one must add that the artistic and well-balanced nature of the work is of course its most valuable quality. The songs used are " Dixie " and " The Suwanee River." These are worked into the score in the most delightful fashion, and are sometimes made laughably comic by contrasts between piccolo and bassoon or other orchestral incongruities.

Schelling's other works include a Legende Symphonique that is really a symphony in two contrasted movements. There is a real symphony as well, and he has written also a Ballet Divertissement. His smaller works include an effective violin sonata, a number of songs, and the piano works that one would expect from such a great performer. Chief among the last is a powerful theme and variations, in which the impressive theme is treated with marked variety and truly remarkable strength.

Ernest Richard Kroeger, whose early successes are already chronicled,[1] has followed his orchestral overtures by the suite " Lalla Rookh," which has been given in many places. Still more closely allied to poetry is his setting of Hewlett's " Masque of Dead Florentines," with voices. In this work the great ones of that famous city are announced by a Herald, commented on by the chorus, and allowed to speak for themselves in turn, while the music gives a faithful and striking picture of their lives and characters. The names include Dante and Beatrice, Petrarch and Laura, Boccaccio, Fiammetta, Leonardo da Vinci, the beautiful Simonetta, the wily Machiavelli, the clever Benvenuto Cellini, the gifted Michael Angelo, and others. The music depicts them all with due fidelity and excellent artistic contrast. Mr. Kroeger is still very active in the smaller forms also, the list of his songs and piano works being

[1] See p. 420.

ERNEST RICHARD KROEGER.

impressive for its length as well as its value. He considers as of most interest his " Ten American Character Sketches," " American Tone Pictures," " Twenty Moods," and a theme and variations for piano, while among his recent songs " The Flight of the Arrow," " Memory," and " Annabel Lee " deserve especial mention.

Arthur Whiting, in addition to the Fantasie and other works already described,[1] has produced an overture. His many smaller works now include the attractive and widely known song-cycle " Floriana."

Nathaniel Clifford Page [2] has continued his incidental music with that written for " The Japanese Nightingale," in 1903.

Henry Schoenefeld,[3] of Rural Symphony fame, has increased his compositions by a piano concerto, a violin concerto, and other pieces.

Henry Holden Huss [4] goes on in his or-

[1] See p. 283.   [2] See p. 139.   [3] See p. 128.   [4] See p. 291.

chestral career with " The Recessional," for mixed chorus, orchestra, and organ. A string quartet and a violin sonata have found a cordial welcome also. Of his new songs, " Before Sunrise " has an effective rippling accompaniment, " Ich Liebe Dich " shows the intensity of the German Lied in its repeated chords, the " Wiegenlied " is attractively soothing, and " It was a Lover and His Lass " is made pleasingly melodious. Most interesting of his recent piano pieces is the Poem " La Nuit," full of nocturnal beauty and mystery. Of the six pieces in op. 23, the Etude Romantique brings expression to the study of triplets, two Intermezzi echo the Brahms style, and a Polonaise Brillante has its steady rhythm ornamented by brilliant runs. Other piano works by Huss are the Valse, Nocturne, and Gavotte, op. 20, and the Minuet and Gavotte, op. 18.

Harry Rowe Shelley,[1] whose first sym-

[1] See p. 304.

phony Mr. Hughes calls virile, has produced a second work in symphonic form, which wins favorable mention.

Rubin Goldmark,[1] nephew of his great foreign namesake, began, as already described, by gaining a name in chamber music. His later chamber works have won prizes, one of which was given by the Federation of Music Clubs. He has kept active in the smaller forms, while a work of larger dimensions is his symphonic poem " Samson and Dalilah." One must have ability to treat such a subject, for Saint-Saens has given us glorious music in his opera of the same title. Goldmark's music stands the comparison well. It is of course dramatic and orchestral in style rather than lyric. It is marked by well-chosen contrasts of material and masterly orchestration.

[1] See p. 278.

CHAPTER II.

In the last few years, Henry F. Gilbert has become a prominent figure among those who believe in working up the native music. This is reflected in his best-known orchestral work, the Comedy Overture based on negro themes. He had planned an opera, in which the libretto, taken from the Uncle Remus stories, was to be set to music founded on negro themes. The opera was abandoned, but Gilbert utilized the themes in the overture, which was partly rewritten. The overture is based on three four-measure phrases and one passage of eight bars. The first two short bits are taken from Charles L. Edwards' book " Bahama Songs and Stories; " the

496

eight-bar phrase is the old Mississippi song " I'se gwine to Alabammy, oh; " while the first four bars of the negro " spiritual " known as " Old Ship of Zion " form the subject of a fugue, which is used in contrast to the lighter comedy element that precedes and follows it. The overture as a whole is bright and interesting. The chief criticism against it lies in the fact that it does not emphasize the negro flavor, for example, in the same way that Dvořák's New World Symphony does. The single first movement of the latter, though in strict sonata form, gives much longer themes than four-bar phrases, and somewhat more characteristic ones. The Gilbert work is interesting *per se*, but it does not proclaim its negro character from the housetops.

Gilbert's other published works are, in large part, a Legend and a Negro Episode for orchestra, five Indian Scenes for piano, " The Island of the Fay," after Poe, also for piano, and a number of songs. Among the latter is " The Pirate's Song," a strongly rhythmic minor strain to Stevenson's " Fifteen Men on the Dead Man's Chest." " The Lament of Deirdré " is another effective work, with exotic flavor. " Orlamonde " has the true shadowy effect of Maeterlinck, while " Zephyrus " and the " Faery Song " show a marked lightness of touch. Of the Celtic Studies, two Songs to the Wind are highly poetic, " My Heart is Heavy " sounds a mournful note, while the Skald's Song is a humorous account of Irish-Danish battles. " Salammbo's Invocation to Tanith " is another powerfully dramatic affair, published for piano but set also for orchestra. Two South American Gypsy songs include " La Zambulidora," a lyric of youth and love, and " La Montanera," in praise of the free life of a mountain maid. The " Fish-Wharf Rhapsody " is an unusual affair, strong in its praise of freedom from conventionality. In

manuscript Mr. Gilbert has three more or-
chestral works, — an Americanesque (on
" Old Zip Coon," " Dearest Mae," and " Rosa
Lee "), a set of three American Dances in
Ragtime, and a fantastic symphonic poem
" The Dance in Place Congo," based on
Cable's story of that title.

Arthur Mansfield Curry was born at
Chelsea, Mass., in 1866. He studied violin
with Kneisel and composition with Mac-
Dowell. He has been active as chorus-
master and conductor, as well as teacher of
violin and composition. His symphonic
poem " Atala " was given at Boston in 1911.
It is based on Chateaubriand's work of that
name, and deals with the life of Atala,
daughter of an Indian chief. She loves
Chactas, a Spanish-bred Indian captive, and
flees with him. But Atala has once taken a
vow of celibacy, so that she hesitates to give
way to her love. The pair wander through
various forest adventures, finally reaching

a priest's home. Here Atala takes poison, just as the priest is about to tell her that the church would not be so harsh as to make her keep her vow. The score opens with a solemn introduction, followed by themes typical of the freedom of Chactas and the love of Atala. A later theme typifies her vow. There is an orchestral storm in the forest, clearing to a pastoral scene in which the priest's bell and his organ tones are heard. The work ends with the theme of Chactas alone. Mr. Curry originally intended to write an opera on this subject, but began to doubt the stage value of the story. His other works include an overture, " Blomidon," a manuscript Elegie in overture form, a Celtic legend, " The Winning of Amarac," for a reader, a woman's chorus, and orchestra, shorter works for chorus and solo voices, and some piano pieces.

William Edwin Haesche was born at New Haven in 1867. He studied violin with

Listemann, piano with Perabo, and composition with Parker. He has been for some time one of the musical staff at Yale College, and conductor of the New Haven Choral Union. His compositions have been largely orchestral. His " Forest Idyl," almost the only one of these that is published, is a grateful work, full of expressive beauty. Horns are used frequently to give the sylvan suggestion, while dainty rippling triplets portray the rustling of the forest. The themes are worked up to good climaxes, and used with strings and woodwind in skilful antiphonal fashion. Haesche's other orchestral works include a tone poem " The South," a symphonic poem " Fridjof's Saga," an overture " The Springtime," a symphony in A-flat, a symphonietta, and the orchestral cantatas " The Haunted Oak of Nannau " and " The Village Blacksmith." His smaller works consist of songs, piano pieces, and violin works. The latter are the most numerous, including a spirited " Souvenir de Wieniaw-ski " in mazurka form, a rhythmic Country Dance, a Characteristic Suite consisting of five numbers entitled Española, Polonaise, Air, Bagdad, and Czardas, a brilliant Hungarian Dance with 2-4 czardas effect, and a suite entitled " Eyes of Night." His Legende for violin, 'cello, and piano shows excellent interweaving of the instruments. " Young Lovel's Bride " is an effective work with chorus. Among the solo songs are a joyous " Love Song " and the rhythmic " Swing High and Swing Low."

Arne Oldberg was born at Youngstown, O., in 1874. He studied piano with Hyllested in Chicago, and with Leschetizky, starting to train himself in composition while with the latter at Vienna. Study in Chicago and Munich prepared him further for creative work, and he now spends much time composing when not teaching at the Northwestern University. He is very strict with himself, and holds that his representative work begins only with op. 15. Before that he wrote piano pieces, three string quartets, a piano trio, a concerto for 'cello and orchestra, a piano concerto, an overture, two symphonies, and a string suite. The list of his later works of larger dimensions is as follows: —

Op. 15, string quartet in C minor.

Op. 16, piano quintet in B minor.

Op. 17, piano concerto.

Op. 18, woodwind quintet (with piano).

Op. 19, horn concerto in E-flat.

Op. 20, orchestral variations.

Op. 21, overture " Paolo and Francesca."

Op. 22, four songs for contralto and orchestra.

Op. 23, symphony in F minor.

Op. 24, quintet in C-sharp minor.

Op. 29, Festival Overture.

Op. 32, organ concerto.

Op. 33, symphony in C minor.

Many of these have been heard frequently

in our larger cities, especially opp. 15, 16, 17, 21, 24, and 29. The composer's piano works include an interesting sonata, some strong variations, a Legend, an Arabesque, an Intermezzo, and a set of Miniatures.

Still younger than Oldberg is Arthur Shepherd, who was born at Paris, Idaho, in 1880. At twelve he came to the New England Conservatory, studying various branches, which included composition with Goetschius and Chadwick. He joined the faculty of that institution in 1909, after having taught for some years in Salt Lake City. He won the Paderewski prize in 1902 with his Overture Joyeuse, and in 1909 he was awarded two prizes by the National Federation of Music Clubs, one for his piano sonata, and one for his song " The Lost Child." He has continued in the larger forms with a Humoreske for piano and orchestra, an overture " The Nuptials of Attila," and the large orchestral cantata " The City in the Sea."

His piano sonata, in F minor, is hailed as a really remarkable work. The first movement, Allegro con Fuoco, has a slow introduction, a strong chief theme using the introduction idea, and a side theme of the expected tranquillity, with a powerful development. The ensuing Andante Sostenuto, in triple time, is like a dirge, with occasional bursts of lyric feeling. The third movement, Allegro Commodo, has a lively second theme (Giocoso), which is altogether spontaneous and effective. The work is very modulatory in character, and somewhat free in form, wherein it reflects the modern spirit. But radicalism is here only a means to an end, the end attained being the creation of virile, forceful music. Shepherd's other piano compositions include a Theme and Variations, a Mazurka, and a Prelude. For voice he has composed a motet with mixed chorus and baritone solo, "The Lord hath brought again Zion." His songs include " A Star in the Night," an ecstatic " Rhapsody," a smooth " Nocturne," the beautiful and brilliant " Adieu," the passionate and Debussy-like " Youth's Spring Tribute," the broad prayer entitled " Sun-Down," and several others. His " Marsyas " is a recent symphonic poem.

Philip Greeley Clapp, who was born at Boston in 1888, is one of those musical youngsters who strive to outdo their predecessors. His symphony in E minor, given during the season of 1913–14 at Boston, is a result of this tendency. It is a large work, with four long movements and many changes of tempo. It is scored for full modern orchestra, and abounds in effects that are original, if not highly significant. The modernists to-day, able to use new orchestral combinations and an enlarged and enfranchised system of harmony, can create music of some interest almost as a matter of routine. We listen to their tone-colors and new chords, and find that these are the chief characteristics of much modern music. But there is still a need for inspiration, and orchestral technique does not always imply inspiration. That is why so many of the works of Holbrooke, Scriabine, Delius, Schoenberg, and others of the sort, are heard once and laid aside. They are merely exercises in modernism, without the inspiration that should go into any real art work. Mr. Clapp's symphony is based too much on this experimental style; and it caused some of the musicians to say that they had not met with so much meaningless difficulty in thirty years. One performer may not see the purport of a work as a whole, but the symphony was no more successful with the audience. As modern works go, Mr. Clapp's is as good as many another, but the school itself has its defects. The composer numbers among his other productions the tone-poem " Norge," a Dramatic Poem for trombone and orchestra, the orchestral prelude " In Summer," a string quartet, and the chorus "O Glad-some Light."

Percy Lee Atherton was born at Rox-bury, Mass., in 1871. He studied music at Harvard, with Rheinberger and Thuille at Munich, and with O. B. Boise. Atherton's orchestral works, mostly in manuscript, are a Symphonic Andante, a Symphonic Scherzo, an Intermezzo, a beautiful tone-poem "Noon in the Forest," and a Scherzino for strings. He has entered the comic opera field with "The Maharajah" and "The Heir-Ap-parent." His other works include two violin sonatas, a suite for violin (all with piano), a Romanza and Rondo for the same two instruments, several piano pieces, and about fifty songs.

Arthur Farwell, mentioned only briefly in the earlier text,[1] is now a prominent figure. He was born at St. Paul in 1872, and studied composition with Humperdinck, Pfitzner,

[1] See p. 348.

and Guilmant. The time that he has left, after fulfilling his duties as supervisor of municipal and school music in New York and elsewhere, is devoted to the cause of native music. By native we may here understand Indian. Even his " Cornell " Overture, which would naturally be based in part on college songs, contains some Indian melodies. The " Love Song," from an unfinished suite, is more general in its style. So, too, are the Symbolistic Studies, and some of his songs, such as the spirited " Drake's Drum," the attractive "Love's Secret," the solemn " Requiescat," or the broad " Hymn to Liberty " for quartet. For the rest, Indian subjects and melodies prevail. " Dawn," " The Domain of Hurahan," and the " Navajo War Dance " are orchestral pictures. Such songs as the cowboy's " Lone Prairie," the two Negro Spirituals, and the two Spanish-Californian folk-songs, are also rather local in color. For piano, however, Farwell has produced one Indian work after another. These include " American Indian Melodies," " Owasco Memories," " Dawn," " Ichibuzzhi," " Pawnee Horses," " Impressions of the Wa-Wan Ceremony," and piano versions of the orchestral numbers.

Indian music is impressive enough in its way. Natalie Curtis says that when the Indians chant together, in the depths of the forest or on the boundless spaces of prairie, their music becomes infinitely effective, even though it is only a unison melody that they sing. But few of us have heard this music under these conditions. The average Eastern musician has to take his Indian melodies from a book, where they may seem rhythmic and effective enough, but are not truly folk-music. In other words, the average man will not recognize Indian music when he hears it; while he will recognize the negro style of music. The latter, therefore, is the true American folk-music, as Dvořák

showed in his " New World " Symphony.
The lack of harmony in the Indian music is

ICHIBUZZHI.[1]

ARTHUR FARWELL OP.13.

another point that tends to prevent its becoming national. Melody is fairly easy to

handle, but harmony is often the individual language of a composer. In the case of Cadman, we find his work great because of the harmonic beauty he puts into it; and his " Songs to Odysseus," with original themes, hold one's attention fully as much as his settings of Indian melodies. In founding a native school, then, Farwell's work is bound to fail; it must be judged as music, without reference to its source. On this basis Farwell has done very interesting work; but we do not recognize its Indian qualities unless we are told about them. The same is true even of MacDowell's Indian Suite, which is recognizable as Indian chiefly in the concert program books.

Otis Bardwell Boise, who has taught so many of our young students, was born at Oberlin, O., in 1845, and died in 1912. Studying at Leipsic and Berlin, he became a teacher at New York, then in Berlin, and finally at the Peabody Conservatory in Baltimore. Known chiefly by his teaching, he has also composed a number of dignified orchestral works, including a symphony, two overtures, and a piano concerto.

At the other end of the country is Henry Bickford Pasmore,[1] who was born at Jackson, Wis., in 1857, but is now identified with San Francisco. He, too, studied in Leipsic. He has been organist and teacher, and has composed a march, an overture, masses, and smaller works. His songs are often highly effective, " My Love Dwelt in a Northern Land " being a striking bit of monochromatic work.

David Stanley Smith was born at Toledo in 1877. He studied at Yale with Parker, composing a Commencement Ode for chorus and orchestra. After a year and a half with Widor, he returned to America to become assistant professor of music at Yale. His compositions consist in part of a symphony,

[1] Mentioned on p. 272.

given and highly praised by Stock in Chicago;
" The Fallen Star," for chorus and orchestra,
which gained the Paderewski prize in 1909;
incidental music for the play " Robin Hood,"
given at Yale; a Fugue for orchestra and
organ; an Overture Joyeuse; an Allegro
Giocoso for orchestra; two contrasted pieces,
" L'Allegro " and " Il Penseroso; " a Symphonic Ballad; " The Djinns," for chorus
and orchestra; and " Prince Hal," a symphonic sketch. His piano trio has been given
by the Adamowskis, and his string quartet
is a valued number in the Kneisel repertoire.
His Christmas Cantata " The Logos " is a
work of much charm, and " The Wind-Swept
Wheat," another choral work, shows marked
beauty. His songs include an exquisite
" Cradle Song," the quaint garden picture
" Gold and Purple," a beautiful setting of
Phoebe Cary's " The Rose," a fiery " Rom-
any Love Song," the smooth lyric " When
Stars are in the Quiet Skies," the joyous

" Song of the Four Seasons," and others of equal value.

Rossetter Gleason Cole was born near Clyde, Mich., in 1866. His studies at Ann Arbor enabled him to compose the cantata " The Passing of Summer." After further work in Berlin, where he won a composition scholarship in the Royal Academy, he became professor of music at Ripon and Iowa Colleges, and later at the University of Wisconsin. He has devoted himself to composition since then, working in various forms. He has composed a strong Ballade for 'cello and orchestra, and the orchestral melodrama " King Robert of Sicily." Cole deserves praise for working in the latter form, which has not yet received the attention it deserves. The " Manfred " of Schumann and the " Enoch Arden " of Strauss are certainly effective enough to be held as good models, yet few composers enter this field; except, perhaps, in Bohemia, where Fibich's " Hip-

podamia " blazed the path. Cole produced
an earlier melodrama with piano, " Hiawatha's Wooing," but greater success was in
store for " King Robert," which has been
given widely in various arrangements. Cole's
piano works include two early Novelettes,
one with striking rhythm and the second
worked up in broad chord passages. Of
charming melodic effect are the five sketches
" From a Lover's Notebook," published in
Germany. " In Springtime " is a more recent
work. For violin and piano Cole has written
an admirable sonata and a number of less
ambitious pieces. For organ he published
an Allegro Quasi Marcia, an Andante Religioso, and other numbers. Most successful
among his songs have been " Auf Wieder-
sehen," " Dearie " (or " Absence "), and
" My True Love Hath My Heart," though
the composer does not rate them as his most
artistic productions. The latter might include " A Kiss and a Tear," " May Song,"

" If Thou Wert Nigh," and the rich " Halcyon Song." Cole's work at its best shows a depth of feeling and a tenderness that is of caressing appeal.

Edwin Grasse, famous as a violinist and violin teacher, was born at New York in 1884. The great misfortune of blindness did not prevent his studying at Brussels and becoming a prominent musical figure on his return. He has composed a symphony, a suite, a violin concerto, two piano trios, and several pieces for piano and violin.

Another violinist-composer is Eugene Gruenberg, of Boston, who has composed a symphony, a suite, and many smaller works.

Arthur Hartmann, the famous concert violinist, considers himself an American, for he came to this country from Hungary at the mature age of two months. A pupil of Loeffler, he is naturally devoted to modernism, and his effects are always original. He is best known as a composer by his male and mixed choruses with orchestra. Some of his songs are striking enough, as, for instance, the declamatory "Ballade;" but "A Child's Grace," though it might suit a Willy Ferrero who conducts at the age of seven, is rather too modulatory for the average child.

Among the pianist composers, Sigismund Stojowski takes high rank. Now a teacher in New York, he was born in Poland, and studied at Cracow and Paris. He numbers among his compositions a symphony, a suite, a piano concerto, violin sonatas, and many piano pieces.

Mme. Helen Hopekirk, a leader among the women pianists, has been active in composition also. Her concerto and Concertstück for piano and orchestra are works of which any American might be proud. In the smaller forms she has written a violin sonata, some dainty songs, and "Iona Memories" for piano, the two latter items testifying to her remembrance of her Scottish birth.

Mrs. Beach [1] has continued her work in the large forms with a piano concerto, which she has often played herself. " The Sea Fairies " and " The Chambered Nautilus " are cantatas for women's voices, showing an admirable balance between strength and tonal beauty. The accompaniment is for either piano or orchestra. Her op. 67 is an effective piano quintet. For piano she has composed the Variations on a Balkan Theme, which becomes a striking recital number in her hands; a somewhat lighter Suite Française; a Scottish Legend and Gavotte Fantastique; and Four Eskimo Pieces. The last are based on real Eskimo folk-songs, and are primitively strong and rhythmic. Their titles are " Arctic Night," " The Returning Hunter," " Exiles," and " With the Dog Teams." Mrs. Beach's " Three Browning Songs " and " Two Mother Songs " have been well known for some time. More re-

[1] See p. 426.

cent are the three songs of op. 71, consisting of a harp-like " Prelude " depicting sunrise, the somewhat declamatory " O Sweet
Content," and the pastoral lyric " An Old
Love Story."

Margaret Ruthven Lang [1] has continued
her work chiefly as a song writer, though she
keeps three orchestral overtures to her credit,
and may have more in manuscript. She has
produced some admirable children's songs,
her op. 39 consisting of ten of these, and
there is " Grandma's Song Book," in addition. Perhaps her settings of Edward
Lear's limericks may please the children,
but they appeal also to children of a larger
growth. Of her serious songs, " Summer
Noon " is a quiet but effective picture, one of
a set of six that includes " The Hills o' Skye,"
" Tryste Noel," and the strong " North-
ward." Of the four in op. 38, the effective
" Orpheus " and the unusual " Song in the

[1] See p. 432.

MARGARET RUTHVEN LANG.

Songless " seem the most striking. " Love is Everywhere," no. 4 in op. 40, carries one along in its grateful enthusiasm, while " A Song of the Gypsies," in op. 50, is another interesting and original bit.

Among the organist-composers, Albert Augustus Stanley was born at Manville, R. I., in 1851. After study with Reinecke and Richter, he returned to Providence, and later on to the University of Michigan as professor. He has composed a symphony entitled " The Soul's Awakening," the symphonic poem " Attis," an Ode for the Providence Centennial, and many smaller works for organ and for voice.

John Spencer Camp was born at Middletown, Conn., in 1858. Studying in America when Dvořák was here, he became a conductor and organist at Hartford, composing orchestral works, cantatas, a string quartet, piano and organ pieces, and both sacred and secular songs.

John A. Broekhoven, born at Beek, Holland, in 1852, has been for many years a teacher of counterpoint at the Cincinnati College of Music. He numbers among his works a Suite Creole for orchestra, a " Columbia " Overture, and smaller pieces.

An influential conductor-composer in Kansas City is Carl Busch, who was born in Denmark in 1862. He has composed a symphony, a symphonic rhapsody, heroic cantatas, violin music, and songs.

Arthur Claassen, renowned in Brooklyn as teacher and conductor, was born in Prussia in 1859. He has composed orchestral works, choruses, and chamber music.

John Powell, of Richmond, has composed a violin concerto that came in for very high praise from Zimbalist when that artist performed the work.

Mortimer Wilson, born in Iowa, is another new name in American orchestral annals. His three-movement " Country Wedding "

Suite, consisting of a Pastoral Dance, Romanza, and festival Finale, was given a favorable hearing at Leipsic. His Symphony in A is a still more recent work. His compositions include another symphony, several other orchestral works, and much chamber music.

Nathaniel Irving Hyatt, born at Lansingburgh, N. Y., in 1865, teaches in Troy, and has composed the " Enoch Arden " Overture, chamber works, and smaller pieces.

Samuel Bollinger, of St. Louis, has many orchestral works hidden away in manuscript. If these fulfil the promise of his Scherzo for piano, they will be well worth while.

Another faithful producer of manuscripts that should bear fruit is Fannie Dillon, known by her Six Preludes for piano.

Among the younger women, Mabel Daniels is rapidly approaching leadership. Of her works, a Ballade for baritone and orchestra was recently included in a MacDowell festival program, along with works of that composer and of the great Européans. Her songs with piano, too, are held highly interesting, and at least one of them has won a prize.

John Nelson Pattison, born at Niagara in 1845, studied with Liszt and others to become a pianist. But he did not neglect composition, writing a " Niagara " symphony and many agreeable piano pieces.

Alexander Hull, born at Columbus, O., in 1887, is one of the best of the modernists. Studying in part with Dr. Hugh A. Clarke, of Philadelphia, Hull is entirely an American product. He has taught much privately, and in the Pacific College also. Most of his works are songs, but " Java " is for full orchestra and piano, and a symphony in D minor is in manuscript. Recently he has worked at an orchestral suite (having written an earlier one for strings and harp), and he has under way the operas " Paolo and Francesca " and " Merlin and Vivien." For piano he has written a sonata, a Book of Sketches, and other pieces. Of the songs, a set of ten constituting op. 16 seem representative. " Within the Convent Close " has a rapid chord accompaniment, glowing with all the strange radiance that a Debussy could obtain. " Blue, Blue Flow'ret " unites the quiet style of folk-music with the most speaking harmonic individuality. " The Argosy " has imaginative words well fitted by its odd 7-4 rhythm, and is another gem of originality. " The Rock " is a weird nature-picture. The " Wanderer's Night Song " (the first of Goethe's, and not that second one which an unwary translator entitled " Another ") is broad and compelling in its style. " Laziness " is another effective number, and it may be hoped that no family troubles resulted from the composer's dedicating it to his sister.

Edward Faber Schneider was born at Omaha in 1872. After studying with Schar-

wenka in New York and Boise in Berlin, he
settled in San Francisco. His symphony
" The Autumn Time " received a San Francisco hearing, and he wrote the music (soli,
chorus, and orchestra) for " The Triumph
of Bohemia," given at one of the " High
Jinks " festival performances of the San
Francisco Bohemian Club. His Romantic
Fantasy and Midwinter Idyl are for piano
and violin, while his other works are chiefly
songs.

Edward Burlingame Hill, son of the Chemistry Professor H. B. Hill of Harvard College,
was born at Cambridge in 1872. He studied
music at Harvard, and with the excellent
teacher and composer Fred Field Bullard.
Hill is now on the musical staff at Harvard.
He has composed two pantomimes to plots
made by Joseph Lindon Smith, and both of
these show much delicacy and originality of
thought. The first is " Jack Frost in Midsummer," the second not yet given. His

three piano sonatas (or at least one of them) helped him to win Highest Honors from the music department at Harvard. Later piano works include the six Country Idyls, gently pastoral for the most part; the strongly effective number " At the Grave of a Hero; " and Four Sketches after Stephen Crane. The last group includes the mocking, carousing " Debils," a broad love-memory, a comical skit on the jingle of three birds talking of a man who thinks he can sing, and the sombre " March of the Mountains." The Three Poetical Sketches, op. 8, are " Moonlight," " A Midsummer Lullaby," and the broad picture " From a Mountain Top." Of Hill's songs, " In Kensington Gardens " has won a name; " Peace at Noon " and " Spring Twilight " are well-contrasted moods; " The Surges Gushed " is a rhythmic marine effect; and " The Full Sea Rolls and Thunders " is a strongly virile affair.

Noble Kreider, born in Goshen, Indiana,

is another of those whose orchestral works
have remained for some time in manuscript.
But he has no reason to complain of the reception accorded to his piano pieces. His
Ballad, op. 2, is a strong and original work,
and a reviewer has said of it, " Its ten pages
of octaves crowding on octaves and chords
sketch an immense story of elemental or
semi-barbarous character, portentous and
powerful." A melodious Nocturne, op. 4,
brings suggestions of Chopin, though the
harmonies used against the expressive melody
are often more modern and dissonant than
those of the great Pole. An Impromptu is
marked by rich harmony, flowing melody,
and interesting phrase-construction. Of the
two Studies, op. 6, the first, with its three-
voiced pattern, is more interesting than the
second, in sixths. The Six Preludes, op. 7,
again suggest Chopin, though decided in their
originality. They are marked in turn by a
delightful lightness, a broad melody in low

positions, an unpretentious but keen harmonic originality, brilliant left-hand work, vague but potent charm of melody, and a final close on an unresolved dissonance in no. 6. As this dissonance follows a cadence, Rupert Hughes calls it rather a " dissolved consonance." The three Moods in op. 9 show an echo of the surging waves, a lotus-eating picture of " The Valley of White Pippins," and a tempestuous storm.

Henry Clough-Leighter has devoted himself to cantatas and songs. He has written also some piano studies and novelettes, in addition to the ballad " Lasca " for voice, piano, and full orchestra. Born at Washington in 1874, he soon showed himself musically gifted under his mother's tuition, and from his fifteenth year has been a professional organist. Of his cantatas, " Christ Triumphant " is a work of rare nobility and loftiness. He has set three other sacred subjects in this form, as well as a " Harvest Cantata "

and " Across the Fields to Anne." These
are published with organ or piano parts, but
the composer has given them orchestral accompaniment as well. He has written about
a hundred choral works, too, more or less
polyphonic in structure, and including settings of the Canticles and Services of the
Anglican Church. " The Day of Beauty "
is a lyric suite for voice, piano, and string
quartet, giving sympathetic pictures of " Radiant Morn," " Silent Noon," and " Starry
Night." " Love-Sorrow " is a cycle for voice,
piano, violin, and 'cello. Cycles for voice
and piano include " A Love Garden," " An
April Heart," " Youth and Spring," and
" Love-Life." His separate songs number
well over a hundred. Most popular among
them is assuredly the richly beautiful lyric
" I Drink the Fragrance of the Rose."

Of American orchestral work in general,
one may speak in high terms. It has difficulties in obtaining hearings, but it is making

its way none the less. Music here, as elsewhere, is in a transition period, often echoing

I DRINK THE FRAGRANCE OF THE ROSE [1]

(Original Key)

CHARLES HANSON TOWNE

H. CLOUGH-LEIGHTER
Op. 19, Nº 1

the more or less experimental work of certain

[1] Copyright, MCMII, by Oliver Ditson Company.

modernists abroad. America has composers as skilled in orchestration as those of almost any other nation. In boldness of effects, too, our radicals are not behind the foreign pioneers. If we are at present composite and cosmopolitan rather than strictly national, there is still time for a distinctly American school to develop. Such a school might well fuse the discordant elements of modern music into a complete whole, which is what the musical world needs at present.

CHAPTER III.

ALTHOUGH the orchestral forms are rightly regarded as the most important, it is quite possible for a genius to manifest itself in other ways. Thus Chopin wrote concertos, but his piano works alone sufficed to place him in the ranks of the immortals. The composers mentioned in this chapter may therefore be quite as gifted as some of those previously described; and probably a number of them will enter the orchestral field, too, in later years.

Benjamin Cutter was born at Woburn, Mass., in 1857, and was much prized as a harmony teacher in the New England Conservatory for many years before his death in 1910. He composed a cantata " Sir Patrick Spens," a Mass, a piano trio, Bagatelles for viola and piano, violin works, songs, and choruses. His Mass, published with organ accompaniment, is a work of full dimensions. The Kyrie shows excellent interweaving of solo voices and chorus; the Gloria begins grandly with chorus; Qui Tollis works up to a great climax by transition from soprano to chorus; the Credo reverses the process, beginning with chorus and ending with strong quartet work; the Sanctus shows due enthusiasm, the Benedictus has real dignity, the Agnus Dei brings expressive solo work, and the Dona Nobis forms a strong finale. This Mass is one of the best works yet produced in America.

John Hyatt Brewer, whose biography is given in the earlier text,[1] has continued as organist and exceptionally gifted chorus leader. As a composer he has won prizes

[1] See p. 331.

from such diverse offerings as Mason and Hamlin, the City of Brooklyn, the Schubert Glee Club, and the Chicago Madrigal Club. He has been active in the American Guild of Organists, the Brooklyn Institute of Arts and Sciences, and other organizations. He really belongs with the orchestral composers, though he keeps his suite hidden away in manuscript. His other recent works follow the lines of his earlier productions.

Another Brooklyn organist and composer is Raymond Huntington Woodman, born there in 1861. He, too, became an organist when fourteen years old, replacing his father when the latter met with an accident. He has also been very successful as a choral conductor, and an active leader in the music department of the Brooklyn Institute. As a composer, he has handled the orchestra as an accompaniment for some of his songs, using the organ to accompany his cantatas. The latter are two in number, — " The

Message of the Star," for Christmas, and
" The Way of Penitence," for Lenten use.
The former is especially happy in its choral
work, beginning with the attractive " There
Shall Come a Star " and ending with the
triumphant " Hail our Redeemer." Woodman's piano pieces include a rhythmic and
lulling Romance, while among his organ
works the bright " Epithalamium," with
quaint five-bar phrases in its middle section,
deserves especial mention. Of his solo songs,
" In San Nazzaro " is an effective cycle
dealing with love and loss as they come to a
young monk. " Give Me the Sea " is a strong
minor picture of longing, while " Wind of
the Downs " is virile in its suggestion of
open air. Woodman has written in all about
fifty songs, and numerous part-songs and
choruses.

Charles Whitney Coombs, already mentioned as a song writer,[1] has continued his

[1] See p. 343.

career as composer and organist in New York. Among his works are the cantatas " The Vision of St. John," " The Ancient of Days," and " The First Christmas," with solo voices, chorus, and organ. Among his songs the best is the intense lyric " My Heart, it was a cup of gold; " while " How Goodly are Thy Tents " is an anthem showing excellent melodic counterpoint.

Another well-known organist-composer is Samuel Prowse Warren.

In his later years, Gerrit Smith [1] entered the cantata field with " David." He also continued his admirable work in the smaller forms that he wrought with so much skill. These Mr. Hughes has described so well that no further comment is needed.

George Balch Nevin, born at Shippensburg, Pa., in 1859, has composed in very many vocal forms, but has been most successful with his church music. His Christ-

[1] See p. 309.

mas cantata " The Adoration " and an Easter work, " The Crucified," represent him at his best; among his secular songs especial mention must be given to " The Bells of Shandon " and " The Song of the Armorer."

Nicholas J. Elsenheimer, born at Wiesbaden in 1866, has for many years been identified with the Granberry Music School, of New York. He has composed the cantatas " Valerian " and " Belshazzar," and many part-songs.

Henry Morton Dunham was born at Brockton, Mass., in 1853. He has been an organist in Boston for many years, and a teacher at the New England Conservatory. He will soon enter the orchestral field with his symphonic poem " Easter Morning." Meanwhile his reputation rests on some valuable organ works. His first organ sonata is a dignified affair, his second remarkably effective, and his third a worthy example of the continuous-movement form. A Fan-

tasia and Fugue, op. 19, is a rapid rush for
the most part. His Fantasia in C minor
shows excellent use of contrast. A Festival
March, op. 15, is worked out with great
breadth. Dunham's other organ pieces include Three Choral Preludes, a Passacaglia,
a Theme and Variations for piano and organ,
and many church works.

Louis Campbell-Tipton, known profession-
ally without the first name, was born at
Chicago in 1877. He has lived for some time
in Paris, but has become well known in Germany also. The reviewer of the " Signale,"
an important periodical, states that " In
many respects he is . . . more interesting
than Debussy, although he may not show
the latter's completeness in the smaller forms.
This comes perhaps from the fact that Campbell-Tipton's musical ideas are larger, and,
consequently, better suited to the larger
forms." Of the Suite Pastorale, for violin
and piano, the same writer says, " All the

movements of this suite bear the marks of a firm hand in the moulding, modern harmonic freedom of an individual character throughout; living, fresh rhythms, and charming tone-colorings, making an interesting work from the first to the last note." A German encyclopedia calls his work " highly colored, vigorous, and dramatic." His chief piano compositions include the aspiring and spirited " Sonata Heroic," some effective Legends, and a suite, " The Four Seasons." The last-named shows bubbling enthusiasm for Spring, languorous calm for Summer, retrospection for Autumn, and a mysterious loneliness for Winter. There is also an early album of ten short pieces, with a bright Scherzetto and an effective Menuet among them. Of his songs, " The Opium Smoker " shows a strong contrast between the dream and the reality; Longfellow's " Hymn to the Night " is set with much breadth; " Three Shadows," with Rossetti's words, is of great intensity;

the Tone-Poems, op. 3, contain admirable pictorial effects, as in " Am winterlichen Meer " or " The Sea Shell; " while the Four Sea Lyrics comprise " After Sunset," " Darkness," " The Crying of Water," and " Requies."

John Alden Carpenter was born at Park Ridge, near Chicago, in 1876. He studied first with his mother, a gifted musician, and later with Amy Fay, W. C. Seeboeck, Prof. Paine at Harvard (where he took Highest Honors with a piano sonata), with Elgar three months, and with Bernhard Ziehn, of Chicago, whom he praises highly. Carpenter is in business, but finds time to toss off compositions that win remarkable eulogies. Chief of these is a sonata for violin and piano, played by Elman. It has an improvisational Larghetto, followed by an energetic and incisive Allegro, with the later movements consisting of a Largo Mistico and a Presto Giocoso. Carpenter's songs are of great variety, ranging from children's work to settings of Verlaine. The former consists of two dainty albums, " When Little Boys Sing " and " Improving Songs for Anxious Children; " and their delicate humor is well indicated by these titles. " Treat Me Nice " is another bit of brightness. Of his four Verlaine songs, the " Chanson d'Automne " is impressively declamatory, " Le Ciel " is broad and effective, " Dansons la Gigue " suggests its subject well, and " Il Pleure Dans Mon Coeur " is sufficiently mournful. " En Sourdine " treats another Verlaine poem. Of the Four Songs for Medium Voice, " Les Silhouettes " is full of variety, " Her Voice " shows a strange intensity, " To One Unknown " is a broad invocation to love, and " Fog Wraiths " has odd modulatory effects. Eight Songs for Medium Voice include a rhythmic " Cradle Song," the smooth " Looking-Glass River," the melodious " Go, Lovely Rose," and the quaint bit of moralizing entitled "Little Fly." Carpenter's work, on the whole, is modern and modulatory, but distinctly and decidedly original.

Harvey Worthington Loomis, rated so highly by Mr. Hughes,[1] has produced an impressive work in his "Tragedy of Death." Its words show a mother's efforts to save her child before Death can take it from the Garden of Souls to Heaven. Undines and Fates also play their part. The music is partly vocal, partly melodramatic, and contains an expressive Intermezzo for piano alone.

Adolph Martin Foerster, whose earlier productions place him in the orchestral class,[2] has devoted his recent work chiefly to songs, with the exception of op. 77, which is a Nocturne and Epigram for organ. His "Ave Maria," with minor-major contrasts, has a violin and organ *obbligato*. Op. 53 is an album of Ten Lyrics, and includes the

[1] See p. 77.   [2] See p. 248.

strangely impressive " Love Seemeth Terrible," the melodious " Sterne Ueberall," the
folk-song-like " Suggestion," an intense
" Farewell " with Byron's words, the beautiful " Water Lily," and others. Op. 57 contains in its Six Songs the smoothly lyric
" Early Spring," an impressive minor setting
of Heine's difficult " Fichtenbaum," a lively
" Forester's Song," and the enthusiastic
Lied " Der Lenz ist da." Most interesting
are the Greek Love Songs, op. 63. There
are nine of them, of which " Bittersweet "
seems pleasingly odd, with its close on the
dominant note, " Time's Revenge " echoes
the ironic spirit of the words, " Rekindling
the Flame " is an effective minor number,
" Purity of Love " is appropriately intense,
and " Love Aflame " a fiery close to the set.
The Garland of Songs, op. 64, deserves note
because it contains a broadly melodious
setting of " The Last Rose of Summer," as
well as the contrasted " Starless Night " and

" Starlit Night." " To the Beloved " and
" Enraptured " are other gems in this set.
Op. 65 contains four love songs, while op. 67,
Child Lyrics, treats five Stevenson poems,
including " Where Go the Boats " and " The
Friendly Cow." In the Second Album of
Lyrics, op. 69, is an artistic version of " Row
Gently Here, My Gondolier," a slow and
majestic " Midnight Reverie," the impressive little tone-picture " Absolved " (depicting a frozen sentry released by death), a
breezy " In March," a remarkably effective
" Swan Song," and the German lyrics " Wo
Ich Bin " and " Durch den Wald." Foerster's later songs include " Gefangen " (here
meaning captivated), " Ein Reif ist gefallen,"
the dramatic " Indian Maid," the Wagner
Albumblatt reminiscence " Calm Be Thy
Sleep," the melodious " My Harp," the
charming " Song of the Woods," and the
tremendously impressive " Alone." In the
last, the loneliness of the eagle, the lion, the

river, and the mountain, are all depicted on
a single note for the voice, and only at the
end, when man sees into Eternity, is there
any change from this monotone.

Herman P. Chelius is a Bostonian (though
of German birth) who is known as pianist,
organist, choral conductor, teacher, and composer. In the last capacity he has produced
a number of piano works and songs, but his
Prelude and Fugue for piano is sufficient by
itself to make a name for him. The prelude
has a running fire of triplets spread between
the hands, and over their rhythmic up-and-
down sweeps are heard expressive chords.
This structure, carried through the work, is
varied harmonically in the most interesting
fashion, the music being clear and logical,
and, at the same time, without any labored
search after novel or abstruse effects. The
fugue, with its running subject echoing the
prelude material, is built up into a most glorious tonal edifice. The exposition is carried

through fully, and the many episodes and
strettos show the true contrapuntal spirit.

Grand Prelude and Fugue [1]
in F minor.

Toward the end the subject and answer are

[1] Copyright, 1907, by Herman P. Chelius.

taken in octaves instead of unison, and made
to finish the work with the most tremendous

FUGUE. [1]

HERMAN P. CHELIUS.

power. It is little wonder that Baermann,

[1] Copyright, 1907, by Herman P. Chelius.

Foote, and other artists called this one of the greatest piano works ever written in America. Other piano pieces by Chelius include a Ballade in F, which Foote calls "beautiful, fresh, and interesting;" a Melodie, a Valse Caprice, a Valse Brillante, the melodious Angelic Vision, a Love Song, a Dance of Gnomes, and many other selections. His violin Romanza is another tuneful work. He has written also a 'cello piece, organ works, songs, and choruses. He is now preparing a set of piano pieces aimed to bring out all varieties of touch.

Frederic Ayres, born at Binghamton in 1876, studied with Kelley in Berlin and Foote in Boston. He, too, has written fugues, but he treats them in freer fashion and with less power. His Two Fugues, op. 9, even show harmonic episodes, though treating the fugal matter. But their material is interesting enough. Ayres has composed a piano trio also, but is best known by his songs. Of his Three Songs, op. 2, the " Spring Song " (Browning) shows a delicate melodic sense, " I Send My Heart Up to Thee " is effective but not individual, while " Bestowal " is apparently simple, but in reality deeply sincere and very strong. " It Was a Lover and His Lass " has a setting of rippling lightness and intricacy, while the Sea Dirge from " The Tempest " is again a strongly poetic work in apparently simple form. " Come Unto These Yellow Sands " has some remarkably original harmonic effects, while " Where the Bee Sucks " is smoothly melodious.

Frank La Forge, who came into public notice as Mme. Sembrich's accompanist, is also a composer in his own right. His Romance and Gavotte for piano are attractive enough, but he has done more in the domain of song. " Am See " is an example of mournful declamation; " An Einem Boten " is a dainty and humorous bit; " The Sheepherder "

has an effective Ostinato figure, giving
a picture of monotony by its repetition; " In
der Abendstille " echoes the mood of that
Strauss gem " Traum durch die Dämmer-
ung; " " Frühlingseinzug " is an enthusiastic specimen of the German Lied; " The
Coyote," with its up-and-down wails, is a
distinctly American subject; " To One Afar "
shows masterly figure treatment; " Spuk " is
duly mysterious and ghostly; " Come Unto
These Yellow Sands " is beautiful, but has too
many sustained notes for its subject; while
" Before the Crucifix " is broadly effective.

Clayton Johns,[1] who still teaches and
writes in Boston in spite of illness, has in
manuscript the music to an old mystery play,
arranged for voice and instruments. He has
added to his piano works an Introduction
and Fugue, an Impromptu-Caprice, a Canzone, a Waltz, and a Promenade, all of which
hold their well-earned popularity. He has

[1] See p. 368.

also issued two technical books, " The Essentials of Pianoforte Playing " and " From Bach to Chopin." But his songs carry farthest with the public. One has yet to hear of a summer hotel in this broad country that has not echoed to " I Cannot Help Loving Thee," or " I Love, And The World Is Mine." These are classics in America, just as much as Nevin's well-beloved " Narcissus " ever was. Johns has set French texts in the dainty " Peu de Chose," the beautiful " Roses Mortes," the quiet " Apaisement," the sombre " Il Pleure Dans Mon Coeur," and the impressive " Un Grand Sommeil Noir." Other effective lyrics of his are " The Scythe Song," " An Old Rhyme," " Through Eastern Gates," " Song of the Trees," " The Lady of the Lagoon," " A Bridal Measure," " When May was Young," " Moon of Roses," and others of the same sympathetic lyricism.

Wilson G. Smith [1] has continued his well-

[1] See p. 395.

liked piano works and songs, and has succeeded in bringing his opus-numbers past

the century mark. The Romanza Appasionata and Simple Story of op. 95 are more appealing than some of his thinly veiled dances, while his recent " Summer Sketches," " Autumn Sketches," and " Moonlight Sketches " have unusual pictorial value. A Danse Arabesque, op. 102, is another work that is far removed from conventionality. In his songs, Smith has become one of a goodly fellowship by setting " The Night Hath a Thousand Eyes; " it should have pretty nearly a thousand composers, also, by this time. " O That We Two Were Maying " is another much-used poem, in setting which the composer was at least following his English namesake, Alice Mary Smith.

Willard J. Baltzell, who refuses to put himself in his own biographical dictionary, is placed by early works among the orchestral composers.[1] Editorial work in Philadelphia and Boston has reduced his later productions to a minimum.

[1] See p. 275.

Daniel Gregory Mason is another exclusively American product, having graduated from Prof. Paine's fostering care, in 1895, to take courses with Chadwick and Goetschius. His compositions include a piano quartet, in manuscript; a violin sonata in G minor; a Pastorale for violin, clarinet, and piano; a strongly effective Elegy in Variation Form for piano; a piano Romance, Impromptu, and the "Birthday Waltzes;" and the delightfully comic Variations on Yankee Doodle, in the style of different composers. His Four Songs, op. 4, consist of the broadly effective "Ah, Wherefore Wait," the lyrical "I Sang My Love a Song," the melodious "Ah, Little Stars, Look Smilingly," and the dainty "O Singing Birds." He has set also five children's songs from Stevenson.[1]

John Beach started out as one of the furi-

---

[1] Mason's recent music for the Cape Cod Pageant has placed him among the orchestral composers.

ous modernists, to whom the tonic and dominant chords seem as relics of a prehistoric age.
After recent study with Gedalge, he has
started two operatic ventures, one the two-
act " Jorinda and Jorindel," and the other
a short curtain-raiser from " Pippa Passes."
He has in manuscript a setting of Kipling's
" Gypsy Trail " for baritone and orchestra.
His published works include the " New Orleans Miniatures " and " A Garden Fancy "
for piano, the dramatic monologue " In a
Gondola," and several songs, of which " The
Kings " is a vigorous protest against fate.
But his works are so extreme that they become
doubtful in value.

Benjamin Lincoln Whelpley,[1] who now
lives in Boston, is one of the conservatives.
He has entered the orchestral field with an
Intermezzo, but is best known by his songs
and piano pieces. The latter are about a
score of little tone-pictures, such as the deli-

[1] See p. 375.

cate " In the Garden," the flute-like " Serenade," or the dainty " Will o' the wisp " of op.
4. His Two Preludes, op. 15, are for violin,
'cello, and organ, the second being especially
broad. His songs include the minor plaint
" I Know a Hill; " the attractive " Forest
Song; " three melodious lyrics with words
from Tennyson's " Maud; " and two songs
from " The Princess," of which " The
Splendor Falls on Castle Walls " is well conceived, in spite of the fact that no composer
can really do justice to that famous outburst
of song.

G. Marscal-Loepke is really Grace Marshall,
who has been for some years the devoted and
helpful wife of Clough-Leighter. She was
born near Nineveh, Indiana, in 1885. After
finishing studies in Boston in 1907, she began
composing piano pieces and etudes, songs,
part-songs, and choruses. " The Prince of
Life " is one of her cantatas, and she has
written numerous anthems. For juvenile

students her little sets " To Nod-Land,"
" In the Woodland," " Childhood Joys," and
" Little Wood Folk " are decidedly suitable
and interesting. More ambitious are a
broadly melodious Nocturne, a brusque Humoreske, and a Polka-Caprice. Her vocal
works range from the strong " War Song of
the Vikings " to the usual treatments of
spring and love, " I Did Not Know " being
an especially good example of the last subject.

Charles Fonteyn Manney, mentioned for
his graceful songs,[1] is now another prolific
Boston worker. He has published sacred
cantatas, such as " The Resurrection; "
anthems, of which " I Heard a Great Voice "
is a good example; part-songs, like " Snowflakes; " and the expected piano pieces and
solo songs. Of the latter, the cycle " A
Shropshire Lad " gives a good portrayal of
varying moods. " Parted Presence " is a
full-voiced lament, while " O Captain, My

[1] See p. 348.

Captain " is another compelling bit of strength. " My Heart is Sair For Somebody " is not entirely Scotch, but few composers ever do really improve on the Scotch tunes. " Des Müden Abendlied " and the " Chanson d'Automne " deserve special mention for their power.

James Cartwright Macy, born at New York in 1845, is an earlier cantata composer, who is known also by his writings.

Leonard Liebling is another man known widely by his writings and periodical work. He has composed some piano works, however, such as the smooth Romance Cantabile, the syncopated Reverie Poetique, and the bright Petite Valse.

Arthur Reginald Little has composed as much as his name implies, but his work is of good quality. His " Ulalume," based on Poe's poem, is a piano selection that has some very pregnant themes, and is admirably grateful to the performer.

Francis Hendriks is another rising piano composer.

Edgar Thorn, who wrote some attractive piano pieces and songs, is now known to be a myth. When it was a question of helping a certain nurse in the MacDowell home, that composer wrote the pieces under the pseudonym, and let the nurse draw the royalties.

Alvah Glover Salmon, born at Southold, N. Y., in 1868, has become known through his lecture-recitals. He has also composed about a hundred works in various forms, but mostly for piano.

Frank Lynes, born at Cambridge in 1858 (he died in 1914), was an organist who composed many very well-known songs and piano pieces.

John P. Marshall, organist of the Boston Symphony Orchestra, has composed organ works and songs.

Charles Henshaw Dana, who died at

Worcester, was another organist who composed church music and songs.

George Albert Burdett, born at Boston in 1856, has composed organ works, piano pieces, and anthems.

Charles Arthur Havens is another song and anthem composer.

Everett E. Truette, born at Rockland, Mass., in 1861, is a Guilmant pupil who was active in founding the American Guild of Organists. He has composed organ works and anthems.

In the domain of teaching pieces, C. W. Krogmann, of Danvers, has done much excellent work for piano, as well as for voice.

Mrs. John Orth (L. E. Orth) is another very successful composer of teaching pieces, of which she has published over three hundred for piano, and very many light, pleasing songs.

Of those who rest their reputation only on songs, Rupert Hughes himself is one. His Riley Album, containing ten songs, is full of unusual effects, made with the simplest of means. "A Scrawl" and "The Little Tiny Kickshaw" prove this in sympathetic fashion. "Billy Goodin" is a rhythmic bit of taunting, while "Coffee Like His Mother Used to Make" is another example of appealing simplicity. Hughes has also written a dramatic Scena entitled "Cain," to his own words. Cain is represented as dashing through the night and storm in a frenzy of remorse. When given in Chicago, this was called the most important novelty of its season, and it had such a strong effect that one woman was temporarily driven into hysterics. It is a work of harmonic liberty, having very daring thirteenth chords that contain every note of the diatonic scale. But in spite of this success, Hughes has turned to literature, and is now known as the author of such diverse works as "The Musical Guide," the strong story "Miss 318," and stage plays.

WILSON G. SMITH.

A composer whose songs sometimes show a most tremendous strength and unusual originality is Sidney Homer. Born in Boston in 1864, he studied with Chadwick and Rheinberger, and in turn taught singing. Some of his compositions seem inimitable, and the hearer unconsciously thinks, as with works of genius, " I could never have done that." Such are the noble " Prospice," the monotonous but intense " Song of the Shirt," the defiant " To Russia," the pathetic " How's My Boy," and the ironic " Pauper's Drive." In a lighter style are the Lyrics from Singsong and the Bandanna Ballads, while more earnest again are " A Woman's Last Word," " My Star," " There's Heaven Above," " The Eternal Goodness," and " The Song of the Watcher."

Mary Turner Salter is another composer whose songs show exceptional vigor and originality. She was born at Peoria, Ill., in 1856. She married Sumner Salter, for many years musical director at Williams College. She was a singer at first, and was led into composition by her habit of musing and improvising at the piano. She has written some part-songs, but most of her work is for solo voice. " The Cry of Rachel " (" Death, Let Me In ") is a tremendously strong work, and Schumann-Heink, who sings it often, rates it with the world's most dramatic songs. In most utter contrast is " The Chrysanthemum," in which that flower gets angry and wishes it had no hair. The Songs of the Four Winds are naturally varied, that of the East Wind again showing power. Settings of Carman's " Lyrics from Sappho," " A Night in Naishapur," and " From Old Japan " are works of compelling intensity. The " Outdoor Sketches " are more familiarly beautiful. Like real Lieder are the German songs " Für Musik," " Die stille Wasserrose," and " Der Schmetterling." " Sleep, little lady " is a charming lullaby. " Contentment,"

" The Lamp of Love," " Goodnight," " A Water Lily," and " Serenity " are attract-

SERENITY[1]

ive in expected ways, while " The Song of Agamede " is another unusual bit.

[1] Copyright, MCMIV, by Oliver Ditson Company.

Gena Branscombe is another much-prized song composer. Such cycles as the charming " Lute of Jade " or the open-air love-songs of " The Sun Dial " show a remarkable faculty for finely-chiseled lyric expression. Her songs are most tenderly poetic and beautiful.

Among other women, Marguerite Melville, who married and settled abroad, deserves mention for compositions in various forms, while Edna Rosalind Park stays in her own country to compose songs.

Arthur H. Ryder, born at Plymouth in 1875, became an organist after studies at Harvard and in London. Of his songs at hand, " Gray Rocks and Grayer Sea " is a strongly effective bit of monochromatic work, " A Voice on the Winds " is weirdly original, " Robin Hood's Goodnight " is charmingly lyrical, and " Yvonne " is of noble breadth. He has written also sacred quartets and choruses. His " Midsummer Lullaby " is a beautifully rhythmic piano piece, while " A June Idyl " consists of three tone-pictures for violin and piano.

William Spencer Johnson, born at Athol, Mass., in 1883, has published about thirty songs, and composed many more. Of these, " A Lyric of Autumn " is strongly virile, " Impatience " shows the rhythmic beat of passionate eagerness, " A Gypsy Song " has mandolin-like arpeggios, the " Menuet " is a strange minor plaint of past joy and present sorrow, and " Beneath her Window " has a rippling accompaniment and flower-like themes. Three Verlaine Silhouettes consist of " Mandolin," " Fantoches," and the strongly varied " Pantomime." Eight songs called " The Little Past," with charming words by Josephine Preston Peabody, are dainty in the extreme. One of these, " The Green Singing Book," indulges in the realistic trick of having the voice part sung through, and then sung back with the book held upside down. Other published songs by Johnson are the poetic and languorous " June," " The Piper " (Peabody words again), the poignant " Rain," the broad " Friendship," the indolent " Barcarolle," and a delicate setting of Hugo's " Hark, Through the Quivering Twilight."

Victor Harris, already mentioned for his lyrics,[1] has written a number of new songs, including the melodious " In the Garden," the sincerely sweet " I Shall Know You," the rollicking " Man's Song," the dainty " April," the poetic " Summer Wind," the strongly expressive " A Little Way," the bright " Lady Laughter," the sympathetic " The Prince Will Come," and the characteristic " Way Down South."

William Arms Fisher has been mentioned as a Boston worker.[2] His compositions still consist almost wholly of songs. Among these, " Sweet is Tipperary " is one of the com-

[1] See p. 336.   [2] See p. 371.

poser's favorites; " As Once in May " is the same poem that Strauss set in " Allerseelen," and the American setting, though different, is still adequate; " O Risen Lord," one of several good sacred songs, has a violin *obbligato;* " Under the Rose " is a dainty affair; of the three lyrics by Arlo Bates, " When Allah Spoke " is extremely broad and effective; and " The Rose of Ispahan," in the same set, is rhythmically charming. " As Drooping Fern," " A Song of Joy," and " For Love's Sake Only " are poetic bits, while " Gae to Sleep " is pleasing enough, if not too characteristically Scotch.

Hallett Gilberté, whose last name was once Gilbert, has made a great success in New York and other places with his songs. Most popular among them is " Ah, Love, But a Day."

Harriet Ware is a successful song composer as well as a pianist. She has to her credit a strong setting of Markham's " The Cross," a real " Hindu Slumber Song," the plaintive " Last Dance," the intense " Wind and Lyre," a rhythmic " Boat Song," and the poetic cycle " A Day in Arcady."

Mrs. Mary Carr Moore has composed songs, and has in manuscript the opera " Narcissa," based on the true story of Narcissa Prentiss, who married Marcus Whitman, went to the Pacific Coast with him as a missionary, and was massacred there by Indians.

Lola Carrier Worrell was born in Michigan, but has passed most of her life in Denver. Her songs are praised by such leaders as Foote and Cadman, and such singers as Gadski, Homer, and Fremstad. Of those printed works at hand, " In a Garden " is a bit of rapid daintiness, " Waiting " is broadly lyrical, " It is June " is another bit of tonal enthusiasm, the " Autumn Bacchanal " is delightfully cheering, " Hohe Liebe " is in the Lied style, and " The Song of the Chimes " is a smooth lullaby.

Other American song composers include Stephen Townsend (" The Night hath a Thousand Eyes "), Natalie Curtis (songs from " A Child's Garden of Verses "), Albert A. Mack (" Forever and a Day "), W. H. Neidlinger (" Serenade "), Winthrop L. Rogers, William Armour Thayer, Stuart Mason (two French songs), Emiliano Renaud, Gertrude Sans-Souci, J. C. Bartlett, Fay Foster, William C. MacFarlane (" Cloister Roses," " The Lover's Shallop," etc.), Hamilton C. MacDougall, H. J. Stewart (the effective " Yosemite Legends "), Walter Rummel, John A Loud, W. Franke-Harling, Albert Ross Parsons, and Malcolm Dana Mac-Millan.

Other names, which should certainly be included for various reasons, are Newnham, W. H. Dayas, Brainard, Dial, Arnold, F. Addison Porter, Alexander Russell, Henry Eichheim, Carl Engel, Benjamin Lambord, Henry Waller, William Schuyler, Chester

Ide, Eleanor Freer, Fanny Knowlton, Caroline Walker, and William McCoy, many of whom have had works published by the patriotic Wa-Wan Press. If still other names might have been treated in this section, the writer hopes that this sentence will be taken as an apology to anyone feeling unjustly omitted, as reasons of space have to be taken into consideration. The length of the list, however, and the number of recent names covered here, will add renewed proof to the fact that music is cherished in our country. If we have as yet no commanding genius of the first rank, we may console ourselves with the fact that most other countries, also, have none. Geniuses are few and far between; but there is no reason why the next member of the score or so of great masters should not appear in these United States.

THE END.

INDEX.

———•———